A Comprehensive and Practical User's Handbook to
Natural Healing.

D0469817

21ST CENTURY

NATURAL MEDICINE

by

Dr. Douglas Lobay, N.D.

A Modern and Scientific Guide to the Use of Diet,
Vitamins, Minerals and Herbal Medicines in the
Treatment of Common Diseases.

Published by
Apple Communications
Kelowna, B.C.

Disclaimer: The information presented here in this book is for educational purposes only and is not intended as a substitute for proper medical care. Individuals should seek out proper medical care from licensed health care practitioners for appropriate diagnosis and treatment.

Canadian Cataloguing in Publication Data
Lobay, Doug, 1965 -
21st Century Natural Medicine

Includes Index

1. Naturopathy - Handbooks, manuals, etc. 2. Medicine - Natural
Treatment 3. Alternative medicine
I. Title RZ 430.l73   1992
615.5'35"   92-10653

Acknowledgements

I would like to thank:

Mom and Dad
Arlene and Jim
Lisa McNally for cover design
Dr. Gaetano Morello
Dr. Michael Murray
Dr. Kim Vanderlinden
Dr. Julian Vigliotti
and of course, Natalie

Dedication

To my parents for all their love and support.

Success

"To laugh often and much; to win the respect of intelligent people and the affection of children; to earn the appreciation of honest critics and endure the betrayal of false friends; to appreciate beauty, to find the best in others; to leave the world a bit better, whether by a healthy child, a garden patch or a redeemed social condition; to know even one life has breathed easier because you have lived. This is to have succeeded."

Ralph Waldo Emerson

Table of Contents

Preface

The purpose of "21st Century Natural Medicine" is to provide a modern and scientific guide to the use of lifestyle changes, diet, vitamins, minerals, food supplements and herbal medicines in the treatment of common diseases. I wanted to present an enjoyable and informative book designed to educate others about the virtues of natural medicine. In the past many individuals have argued that there is no scientific basis to naturopathic medicine or the therapies that this branch of medicine employs. When I decided to attend Bastyr College of Natural Health Sciences to study naturopathic medicine, I wanted to prove to myself that naturopathic therapies were effective and that there was substantial scientific literature to support this.

Early in my career I was fortunate enought to have Dr. Michael Murray as a teacher at Bastyr College. Dr. Murray taught herbal medicine at the college and used documented evidence from the scientific literature to support the claims he made. Dr. Murray along with Dr. Joe Pizzorno wrote "The Textbook of Natural Medicine" the first fully referenced textbook on natural medicine written from a scientific perspective. Dr. Murrays's contribution to the modern practice of naturopathic medicine is invaluable.

As a student I spent countless hours at the University of Washington Medical Library photocopying articles from various medical journals. I was surprised at the amount of documented scientific evidence there was for the use of natural therapies. I learned that many of the traditional methods of healing did indeed have merit and the scientific literature abounded with research supporting many of these methods. Prestigious medical journals like "The New England Journal of Medicine" and "The Journal of the American Medical Association" had many articles on the therapeutic effects of diet, vitamins, minerals, food supplements and herbal medicines on disease. From this research I began to write "21st Century Natural Medicine."

Rather than be a radical alternative to conventional medicine I view natural medicine as a complement to the conventional route. Drugs and surgery are strong tools of medicine and definitely do have their place in the treatment of disease. Surgery and drugs have saved many lives and should be respected. However, there is widespread misuse of these powerful tools and in many cases gentler and very effective natural therapies are available for treatment of common diseases. Rather than be at odds with conventional medical doctors, I believe that we should all work together to provide the best medical care available to all individuals regardless of whether it is natural or not. In many cases natural medicines can prevent or alter to course of many diseases and offer much less risk of side effects than conventional medications.

Let's bridge the gap between folk medicine and modern science and strive for excellence in health. The future of naturopathic medicine looks very bright. I believe that natural medicine will undoubtedly play a part in modern medicine of the 21st Century. I hope you enjoy "21st Century Natural Medicine". Live with passion and joy.

Douglas Lobay, Kelowna, B.C.

21st Century Natural Medicine

"The doctor of the future will give no medicine, but will interest their patients in the care of the human frame, in proper diet and in the cause and prevention of disease." Thomas A. Edison

Naturopathic medicine is a separate and distinct branch of medicine based upon the following principles of practice:

The Healing Power of Nature (Vis Medicatrix Naturae). Vis Medicatrix Naturae acts powerfully through healing mechanisms in the body and mind to maintain and restore health. Naturopathic physicians work to restore and support these inherent healing systems when they have broken down, by using methods, medicines and techniques that are in harmony with natural processes.

First Do No Harm (Primum non nocere). Naturopathic physicians prefer non-invasive treatments which minimize the risks of harmful side effects. They are trained to know which patients they can treat safely and which ones they need to refer to other health care practitioners.

Find the Cause (Tolle Causum). Every illness has an underlying cause, often in aspects of lifestyle, diet or habits of the individual. A naturopathic physician is trained to find and remove the underlying cause of a disease.

Treat the Whole Person. Health or disease comes from a complex interaction of physical, emotional, dietary, genetic, environmental, lifestyle and other factors. Naturopathic physicians treat the whole person, taking these factors into account.

Preventive Medicine. The naturopathic approach to health care can prevent minor illnesses from developing into more serious or chronic degenerative diseases. Patients are taught the principles with which to live a healthy life; and by following these principles they can prevent most major illnesses.

History

As a distinct health care profession, Naturopathic medicine is almost 100 years old. Its roots go back through medical history to the healing wisdom of many cultures and times. At the turn of century, practitioners of a variety of medical disciplines combined natural therapeutics in a way they hadn't been combined before and joined together to form the first naturopathic medical societies. Naturopathic medical conventions in the 1920's attracted more than 10,000 practioners. Earlier in the century there were more than 20 naturopathic medical colleges and naturopathic physicians were licensed in a majority of North America.

Naturopathic medicine experienced a decline in the 1940's and 1950's with the rise and popularity of pharmaceutical drugs, technological medicine and the idea that drugs would eliminate all disease. It has experienced a resurgence in the last two decades, as a health conscious public began to seek out alternatives to conventional medicine. As a body of knowledge, naturopathic medicine continues to grow and evolve. It incorporates those elements of scientific modern medicine that forward the knowledge of the mechanisms of natural healing and therapeutics, especially in the fields of diagnosis, immunology, clinical nutrition, botanical medicine and other clinical sciences. As an organized profession, naturopathic medicine is committed to on-going research and development of its science.

The Naturopathic Physician

Naturopathic physicians (N.D.'s) are general practitioners trained as specialists in natural medicine. They are educated in the conventional medical sciences, but they are not orthodox medical doctors (M.D.'s). Naturopathic physicians treat disease and restore health using therapies from the sciences of clinical nutrition, herbal medicine, homeopathy, physical medicine, exercise therapy, counselling, oriental medicine, acupuncture, natural childbirth and hydrotherapy. They tailor these approaches to the needs of the individual patient. Naturopathic medicine is effective in treating most health problems, whether acute or chronic. Naturopathic physicians cooperate with all other branches of medical science, referring patients to other practitioners for diagnosis or treatment when appropriate. In practice, naturopathic physicians perform physical examinations, laboratory testing, gynecological exams, nutritional and dietary assessments, metabolic analysis, allergy testing, X-ray examinations and other modern diagnostic tests. They are the only primary health care practitioners clinically trained to the needs of the individual based on a philosophy that acknowledges the patient as a participant.

The naturopathic physician has a Doctor of Naturopathic Medicine (N.D.) degree from a four year graduate level naturopathic medical college. In states and provinces where they are regulated, naturopathic physicians must pass either a national or a state/provincial level board examination and their actions are subject to review by a state/provincial Board of Examiners.

Another Kind of Doctor

Naturopathic physicians are the only primary care physicians clinically trained in a wide variety of medical systems. Some of the natural therapies practiced by naturopathic physicians are:

Clinical Nutrition. Nutrition and the therapeutic use of foods have always been a cornerstone of naturopathic medicine. A growing body of scientific knowledge in this area is reflected in numerous professional journals of nutrition and dietary sciences, validating the naturopathic approach to diet and nutrition. Many medical conditions can be treated as effectively with foods and nutritional supplements as they can be by any other means, but with fewer complications and side effects. Naturopathic physicians receive more than 140 classroom hours in clinical nutrition, while in contrast most medical doctors receive fewer than 20 hours.

Homeopathic Medicine. This powerful system of medicine is more than 200 years old and is widely accepted in other countries around the world. The Royal Family of England uses a homeopathic physician. Homeopathic medicines act to strengthen the body's innate immune response; they seldom have side effects. Some conditions that conventional medicine has no effective treatment for, respond well to homeopathy.

Botanical Medicine. Many plant substances are powerful medicines, with advantages over conventional drugs. They are effective and safe when used properly, in the right dose and in the proper combinations with other herbs and treatments. A resurgence of scientific research in Europe and Asia is demonstrating that some plant substances are superior to synthetic drugs used in clinical situations. Naturopathic physicians are trained in both the art and the science of botanical medicine.

Physical Medicine. In the last 100 years, various methods of applying treatments through the manipulation of the muscles, bones and spine have been developed in North America. Naturopathic Medicine has its own techniques, collectively known as naturopathic manipulative therapy. Physical medicine also includes, but is not limited to, physiotherapy using heat and cold, gentle electric pulses, ultrasound, diathermy, hydrotherapy and exercise therapy.

Natural Childbirth. Some Naturopathic physicians provide natural childbirth care in an out-of-hospital setting. They offer pre-natal and post-natal care using the most modern diagnostic techniques. When natural childbirth is not medically indicated, because of high risk, patients are referred for appropriate care.

Oriental Medicine. Naturopathic physicians are trained in the fundamentals of oriental medicine and diagnosis and many use acupuncture, acupressure and oriental botanical medicine in their practices.

Counselling and Stress Management. Mental attitudes and emotional states can be important elements in healing and disease. Naturopathic physicians are trained in various psychological techniques, including counselling, nutritional balancing, stress management, hypnotherapy, biofeedback and other methods.

Minor Surgery. This includes repair of superficial wounds, removal of foreign bodies, cysts and other superficial masses with local anaesthesia as needed.

The future of natural medicine, including botanical medicine, has entered a new and exciting era. The therapeutic value of natural medicine is being validated by scientific research. The future of natural medicine, looks very bright and undoubtedly will play a major part of medicine in the 21st century.

References

(1) American Association of Naturopathic Physicians (AANP) brochure, Naturopathic Medicine: What it is...What it can do for you, Seattle, Washington, 1991.

CHAPTER 1

Acne

Acne is a chronic disorder of sebaceous or oil glands of the skin, particularly those on the face, chest and back, where the glands are the largest and most dense.

Acne is estimated to occur in 5 to 10% of the entire population with varying degrees of severity. Acne occurs equally among male and female adolescents, although eruptions are worse among males. Almost all teenagers have acne to some degree which usually resolves by age 20.

Normally sebum or oil from these glands reaches the surface, emptying into the hair follicle and flows along the hair shaft. The earliest sign of acne is the comedone, a plug formed by impaction of the opening of the duct by hard material and dried oil. The plugs are visible as closed comedones or whiteheads and if the surface is darkened, open comedones or blackheads, not due to dirt as erroneously believed, but rather due to oxidation of melanin and oil in the plugs. Comedones become inflammed as friendly bacteria, normal residents within the duct and gland proliferate within obstructed glands and produce reddening in the area.

The underlying cause of acne is unclear, but several events partici- pate in its development. These include proliferating sebaceous glands and increased production of sebum, under the stimulation of male sex hor- mones as puberty occurs, obstruction of the sebaceous glands with proliferation of bacteria, followed by development of inflammation and characteristic pimples of acne. Genetics is believed to play a role in the development and the seriousness of the disease. Topical medication, face care, factors that improve or worsen acne, or other medical conditions or medications should be considered in the evaluation of acne. Acne can be produced or exacerbated by drugs, including steroids, testosterone, phenytoin, and external irritants.

Conventional medical treatment of acne includes the use of antibi- otics, cortisone, Retin-A, Accutane and topical creams. No single treatment is effective for all patients with acne. The overall goal is to reverse and prevent plugging of sebaceous ducts, as well as to prevent and reduce inflammation of sebaceous glands and the surrounding tissue.

Lifestyle

Stop scrubbing areas affected hard. Stop using antibacterial soap, because it will decrease friendly bacteria and increase proliferation of disease causing bacteria. Stop using oil-based cosmetics which can obstruct sebaceous ducts and form plugs. Stress is known to aggravate acne. Stressors should be identified and reduced. Stress reduction techniques including meditation, deep breathing exercises, biofeedback, yoga and exercise should by utalized.

Diet

The standard american diet, high in refined carbohydrates, fats and calories, is associated with an increased incidence of acne. After World War II, Eskimos who changed from their traditional diet to western diets developed a number of new diseases including acne. Increased dietary fat is associated with increased sebum production. A low fat diet may benefit individuals with acne. Food sensitivities and allergies can cause and worsen existing acne. A food sensitivity or allergy test may be necessary to identify offending foods. Avoid foods such as white sugar, refined carbohydrates, milk, cheese, coffee, tea, chocolate, alcohol, soft drinks, fats and oils, citrus fruits, nuts, corn and processed foods. Increase consumption of whole, unprocessed foods, fiber, complex carbohydrates, vegetables and fruits.

Vitamins and Minerals
(Daily unless otherwise stated)

Vitamin A - 10,000-50,000 IU. Necessary for the development and maintenance of healthy skin. Vitamin A analogs are the basis of conventional drugs such as Retin-A, routinely used to treat acne. Doses greater than 50,000 IU's per day are often recommended, but are best administered under medical supervision. Vitamin A is potentially toxic at high doses and can cause liver damage.
Folic Acid - 400-800 mcg. Helps to improve symptoms of acne.
Biotin - 400-800 mcg. May be deficient and supplementation helps to improve symptoms of acne.
Inositol - 100-200 mg. Important for hair and skin nutrition and helps to improve the breakdown of fats.
B-complex - 25-100 mg. Helps the body respond to stress and may reduce stress related acne breakouts.

Vitamin B6 (Pyridoxine) - 25-100 mg. Used in many enzymatic processes in the body and is involved in the breakdown of toxins in the liver. Supplementation may help to improve symptoms in those individuals with premenstrual acne.

Vitamin E - 400-1000 IU. A powerful antioxidant and anti-inflammatory that helps to prevent inflammation and damage to the skin. Important for proper skin nutrition.

Zinc - 25-50 mg. May be deficient and supplementation may improve symptoms of acne. It activates enzymes that eliminate toxins in the blood.

Chromium - 200-400 mcg. Important in regulating blood sugar levels and abnormal blood sugar levels have been observed with individuals with acne.

Sulfur - 600-1200 mg. Helps to eliminate toxins in the liver and has potent antibacterial action. Topical application is effective and is a common constituent in many topical acne preparations. Excess sulfur may cause drying and flaking of the skin.

Food Supplements
(Daily unless otherwise stated)

Omega-3 oils (flaxseed, fish oil) - 1000-3000 mg. A rich source of essential oils that are utalized by the skin. Also involved in fat metabolism and decreases inflammation of the skin.

Omega-6 oils (evening primrose, borage oil) - 1000-3000 mg. A rich source of essential oils that are utalized by the skin. Also involved in fat metabolism and decreases inflammation of the skin.

Bromelain (1200 m.c.u.) - 600-1200 mg. Has strong anti-inflammatory activity and protein digesting ability that helps to eliminate plugged glands.

Herbal Medicines

Specific plants and plant derivatives may be useful in treating acne. Plants that have been traditionally used to treat acne include **Burdock (Arctium lappa), Chaparral (Larrea tridentata), Cleavers (Galium aparine), Dandelion (Taraxacum officinale), Goldenseal (Hydrastis canadensis), Red Clover (Trifolium pratense), Sarsaparilla (Smilax officinale)** and **Yellow dock (Rumex crispus).** Although the constituents of these plants differ they are collectively known as alteratives or blood cleansers. They help to improve elimination of wastes and toxins through the skin, urine and other avenues. A popular combination used to treat acne includes Burdock, Cleavers, Red clover and Yellow dock. One or more of these herbal medicines may be consumed as a tea, tincture, fluid extract, solid extract or supplement.

Highly Recommended

Vitamin A / vitamin B-complex / vitamin B6 / vitamin E / chromium / sulfur / Burdock / Cleavers / Red clover / Yellow dock.

CHAPTER 2

Aids

AIDS or Acquired Immune Deficiency Syndrome is caused by a virus and is characterized by immune deficiency, opportunistic infections, malignancy and nerve degeneration.

HIV or Human Immunodeficiency Virus is the virus that causes AIDS. However, not all individuals with HIV have AIDS. AIDS is a serious condition of severe immune depression that some, but not all, individuals with HIV infection develop. Currently approximately 20 to 40% of HIV positive individuals develop AIDS.

AIDS is characterized by severe immune system dysfunction. The target of HIV is a white blood cell of the immune system called the lymphocyte. HIV infects a specific lymphocyte cell called a T-helper cell. The normal function of the T-helper cell is to "help" the rest of the immune system to function and respond to infection. Another lymphocyte cell is called the T-suppressor cell and whose function is to "suppress" immune system function. Suppressing immune function is important in preventing auto-immune reactions in which the immune system attacks parts of the body. In a normal person the T-helper cells and the T-suppressor cells are in a ratio of 2:1. In an individual with AIDS the T-helper cells are drastically decreased. Subsequently, the T-suppressor cells are increased. This prevents proper immune function and prevents the body from responding to infection.

AIDS may have a sudden or gradual onset. Symptoms include fever, night sweats, fatigue, malaise, general tiredness, muscle pain, joint pain, sore tongue, headache, sore throat, swelling of the lymph glands, skin rash, weight loss and diarrhea. Opportunistic infections including Cytomegalovirus (CMV), Epstein-barr virus (EBV), Herpes, Toxoplasmosis, Tuberculosis, Cryptococcus and Candida can develop. Pneumocyctis pneumonia (PCP) occurs in 60% of individuals with AIDS. Tuberculosis can also occur. Chronic, recurrent candida infections of the mouth, skin and digestive system can occur. Kaposi's sarcoma, a connective tissue cancer of the skin, can also develop.

HIV is not transmitted by casual contact or even close non-sexual contact that normally occurs at work, in school or at home. Transmission to another person requires transmission of body fluids containing HIV infected cells. Fluids such as blood, plasma, saliva, semen, tears and vaginal secretions could contain HIV infected cells. At this time transmission of HIV infected cells through tears and saliva has not been reported. Airborne transmission of HIV does not occur.

97% of all individuals with AIDS have one or more of the following risk factors: Homosexual or bisexual males, intravenous drug users, hemophiliacs, blood transfusion recipient, heterosexual contact with HIV infected carrier and children borne to HIV infected mothers.

HIV and AIDS infection may be suspected on history, risk factors and physical exam. However, definitive diagnosis of HIV is based blood tests to determine the presence of the virus. Testing should be confidential at the request of the individual being tested. Counselling individuals about the meaning of HIV infection and AIDS should be mandatory to all those tested.

Currently there is no cure for AIDS. Conventional medical treatment of AIDS focuses on drug therapy to help control the infection. HIV is readily inactivated by heat and commonly used disinfectants such as peroxide, hibitane and alcohol. Drugs such as AZT, Zidovudine and DDI are presently used and help to inhibit the replication of the virus. A search for the development of a vaccine for preventing AIDS is widespread. Side effects of AZT use include anemia, skin rash, nausea, vomiting, muscle and joint pain, fever, sweating, double vision, anorexia and constipation. Education plays a very important role in preventing HIV and AIDS.

Lifestyle

Avoid the high risk activities associated with HIV infection and AIDS. Intravenous drug use is strongly discouraged. Safe sex activities should be practiced and the use of latex condoms is strongly recommended. Counselling and support groups play an important in dealing with the fears and reality of HIV infection and are strongly recommended.

Excess stress is strongly associated with the development of disease and can aggravate AIDS and contribute to opportunistic infections. Stressors should be identified and reduced. Moderate exercise, meditation, yoga and biofeedback are excellent ways to reduce stress. Smoking is strongly discouraged and only contributes to poor health, a weakened immune system and the development of opportunistic infections.

Hydrotherapy

Artificial fever treatments may be beneficial. Fever occurs when the body temperature is raised in response to an infection. This is a natural process that helps the body fight infection and stimulates the immune system. An artificial fever treatment is the process in which an individual's body temperature is raised to 39 to 40 degrees celcius (102 to 104 degrees Fahrenheit). The individual is placed in a very warm bath with the water temperature between 42 and 45 degrees Celcius (104-108 degrees Fahrenheit) for 20 to 60 minutes or as long as tolerated. This raises the core body temperature and produces an artificial fever. Hydrotherapy is an excellent way to help induce an artificial fever and stimulate the immune system.

Diet

Avoid white sugar and refined carbohydrates. A high consumption of refined carbohydrates can impair immune response. Decrease consumption of coffee, tea, chocolate and other stimulants. Excess consumption of stimulants can also depress immune function. Limit consumption of alcohol. Decrease consumption of refined and processed foods. Increase consumption of whole and unprocessed foods, fruits and vegetables. Fresh fruit and vegetable juicing may be beneficial.

Vitamins and Minerals
(Daily unless otherwise stated)

Vitamin A - 25,000-50,000 IU. Important for the development of maintenance of the epithelial tissue. Supplementation helps to improve immune function and stimulate T-helper cell response.
Beta-carotene - 100,000-300,000 IU. Precursor to vitamin A without the side effects at high doses. Supplementation helps to improve immune function and stimulate T-helper cell response.
Vitamin B-complex - 50-100 mg. May be deficient. Helps the body respond to stress.

7

Vitamin C - 2000-10,000 mg. Has antiviral effects and supplementation helps to improve immune function and stimulate T-helper cell response.
Zinc - 15-25 mg. Helps to improve immune function and increase T-cell counts. However, high doses of zinc over long periods may actually decrease immune function.

Food supplements
(Daily unless otherwise stated)

Bioflavonoids - 1000-2000 mg. Supplementation helps to improve immune function. Works synergistically with vitamin C.
Catechin - 200-400 mg. A naturally occuring bioflavonoid that may help to improve immune function.
N-acetyl cysteine (NAC) - 500-1000 mg. Has antiviral effects and supplementation may help to improve immune function.
Monolaurin - 250-500 mg. Has immune stimulating properties and supplementation may be beneficial.
Thymus glandular extract - 500-1000 mg. Helps to support and stimulate the thymus gland function, a vital part of the immune system.

Herbal Medicines

Specific plants and plant derivatives may be useful in treating AIDS and improving immune function. **Astragalus root (Astragalus membranaceous), Garlic (Allium sativum), Goldenseal (Hydrastis canadensis), Licorice (Glycyrrhiza glabra), Lomatia (Ligusticum porteris), Purple coneflower (Echinacea angustifolia) and Saint John's wort (Hypericum perforatum)** contain antiviral properties. **St. John's wort (Hypericum perforatum)** contains certain derivatives that have demonstrated antiviral activity against HIV virus. **Shiitake (Lentinus edodes) and Reishi (Ganoderma lucidum) mushrooms** have immune stimulating properties. One or more of these herbal medicines may be consumed as a tea, tincture, fluid extract, solid extract or supplement.

Highly Recommended

Avoid white sugar, refined carbohydrates and processed foods / Eat whole and unprocessed foods / multiple vitamin and mineral complex / beta-carotene / vitamin C / zinc / thymus glandular extract / N-acetyl cysteine / Astragalus / Garlic / Licorice / St. John's wort.

CHAPTER 3

Alcoholism

Alcoholism is a chronic substance abuse disorder and is characterized by repeated and excessive drinking of alcoholic beverages. This addiction can lead to poor health and can interfere with social, economic and personal functioning.

Although the exact prevalence of alcoholism is unknown, a conservative estimate indicates that 5 to 10% of the adult population may have problems with alcohol dependence. The vast majority of alcoholics do not fit the stereotype of the drunken bum on skid row, but rather are ordinary people who constitute a wide cross section of society. 75% of alcoholics do not receive appropriate treatment for this disorder. Yet alcoholism is one of the most treatable of all medical and psychiatric conditions.

Alcohol is a toxic drug that is harmful to all body tissues. Excess use can affect the nervous system and brain, liver, kidneys, heart and digestive system. Liver damage and cirrhosis is the most common consequence of chronic alcoholism. Intellectual impairment can occur in the early stages of the disease and later permanent and disabling brain damage can occur. Digestive disturbances such as esophageal and peptic ulcers are common. Heart disease, stroke and hypertension commonly occur. Habitual drinking may interfere with proper immune function and can lead to frequent infections. Excess alcohol intake can also cause sexual impotence particularly in males. Prolonged and excessive intake of alcohol and vitamin B1 deficiency can cause Wernicke-Korsakoff's syndrome characterized by psychosis and delerium. Newborn infants of mothers who drink during pregnancy are susceptible to fetal alcohol syndrome.

The signs and symptoms of alcoholism include a wide variety of behaviors that vary from individual to individual. These include drinking to the point of drunkenness, drinking alone or in secrecy, using alcohol to relieve insomnia or to help get started in the morning, using alcohol to modify stress, anger and anxiety about personal, family, social or economic problems. Common signs of intoxication include staggering, lack of coordination and balance, emotional lability and incoherence of speech. Other signs include muscle tremors of the hands, rapid heart beat, palpitations, sweating, mood change, restlessness, insomnia or hyperinsomnia and blackouts. A blood alcohol level greater than 80 mg/dl makes a driver legally intoxicated. Blood levels above 200 mg/dl can produce signs of severe intoxication.

There is no universally accepted explanation as to why one person becomes an alcoholic while another does not. Although many alcoholics have no family history of alcoholism, a person who grows up in a family in which one or both parents have an addiction problem with alcohol are at very high risk of becoming an alcoholic themselves. In general, a person is more likely to become an alcoholic if their environment emphasizes drinking, presenting it as a fashionable and indespensable social pastime. Psychological factors play an important role in the development of alcoholism. Unresolved conflicts, loneliness, financial difficulties, social rejection and marital problems contribute to the development of this addiction. Poor diet and nutritional deficiencies caused by excess alcohol intake are common and may contribute to further drinking.

Conventional medical treatment of alcoholism often involves referral of an individual for appropriate counselling and therapy. Alcohol abuse deterrents such as the drug Antabuse (disulfiram) are occasionally prescribed in conjunction with psychotherapy. Muscle relaxants, tranquilizers, and anti-convulsant medication are prescribed for individuals with severe intoxication and withdrawal symptoms.

Lifestyle

Stress can contribute to the development and dependence of alcoholism. Personal, family, social and economic problems should be addressed. Behavior patterns that encourage habitual drinking should be identified and changed.

Counselling and therapy to change behavior patterns that contribute to psychological dependence on this drug are encouraged. Self-help groups such as Alcoholics Anonymous (AA) are strongly recommended. From their own experiences AA members motivate and encourage others to stop drinking. Meetings and discussions give the alcoholic an opportunity to share his or her problems and learn from the experience of others who have had similar problems.

Diet

Avoid alcohol and all products that contain alcohol including sauces and extracts used in cooking. Avoid white sugar and refined carbohydrates, coffee, tea and caffeinated beverages and other stimulants and candy. Hypoglycemia or low blood sugar levels is common in alcoholics. Decrease consumption of refined and processed foods. Increase consumption of fruits and vegetables, complex carbohydrates including whole grains and legumes and whole and unprocessed foods. Food sensitivities and allergies are common in alcoholics. They may induce craving of the foods from which the alcoholic beverage was derived. Alcohol consumption can aggravate the sensitivity and can produce allergic reactions. A food sensitivity test may be beneficial to identify such foods.

Vitamins and Minerals
(Daily unless otherwise stated)

Vitamin A - 10,000-25,000 IU. May be deficient due to poor diet and impaired digestion and absorption. Supplementation helps to improve taste and smell that may be impaired with excessive alcohol consumption.
Vitamin B-complex - 50-100 mg. May be deficient due to poor diet and impaired digestion and absorption. Intramuscular injections may be beneficial.
Vitamin B1 (Thiamine) - 5-10 mg. May be deficient and this deficiency contributes to the development of psychosis and nerve dysfunction.
Vitamin B2 (Riboflavin) - 10-20 mg. May be deficient especially in individuals with liver cirrhosis.
Vitamin B3 (Niacin) - 500-1000 mg. May be deficient. Necessary to activate the enzymes required to breakdown alcohol into harmless byproducts. Deficiency of niacin and nicotinic acid impairs the breakdown of alcohol and contributes to addiction. Supplementation helps to reduce the symptoms of alcoholism and prevent addiction.
Vitamin B6 (Pyridoxine) - 50-100 mg. May be deficient. Deficiency contributes to the development of nerve dysfunction.
Vitamin B12 - 100-250 mcg. May be deficient due to poor diet and impaired digestion and absorption.
Folic acid - 400-800 mcg. May be deficient due to poor diet and impaired digestion and absorption.
Vitamin C - 500-3000 mg. May be deficient and supplementation helps to reduce the effects of alcohol toxicity.

11

Vitamin E - 400-800 IU. May be deficient due to poor diet and impaired digestion and absorption. Helps to prevent fatty degeneration of the liver

Calcium - 800-1200 mg. May be deficient.
Chromium - 200-400 mcg. May be deficient. Helps to regulate blood sugar levels and prevent hypoglycemia and diabetes.
Magnesium - 600-800 mg. May be deficient and deficiency can cause alkalosis, delerium and muscle tremors.
Selenium - 200-400 mcg. May be deficient. Essential for the activity of Glutathione peroxidase, a potent antioxidant that helps to prevent liver cirrhosis.
Zinc - 25-50 mg. May be deficient. Necessary for the enzyme required to breakdown alcohol into harmless byproducts. Also important for taste and smell.

Food Supplements
(Daily unless otherwise stated)

Amino acids (free form) - 4-8 gm or as directed. May benefit individuals with hepatitis and liver cirrhosis.
L-carnitine - 500-1500 mg. Helps to breakdown fats in individuals with fatty degeneration of the liver caused by excessive alcohol consumption.
Catechin - 1-2 gm. A naturally occuring bioflavonoid that helps to prevent liver damage.
Omega-6 oils (evening primrose, borage oil) - 1000-3000 mg. Supplementation may help to reduce the symptoms associated with alcohol withdrawal, prevent liver damage and alcohol related nerve dysfunction.
Glutamine - 1-2 gm. An amino acid used by the brain. Supplementation helps to decrease the desire to drink, decrease anxiety and improve sleep.
Glutathione - 200-400 mg. A powerful antioxidant in the liver that helps to prevent liver damage.
Pantethine - 500-1000 mg. An active form of vitamin B5. Necessary to activate enzymes required to break alcohol down into harmless byproducts.

Herbal Medicines

Specific plants and plant derivatives are useful in preventing liver damage caused by excess drinking. **Artichoke (Cynara scolymus), Dandelion (Taraxacum officinalis), Fringetree bark (Chionanthus virginicus), Greater celandine (Chelidonium majus), Milk thistle**

(Silybum marianum) and Tumeric (Curcuma longa) contain substances that help to prevent liver cirrhosis and promote regeneration of liver cells. One or more of these herbal medicines may be consumed as a tea, tincture, fluid extract, solid extract or supplement. Please, note that many tinctures are alcohol based and should be used with discretion.

Highly Recommended

Eat whole and unprocessed foods / multiple vitamin and mineral complex / vitamin B-complex / vitamin B1 / vitamin B2 / vitamin B3 / chromium / magnesium / glutamine / Milk thistle.

CHAPTER 5

Alzheimer's Disease

Alzheimer's disease refers to a syndrome characterized by intellectual and cognitive deterioration, memory loss, dementia, and neurological degeneration of the brain.

Alzheimer's disease is estimated to affect 5 to 10% of the population over the age of 65 years and up to 20% of the population over 80 years of age. This disease rarely occurs in individuals younger than 65 years of age. It is estimated to affect 1 to 3 million people in North America and affects males and females equally.

Symptoms of Alzheimer's disease include recent and long term memory loss, intellectual deterioration, cognitive impairment, motor and sensory impairment, inappropriate behavior, aggressive behavior, sleep disturbances (either insomnia or excessive sleep), urinary incontinence, fecal incontinence, appetite disturbance, muscle incoordination and weakness and nervous system impairment. Approximately 75% of individuals with this disease develop seizure activity. As the disease progresses there may be need for total care and the patient is often bedridden, requires catheterization and frequently develops contractures and skin problems.

In Alzheimer's disease there is a marked loss of an enzyme called choline acetyltransferase (CAT) which is responsible for the formation of the brain neurotransmitter, acetylcholine. A 30 to 50% loss of CAT activity has been detected in individuals with Alzheimer's disease. There is also marked brain atrophy in individuals with this disease. Other physiological aspects of Alzheimer's disease include reduced brain blood flow, characteristic EEG (electroencephalogram) and decreased brain metabolism.

The exact cause of Alzheimer's disease is still unknown. The variety of theories suggest that Alzheimer's disease is multifactorial in origin. Heredity is believed to play a role in the development of this disease. It occurs in certain families suggesting a possible genetic connection. It also occurs at a higher rate in individuals with Down's syndrome and in individuals with a specific fingerprint pattern. Viral infection of the brain and nervous system may also cause this disease.

14

This disease may be the result of previous viral infection or a slowly developing virus. Excessive intake of aluminum and silicon is strongly linked to development of this disease. Aluminum and silicon deposits have been detected in the affected portions of the brains of patients with Alzheimer's disease. However, these deposits may be a result of the disease and rather than a causative factor.

Diagnosis of Alzheimer's disease is made by examination of brain tissue, computed tomography (CT scan) and magnetic resonance imaging (MRI). Approximately 80% of dementia is caused by Alzheimer's disease or another irreversible dementia. However, 20% of dementia is caused by a reversible condition and it is imperative to get a thorough examination.

Conventional medical treatment of Alzheimer's diseases focuses on drug therapy to help retard the disease progression and provide symptomatic relief. Presently there is no cure for this disease.

Lifestyle

Avoid excessive exposure to aluminum and silicon. Avoid cooking with aluminum cookware, aluminum containing deodorant, aluminum containing toothpaste and aluminum silicates used as a thickener and binder in certain bakeries. Avoid exposure to other toxic heavy metals including lead, mercury, and cadmium.

Diet

A well balanced diet emphasizing whole, unprocessed and unrefined foods is recommended. Refined carbohydrates, sugar, fat and alcohol should be decreased. Complex carbohydrates, fruit and vegetables and fiber should be decreased. The diet should include a wide variety of foods to maintain proper nutrition and prevent nutritional deficiencies.

Vitamins and Minerals
(Daily unless otherwise stated)

Vitamin A - 10,000-25,000 IU. A potent antioxidant that helps to prevent free radical damage to nerve cells of the brain.

15

Vitamin B-complex - 50-100 mg. May be deficient and supplementation helps the body respond to stress.

Vitamin B6 (Pyridoxine) - 25-50 mg. Is often deficient in elderly individuals and parallels a deficiency in dopamine receptors in the brain.

Vitamin B12 - 50-100 mcg. May be deficient. Deficiency is associated with depression, confusion, memory deficits, mental slowness and neurological deficits. Supplementation helps to improve nerve cell function.

Folic acid - 400-800 mcg. May be deficient. Deficiency is associated with organic brain syndrome and symptoms of deficiency include apathy, disorientation and dementia.

Vitamin C - 500-2000 mg. May be deficient and deficiency is characterized by senile dementia. Also acts as a natural chelator that binds environmental and food toxins and prevents their absorption into the body.

Vitamin E - 400-800 IU. Is often deficient in Alzheimer's patients. Vitamin E is a potent antioxidant that helps to prevent free radical damage to nerve cells of the brain.

Selenium - 200-400 mcg. A potent antioxidant that helps to prevent free radical damage to nerve cells of the brain.

Zinc - 25-50 mg. May be deficient and is required for many enzyme processes that occur within nerve cells of the brain.

Food Supplements
(Daily unless otherwise stated)

Fiber - 10-30 gm. Increases stool transit time and binds environmental and food toxins and prevents their absorption into the body. Helps to bind aluminum and prevent its absorption into the body.

Lecithin (Phosphatidyl choline) - 10-40 gm. A natural source of choline that is used by the brain to make the neurotransmitter, acetylcholine. Supplementation appears to be useful in retarding the rate of disease progression. However, it does not appear to improve symptoms of this disease.

Herbal Medicines

Specific plants and plant derivatives may be useful in treating Alzheimer's disease. **Calabar bean (Physostigma venenosum), Chinese ginseng (Panax ginseng), Ginkgo (Ginkgo biloba) and Siberian ginseng (Eleutherococcus senticosus)** are useful plants in treating this

16

disease. One or more of these herbal medicines may be consumed as a tea, tincture, fluid extract, solid extract, or supplement.

Highly Recommended

Avoid dietary and environmental aluminum sources / multiple vitamin and mineral complex / vitamin B-complex / vitamin B-6 / vitamin C / fiber / lecithin / Ginkgo biloba.

CHAPTER 5

Asthma

Asthma is a condition marked by recurrent attacks of difficult breathing and wheezing due to spasmodic constriction of the bronchi. It also known as bronchial asthma. Attacks vary greatly from occasional periods of difficult breathing and wheezing, to severe attacks that produce suffocation and require immediate medical treatment. An acute attack that lasts for days or weeks is called status asthmaticus

Asthma occurs in approximately 3% of the population with varying degrees of severity. It occurs equally in males and females and tends to occur in children and young adults.

Asthma can be classified into three types, according to causative factors. Extrinsic asthma is due to an external allergy and represents the most common type of asthma. Usually the offending allergens are suspended in air in the form of pollen, dust, cigarette smoke, automobile exhaust and animal dander. Intrinsic or non-allergenic asthma is due to an underlying, chronic or recurrent infection of the bronchi, sinuses, tonsils or adenoids. There is evidence that this type of asthma develops from a hypersensitivity to the bacteria causing the infection. The third type of asthma, the mixed type, is due to a combination of extrinsic and intrinsic factors. Attacks can be precipitated infections, emotional factors such as stress and exposure to non-specific irritants.

A typical asthmatic attack is characterized by difficult breathing and wheezing due to restricted airflow. The affected individual assumes a classic sitting posture, leaning forward, so as to use all the muscles of respiration. The skin is usually pale and moist with perspiration and in severe attacks the lips and nailbeds may be blue. In early stages of the attack, coughing may be dry, but as the attack progresses, the cough becomes more productive of a thick, mucoid sputum. Asthma is a chronic condition with an irregular pattern of remissions and exacerbations.

The exact cause of asthma is unknown. There is an inherited tendency toward the development of extrinsic asthma. It is related to a hypersensitivity reaction of the immune system. The affected individual often gives a family history of allergies of one kind or another and a

18

personal history of allergic disorders. Secondary factors affecting the severity of an attack or triggering its onset include events that produce emotional stress, exercise, environmental changes in humidity and temperature and exposure to noxious fumes or other airborne allergens.

Conventional medical treatment of asthma focuses on drug therapy to prevent bronchial spasm. Ventolin, Proventyl, Alupent and Metaprel relax bronchial smooth muscle and may consumed orally or as an inhalant. Theophylline and caffeine also relax bronchial smooth muscle. Cortisone, Intal and Atropine are other classes of drugs that have been used to treat asthma.

Lifestyle

Stress and emotional factors can aggravate asthma. Stressors should be identified and reduced. Environmental sensitivities and allergies should be identified and eliminated. Common environmental allergens include pollen, dust, molds, animal dander, automobile exhaust and other pollution, cigarette smoke, pesticides, herbicides, perfumes and other inhalants. Breathing exercises that increase the use of the diaphragm and promote deep breathing should be practiced. Meditation can be used to relax bronchial muscle spasms.

Diet

Avoid sugar, refined carbohydrates, wheat, excess dairy products, eggs, corn, nuts, chocolate, citrus fruits and any other foods that evoke an allergic response. Food sensitivities can trigger an asthmatic attack. Monosodium glutamate (MSG), sodium bisulfite, tartazine, acetylsalicylic acid, sulfur dioxide, sodium benzoate and other additives have been known to trigger asthmatic attacks. Avoid all processed and refined foods. Increase consumption of whole, unprocessed foods. Sensitivity to tap water can also trigger an asthmatic attack.

Vitamins and Minerals
(Daily unless otherwise stated)

Vitamin A - 10,000-25,000 IU. Necessary for proper development and maintenance of the connective tissue lining the lungs.

19

Vitamin B-complex - 50-100 mg. May be deficient and supplementation may be help the body respond to stress.

Vitamin B6 - 50-200 mg. May be deficient and supplementation may improve symptoms associated with asthma.

Vitamin B12 - 500-1000 mcg. Supplementation may reduce symptoms associated with asthma. Intramuscular injections may be beneficial.

Vitamin C - 500-3000 mg. Important in development and maintenance of connective tissue of the lungs. Helps to stabilize histamine levels in the body and prevent bronchial constriction.

Vitamin E - 400-1200 IU. A potent antioxidant and has antihistamine properties.

Calcium - 800-1200 mg. Helps to relax bronchial smooth muscle and increases air supply to the lungs.

Magnesium - 600-1000 mg. Helps to relax bronchial smooth muscle and increases air supply to the lungs.

Manganese - 1-2 mg. May be deficient and supplementation may be beneficial.

Zinc - 10-25 mg. Important in immune function and supplementation may be beneficial.

Food Supplements
(Daily unless otherwise stated)

Adrenal glandular extract - 500-1000 mg. Supports adrenal gland function. Has anti-inflammatory and antihistamine effects.

Bioflavonoids - 1-2 gm. Naturally occuring compounds that help to stabilize connective tissue lining the lungs and stabilizes cells that release histamine and cause allergic reactions. Works synergistically with Vitamin C.

Quercitin - 50-100 mg. A naturally occuring flavonoid. Helps to stabilize cells responsible for histamine release.

Omega-3 oils (flaxseed, fish oil) - 1000-3000 mg. A rich source of essential oils that reduces inflammation and allergic attacks.

Omega-6 oils (evening primrose, borage oil) - 1000-3000 mg. A rich source of essential oils that reduces inflammation and allergic attacks.

Digestive Enzymes and/or Hydrochloric acid - 1-2 capsules with each meal. May be deficient and can contribute to food sensitivities and food allergies. Supplementation helps to improve digestion and absorption of food.

Herbal Medicines

Specific plants and plant derivatives may be useful in treating asthma. Many plants have been used traditionally to treat asthma. **Ma Huang (Ephedra sinica)** contains ephedrine that is widely used as a bronchodilator, anti-allergic and nervous system stimulant. Ephedrine relaxes bronchial smooth muscle and improves breathing. **Anise (Pimpinella anisum), Bloodroot (Sanguinaria canadensis), Cayenne (Capsicum frutescens), Coltsfoot (Tussilago farfara), Elecampagne (Inula helenium), Grindelia (Grindelia camporum), Indian tobacco (Lobelia inflata), Licorice (Glycyrrhiza glabra), Mullein (Verbascum thapsus), White horehound (Marrubium vulgare), Wild cherry bark (Prunus serotina), and Yerba santa (Eriodyctium)** represent a combination of antispasmodics, expectorants and demulcents that have been used to treat asthma. A popular combination used to treat asthma includes Ephedra, Grindelia, Lobelia and Licorice in equal parts. One or more of these herbal medicines may be consumed as a tea, tincture, fluid extract, solid extract or supplement.

Highly Recommended

Avoid stress / avoid food and environmental allergens / vitamin B-complex / vitamin C / calcium / magnesium / adrenal glandular extract / omega-3 oils / omega-6 oils / Coltsfoot / Ephedra / Grindelia / Lobelia / Licorice / White horehound.

21

CHAPTER 6

Atherosclerosis

Atherosclerosis is the term used to describe the abnormal thickening of an artery due accumulation of cholesterol, fat and lipids. The word atherosclerosis comes from the Greek word "athere" meaning soft, fatty and gruel-like and "sclerosis" meaning hard. These terms are descriptive of the material deposited on the inner lining of the artery wall.

Atherosclerosis is estimated to affect 20 to 40% of the population. Its incidence increases with advanced age and is estimated to affect 50 to 70% of the population over 65 years of age. It occurs slightly more commonly in males than females, although both sexes are equally at risk for developing atherosclerosis.

In the normal artery, the artery wall is tightly packed with cells that allow for the smooth passage of blood and protects against harmful substances from circulating in the blood stream. The inner lining of the artery is surrounded by muscle tissue. In the earliest stages of atherosclerosis, fatty streaks form along the inner lining. Later, plaques of newly formed muscle cells filled with cholesterol build up and protrude in the opening of the blood vessel. These deposits cause narrowing of the opening of the blood vessel and hardening of the muscle wall. This leads to a decrease in the rate at which blood can flow through the artery. The eventual outcome of this process is that the artery can become completely occluded and depending on the location of the occlusion can lead to a heart attack or stroke.

Cholesterol is the single most significant indicator of atherosclerosis. An individual with a total blood cholesterol level greater than 6.2 mmol/l (200 mg/dl) is at high risk for the development of atherosclerosis, heart attack and stroke. Cholesterol was found to consist of several different types depending on its density. LDL (low density lipoprotein) cholesterol, commonly termed "bad cholesterol", is strongly associated with the development of atherosclerosis. LDL transports cholesterol and fats from the liver and digestive system to the arteries where it can be deposited and form plaques. A high LDL count greater than 4.2 mmol/l is associated with increased atherosclerosis. HDL (high density lipoprotein) cholesterol, commonly termed "good cholesterol", is inversely associated with the development of atherosclerosis. HDL transports cholesterol and fats from the arteries and takes it back to the liver where it can be disposed of. A high HDL count greater than 0.9 mmol/l is beneficial.

The exact cause of atherosclerosis is not entirely known and is most likely a combination of factors. Heredity seems to play a role. Other risk factors include hypertension, elevated cholesterol and fats, cigarette smoking, diabetes and obesity. Other presumed risk factors include physical inactivity, certain types of behavioral patterns and personality traits and hardness of the drinking water.

Conventional medical treatment of atherosclerosis focuses on the use of cholesterol reducing medication. Drugs such Questran (cholestyramine), Mevacor (lovastatin), Lopid (gemfibrozil), Lorelco (probucol), Atromid (clofibrate) and Colestid (colestipol) are commonly prescribed. Side effects of these drugs include allergic reaction, liver and kidney dysfunction, peptic ulcer, anemia, constipation, diarrhea, nausea, vomiting, headaches, gall stones, biliary disease and vitamin A, D, E, K and folic acid deficiency.

Lifestyle

Physical and emotional stress can accelerate atherosclerosis. Stressors should be identified and reduced. Exercise is a great way to reduce stress and increase blood circulation. Consistent exercise can reduce total cholesterol and LDL levels and increase HDL cholesterol. Exercise should be a part of daily routine. A daily walk for 30 minutes or longer is suggested. Other aerobic activities including bicycling, swimming, running, hiking and cross country skiing are excellent exercises. Tobacco smoking is strongly associated with accelerated atherosclerosis and is strongly discouraged. A conscious effort to quit smoking should be encouraged.

Diet

Strictly avoid sugar, refined carbohydrates, fats and oils, especially saturated fats from meat and meat products, butter, nuts, margarine, coffee, tea, carbonated beverages, chocolate, milk, cheese and other dairy products, alcohol and white flour. Avoid fried foods. Steam, bake, broil or boil foods. A moderate alcohol consumption up to 2 ounces per day is beneficial in lowering cholesterol, while higher doses can promote atherosclerosis. Increase consumption of complex carbohydrates including grains, rice, legumes and beans. Increase consumption of foods high in fiber, such as vegetables and fruits.

Vitamins and Minerals
(Daily unless otherwise stated)

Vitamin B-complex - 50-100 mg. Helps the body respond to stress. Supplementation may improve the ratio of unsaturated/saturated fats.

Vitamin B3 (Niacin) - 200-1000 mg. Effective in decreasing total cholesterol, LDL cholesterol and triglycerides and in increasing HDL cholesterol. High doses of niacin may cause dilation of blood vessels and sweating. High doses of niacin may cause abnormalities in liver function and should be administered under medical supervision. Niacinamide is ineffective in reducing cholesterol.

Vitamin B6 (Pyridoxine) - 50-100 mg. May be deficient and may lead to atherosclerosis. Vitamin B6 inhibits platelet aggregation and is required by the liver to breakdown toxins.

Folic acid - 400-800 mcg. Required by the liver to breakdown toxins that are associated with atherosclerosis.

Vitamin C - 500-2000 mg. May be deficient and can cause atherosclerosis. Necessary for healthy connective tissue of the artery wall and may decrease platelet aggregation.

Vitamin E - 400-800 IU. Supplementation may decrease platelet aggregation and increase blood flow.

Calcium - 800-1200 mg. Combines with cholesterol to form calcium soaps that are excreted through the digestive system.

Chromium - 200-600 mcg. Deficiency associated with the development of atherosclerosis. Important in maintaining proper blood sugar levels. Supplementation may reduce total cholesterol.

Copper - 2-3 mg. May be deficient and may lead to atherosclerosis.

Magnesium - 500-1000 mg. May be deficient and deficiency is associated with arterial spasms. Supplementation may reduce total cholesterol, increase HDL cholesterol and inhibit platelet aggregation.

Selenium - 200-400 mcg. A potent antioxidant. Supplementation may help prevent development of atherosclerosis.

Zinc - 25-50 mg. Supplementation may help increase HDL cholesterol.

Food Supplements
(Daily unless otherwise stated)

Brewer's Yeast - 3-6 gm. A rich source of chromium containing glucose tolerance factor (GTF) that impoves sugar metabolism, decreases LDL and increases HDL cholesterol.

Bromelain (1800-2200 m.c.u.) - 600-1200 mg. A proteolytic enzyme derived from the pineapple plant. Increases the breakdown of plaques and cholesterol deposits.

Carnitine - 1500-3000 mg. Improves fat metabolism, lowers cholesterol and increases the heart's ability to breakdown fats.

Chondroitin sulphate - 500-1500 mg. A constituent of the arterial wall. Supplementation forms complexes with LDL and VLDL cholesterol. Decreases formation of plaques and cholesterol deposits.

Fiber - 10-20 gm. Increases intestinal bulk and binds cholesterol and prevents its absorption. Water insoluble fiber such as oat bran, guar gum and pectin are more effective than water soluble fiber in lowering cholesterol.

Omega-3 oils (flaxseed, fish oil) - 1000-3000 mg. A rich source of essential oils. Can reduce total cholesterol, LDL cholesterol and triglycerides, while increasing HDL cholesterol. Reduces platelet aggregation and improves blood flow.

Omega-6 oils (evening primrose, borage oil) - 1000-3000 mg. A rich source of essential oils. Can reduce total cholesterol, LDL cholesterol and triglycerides, while increasing HDL cholesterol. Reduces platelet aggregation and improves blood flow.

Lecithin (Phosphatidyl choline) - 5-10 gm. Improves fat metabolism and supplementation accelerates the regression of plaques.

Herbal Medicines

Specific plants and plant derivatives may be useful in treating atherosclerosis and reducing cholesterol. Phytosterols are cholesterol analogs found in many plants and vegetables which have been shown to reduce total cholesterol. **Alfalfa (Medicago sativa)** is rich in phytosterols that are capable of binding cholesterol and bile salts in the digestive system, thereby preventing cholesterol absorption. Supplementation with **common beans (Pinto, Navy, Kidney)** have been shown to reduce LDL cholesterol. **Eggplant and other vitamin C rich vegetables** have been shown to decrease the formation of cholesterol deposits and plaques. **Garlic (Allium sativum) and Onions** inhibits platelet aggregation, increase plaque and cholesterol deposit breakdown, increases HDL cholesterol and decreases LDL cholesterol. **Ginger (Zingiber officinalis)** inhibits platelet aggregation and decreases the formation of plaques and cholesterol deposits. **Ginkgo biloba** dilates arteries and improves blood flow and may relieve the symptoms associated with cholesterol deposits and plaques. **Gugulipid (Commiphora mukul)** contains phytosterols that decrease LDL cholesterol and increase HDL cholesterol. One or more of these herbal medicines may be consumed as a tea, tincture, fluid extract, solid extract or supplement.

Highly Recommended

Avoid white sugar, refined carbohydrates, fats and oils / vitamin B3 / vitamin C / vitamin E / calcium / magnesium / chromium / fiber / omega-3 oils / lecithin / Alfalfa / Garlic / Ginger / Gugulipid.

CHAPTER 7

Cancer

Cancer is not a specific disease but a group of diseases in which there is a transformation of normal body cells into malignant ones. Malignant cells are unhealthy cells that become progressively worse and if uncorrected, tends to worsen so as to cause serious illness or death. Cancer can affect any organ of the body at any time. Over 150 different types of cancers have been described in humans.

Cancer accounts for 23% of all deaths in North America and is second only to cardiovascular disease as the leading cause of death. One in five individuals will die from cancer. 870,000 new cases of life threatening cancers are diagnosed each year. 450,000 individuals will die from cancer each year. Cancer is the leading cause of death for females between the ages of 35 and 74 years. The leading cancers in females are breast, colo-rectal, lung, uterus and Hodgkins disease and other lymphomas. Cancer is the leading cause of death for males between the ages of 15 and 34 years. The leading cancers in males are lung, prostate, colo-rectal, bladder, Hodgkins and other lymphomas.

Some potentially dangerous cancers appear first in the form of harmless changes in the body's tissues. Their danger lies in the fact that they have a tendency to become malignant. Among these precancerous conditions include sores that appear as thickened white patches in the mouth and on the vulva, some moles on the skin and some chronically irritated areas on the skin or mucous membranes of the mouth and tongue. Polyps also are possible precancers.

There are seven cardinal warning signs of cancer. These signs do not necessarily signify cancer, but should they occur, a physician should be consulted and an examination is advisable. These signs include a change in bowel or bladder habits, a sore that does not heal, any unusual bleeding or discharge, thickening or lump in the breast or elsewhere, indigestion or difficulty swallowing, obvious change in a wart or mole and a nagging cough or persistent hoarseness. Other symptoms depend on the location and type of malignancy present.

Stomach cancer: continued lack of appetite, persistent indigestion, pain after eating, loss of weight, vomiting, anemia.

Cancer of the rectum: changes in bowel habits, such as periods of constipation followed by episodes of diarrhea, abdominal cramps and a sensation of incomplete elimination or a feeling there there is a mass in the rectum, rectal pain and bleeding.

Cancer of the Uterus: increased or irregular vaginal discharges, return of vaginal bleeding after menopause, bleeding between menstrual periods or after coitus.

Cancer of the breast: painless lumps in the breast, bleeding or discharge from the nipple. Many kinds of lumps in the breast are innocent, but since this form of cancer is now the leading cause of death from cancer among women, any breast nodule or tumor should be examined by a physician.

Skin cancer: sores and ulcers that do not heal, sudden changes in color, size and texture in moles, warts, scars and birthmarks.

Lung Cancer: a persistent cough that lasts beyond two weeks, wheezing or other noises in the chest, coughing up of blood or bloody sputum, shortness of breath not caused by obvious exertion, such as climbing stairs or running, chest ache or pain.

Cancer of the mouth, tongue and lips: any sore that does not heal in two weeks, any white patch taking the place of the normal pink color of the tongue or inside of the mouth, hoarseness lasting more than two weeks.

Cancer of the larynx: persistent hoarseness.

Cancer of the kidney, bladder and prostate: bloody urine or reddish or pink urine, difficulty in starting urination, increasing frequency of urination during the night.

Brain tumors and cancers: headaches, changes in vision, dizziness, nausea and vomiting, paralysis.

The exact cause of cancer is not known and many different factors are known to be involved. There is a strong genetic link to the development of cancer. DNA, the genetic code within cells may become damaged. The altered cells pass on inapproriate genetic information to their offspring and begin to proliferate in an abnormal and destructive

28

way. Normally, the cells of which body tissues are made are regularly replaced by new cells. New cells form to repair tissue damage and stop forming when the healing is complete. Why they stop forming is unknown, but clearly the body in its normal processes regulates cell growth. In cancer, cells grow unregulated and do not stop dividing. Malignant cells become progressively deformed and have a strong tendency to spread to other cells and tissues and further divide and spread. The spread and migration of malignant cells is called metastasis.

The immune system undoubtedly plays an imporant role in stopping the growth of cancer cells. It is believed by some that most persons develop many small cancers in their lifetime, but do not develop clinicals signs of cancer, because their immune system destroys malignant cells and prevents their growth.

At least 40 to 60% of all cancers are related to diet and lifestyle. For example, cigarette smoking is related to approximately 90% of all cancers of the lung. Nutritional balance is important in prevention of cancer. Certain foods and food additives contain specific cancer causing chemicals. Nutritional deficiency can lower resistance and increase the risk of certain types of cancers. Studies have shown that a relationship exists between obesity and cancer and between dietary excess, particularly the consumption of large amounts of fats and certain types of cancers.

Cancer causing agents in our environment include industrial pollutants and radiation. Environmental factors including exposure to aromatic hydrocarbons and amines, alkylating agents, tobacco, wood products, nickel, asbestos, chromates, thorium dioxide, senecio alkaloids, aflatoxins. Other cancer causing agents include arsenic from mining and smelting industries, asbestos from insulation at construction sites and power plants, benzene from oil refineries, solvents and insecticides and products from coal combustion in steel and petrochemical industries. Each year new products that can cause cancer are produced in industrial operations. A major concern is the occupational and environmental hazards these chemicals present to those who work in or live near these areas.

Certain drugs can cause DNA damage, which can cause cancer including diethylstilbestrol and oxymetholone. Excessive exposure to light and UV radiation can cause basal and squamous cell skin cancer. Chronic trauma to the skin can cause skin cancer. Certain parasites such as Schistosoma can cause bladder cancer and Clonorchis can cause pancreatic and bile duct cancer. Increased age and geographical variation are known to be associated with certain cancers. Certain viruses are known to cause cancer including Herpes virus, Cytomegalovirus, Human papilloma virus and Retroviruses.

The diagnosis of cancer can be made by a number of tests and examinations and should be made by a licensed physician. A PAP test should be done for all women over the age of 20 years and for sexually active women under the age of 20. A breast exam should be done by a doctor at least every three years for women. Breast self-examination is encouraged every month. A colon and rectal exam should be a part of a routine physical at the doctor's office.

Conventional medical treatment of cancer includes surgical removal of the tumor and possibly adjacent tissue, radiation therapy, chemotherapy and immunotherapy. The selection of treatment modality is based on the type of cancer, its location and the extent of involvement. Surgical removal of the tumor and the areas to which it has spread is aimed at removal of all cancerous and potentially cancerous tissue. This method of treatment is most successful when the growth is small and localized. Radiation utilizes ionizing radiation to destroy cells by inhibiting their ability to multiply. Radiation is especially effective against rapidly dividing tissues, such as cancerous tissue, but can also damage normal tissue of the body. Chemotherapy is most frequently used on cancer that has spread from its initial origin and cancer that cannot be removed surgically. Chemotherapeutic agents include alkylating agents, antimetabolites, vinca alkaloids, several antibiotics, certain hormones, certain enzymes and certain heavy metals. These agents are usually very toxic and adjunctive therapy to restore the well being of the cancer patient is usually necessary. Immunotherapy is a newer therapy aimed at increasing the body's own defenses and immune system against malignant cells.

Lifestyle

Prevention is the single, most important factor in preventing cancer. Lifestyle changes are most imperative in preventing cancer. Cigarette smoking is the most common cause of lung cancer and is strongly discouraged. All current smokers are advised to start a program to quit smoking. Excess stress is strongly associated with the development of disease and cancer is no exception. Stressors should be identified and reduced. Exercise, walking, meditation, deep breathing, biofeedback and yoga are excellent ways to reduce stress.

Diet

Decrease white sugar and all refined carbohydrates. Decrease consumption of fats and oils, eggs and other foods high in cholesterol and fried foods. Avoid partially hydrogenated oils including margarine, vegetable oils and vegetable shortening. Avoid smoked, pickled and salt cured foods. A high consumption of these foods is associated with increased risk of developing esophagus and stomach cancer. Avoid excess alcohol. A high consumption of alcohol is associated with increased risk of developing cancer of the respiratory and digestive systems. Increase consumption of whole and unprocessed foods, fresh fruit and vegetables. A vegetarian diet (low fat, high fiber) is beneficial in reducing the risk of many cancers. A high fiber diet is especially beneficial for cancer of the colon, intestines, prostate and breast. Increase consumption of garlic and onions. A liberal consumption of garlic and onions may help to inhibit tumor growth especially of the skin.

Increase consumption of pits of the Prunaceae family including apricots, pears, peaches, plums and bitter almonds. They are a natural source of amygdalin or laetrile. Consume 8 to 15 kernels per day. Do not consume more than this or while taking oral laetrile. Laetrile is a cyanide containing compound that can be toxic to the body.

Vitamins and Minerals
(Daily unless otherwise stated)

Vitamin A - 10,000-25,000 IU. A potent antioxidant. Important for the development and maintenance of epithelial tissue.
Beta-carotene - 50,000-200,000 IU. Precursor to vitamin A. Supplementation beneficial for all types of cancer including cervical, ovarian and lung cancer. Can be consumed in high doses without the toxicity of vitamin A.
Vitamin B-complex - 50-100 mg. May be deficient. Helps the body respond to stress. Supplementation may be beneficial.
Vitamin B6 (Pyridoxine) - 25-50 mg. An important part of many enzyme processes.
Vitamin B12 - 50-100 mcg. May be deficient. Supplementation may help to inhibit the action of cancer causing agents. Should be taken concurrently with folic acid.
Folic acid - 400-800 mg. Important for the development, maintenance and repair of epithelial tissue inluding the skin, mouth, cervix and lining of the digestive system.

31

PABA (Para amino benzoic acid) - 200-400 mg. Used to produce folic acid. PABA absorbs ultraviolet radiation and use in sunscreens may help to prevent skin cancer.

Vitamin C - 2000-8000 mg. A potent antioxidant. Important for the development and maintenance of connective tissue. Supplementation helps to block the action of cancer causing agents such as nitrosamines.

Vitamin E - 400-800 IU. A potent antioxidant that helps to prevent free radical damage to the body.

Calcium - 800-1500 mg. Important for the development and maintenance of bones, connective tissue, muscle and the nervous system. Supplementation helps to reduce the adverse effects of bile acids and decrease the risk of colon cancer.

Iodine - 100-300 mcg. Important for the function of the thyroid gland. Supplementation helps to decrease the risk of breast, uterine and ovarian cancers.

Magnesium - 400-800 mg. May be deficient. Supplementation helps to reduce the risk of most cancers.

Phosphorus - 1000-2000 mg. Helps to decrease the risk of colon cancer.

Selenium - 200-400 mcg. May be deficient. A potent antioxidant. Supplementation helps to reduce the risk of cancer of the colon, rectum, prostate, breast, ovarian and leukemia.

Zinc - 25-50 mg. Supplementation helps to reduce the risk of prostate cancer.

Food Supplements
(Daily unless otherwise stated)

Adrenal glandular extract - 500-1000 mg. Helps the body respond to stress and increases energy level.

Benzaldehyde - 50-150 mg. Interferes with the breakdown of sugar and interferes with fermentation within cancer cells. Increases lifespan of red blood cells and prevents their breakdown.

Hydrazine sulphate - 30-60 mg. Interferes with the breakdown of sugar in the liver and prevents fermentation that occurs in cancer cells.

Lactobacillus acidophilus - 2-4 capsules between meals. Beneficial for the development and maintenance of "friendly" bacteria in the intestines. Supplementation helps to reduce the risk of intestine and colon cancer.

Laetrile - 100-300 mg. A cyanide containing chemical derived from apricot pits that is toxic to rapidly dividing cells.

Methionine - 750-1500 mg. Used by the liver to breakdown toxins and buildup of chemicals that are harmful to the body.

Omega-3 oils (flaxseed, fish oil) - 1500-3000 mg. Important for fat metabolism and inhibits enzymes the increase inflammation.

Omega-6 oils (evening primrose, borage oil) - 1500-3000 mg. Important for fat metabolism and inhibits enzymes that increase inflammation.

Polyerga 250-500 mg. A naturally derived immune stimulating protein that may be beneficial in treating certain kinds of cancer.

Phytosterols - 3-6 capsules. Naturally occuring steroid molecules found in plants. Supplementation decreases the risk of developing colon cancer.

Thymus glandular extract - 500-1000 mg. Helps to support and stimulate the function of the thymus gland. This gland is an important part of the immune system and increases immune response.

Wheat grass - 10-20 tabs. A rich source of chlorophyll and high in abscissic acid. Helps to clean the body.

Herbal Medicines

Specific plants and plant derivatives may be beneficial in treating cancer, helping the immune system and improving overall health. The Hoxsey formula is a combination of herbs used to treat cancer that was popularized in the 1920's. **Barberry (Berberis vulgaris), Buckthorn (Rhamnus purshiana), Burdock (Arctium lappa), Cascara amarga (Picramnia artidesma), Chaparral (Larrea mexicana), Licorice (Glycyrrhiza glabra), Prickly ash (Zanthoxylum americanum) and Red clover (Trifolium pratense).** Although the chemical constituents of these plants differ they are collectively known as blood cleansers or alteratives. Their main action is to aid in the elimination of toxins through the lungs, skin, urine and intestines. **Astragalus (Astragulus membranaceous), Korean ginseng (Panax ginseng), Mistle toe (Viscum album), Purple coneflower (Echinacea angustifolia), Reishi mushroom (Ganoderma lucidum), Shiitake mushroom (Lentinus edodes) and Siberian ginseng (Eleutherococcus senticosus)** contain immune stimulating compounds. One or more of these herbal medicines may be consumed as a tea, tincture, fluid extract, solid extract or supplement.

Highly Recommended

Avoid cigarette smoking / Decrease consumption of white sugar, refined carbohydrates, fats and oils / Decrease caffeine containing beverages / Increase fiber intake / vitamin A / beta-carotene / vitamin C / vitamin E / selenium / thymus glandular extract / Chinese ginseng / Mistletoe / Prickly ash / Purple coneflower / Red clover / Siberian ginseng.

CHAPTER 8

Canker Sores

Canker sores are acute, painful ulcerations, less than one centimeter in diameter, that occur on the lips, gums and mouth of an affected individual. Canker sores are also called apthous stomatitis.

Canker sores are estimated to affect 20% of the North American population. They are more common in females than males. Canker sores usually follow a recurrent pattern and usually present as multiple ulcerations. These aggravating ulcers usually heal spontaneously within 10 to 14 days, but they have a high tendency to recur. Exacerbations and remissions are common throughout life.

Canker sores have white centers and are surrounded by red, inflammed borders. These ulcerations may be slightly painful. They tend to localize on the lips, gums and mouth of affected individuals.

Conventional medical treatment of canker sores is limited and provides only symptomatic relief. Oral antibiotics are occasionally prescribed to help prevent active lesions from becoming infected.

Lifestyle

Stress can precipitate and aggravate canker sores. Stressors should be identified and reduced. Exercise and meditation are excellent ways to reduce stress. Poor dental hygiene is associated with the development of canker sores. Daily brushing, flossing and mouthwash are an important part of oral hygiene. Avoid chewing gum, chewing tobacco, smoking and mouthwashes that are high in sugar.

Diet

Food sensitivities and allergies are associated with the development of canker sores. Common food sensitivities include white sugar, chocolate, milk, cheese and other dairy products, tomato, vinegar, lemon and other citrus fruits, pineapple, mustard, spices and wheat. Gluten, a protein from wheat has been singled out as a specific food that can cause canker sores. The elimination of food sensitivities from the diet results in complete remission of ulcerations. A food sensitivity test may be necessary to determine offending foods.

Vitamins and Minerals
(Daily unless otherwise stated)

Vitamin A - 10,000-25,000 IU. Imporant in the development and maintenance of the cells lining the lips, gums and inner mouth. Supplementation helps to speed up healing time.
Vitamin B-complex - 100 mg. May be deficient and helps the body respond to stress.
Vitamin B12 - 100-1000 mcg. May be deficient and supplementation may be beneficial. Intramuscular injections may be beneficial.
Folic acid - 400-800 mcg. May be deficient and supplementation may be beneficial.
Vitamin C - 1000-3000 mg. Important in the development and maintenance of connective tissue. Supplementation helps to improve immune function.
Vitamin E - 400-1200 IU. Decreases pain and inflammation associated with canker sores.

Iron - 10-25 mg. May be low or deficient and supplementation may be beneficial.
Zinc - 25-50 mg. Helps to improve immune function and supplementation may be beneficial.

Food Supplements
(Daily unless otherwise stated)

Adrenal glandular extract - 500-1000 mg. Helps to support and stimulate adrenal gland function which is the main gland responsible for helping the body deal with stress.
Lactobacillus acidophilus - 1-2 capsules. Supplementation helps to prevent bacterial infection and balances the normal bacterial flora in the mouth.

Herbal Medicines

Specific plants and plant derivatives may be useful in treating canker sores. **Barberry (Berberis vulgaris), Calendula (Calendula officinalis), Garlic (Allium sativum), Goldenseal (Hydrastis canadensis), Licorice (Glycyrrhiza glabra), Myrrh (Commiphora molmol) and Saint John's wort (Hypericum perforatum)** may be beneficial. Topical applications of these plant derivatives may be effective in reducing the inflammation associated with canker sores. One or more of these herbal medicines may be consumed as a tea, tincture, fluid extract, solid extract or supplement.

Highly Recommended

Reduce stress / Avoid food sensitivities and allergies / vitamin A / vitamin B-complex / folic acid / Lactobacillus acidophilus / Calendula / Goldenseal / Myrrh.

CHAPTER 9

Carpal Tunnel Syndrome

Carpal tunnel syndrome is a common nerve entrapment disorder of the median nerve that results in pain, burning or tingling sensations in the fingers and hand and sometimes extending to the elbow.

Carpal tunnel syndrome can occur at any age. The disorder occurs most often in middle aged women. It is common in individuals whose work involves repetitive motion of the hands and wrist.

The median nerve is a large nerve that originates in the neck and runs along the anterior aspect of the arm and forearm. It passes into the palm of the hand through a band of connective tissue called the carpal tunnel. The carpal tunnel is formed by the concave arch of the wrist bones and by the tranverse carpal ligament. Carpal tunnel syndrome results when there is nerve irritation caused by pressure of the carpal tunnel on the median nerve.

Symptoms of carpal tunnel syndrome include episodic tingling and numbness in the wrist, hand and fingers. Burning, aching, and prickling sensation can also occur in the fingers or deep in the palm of the hand. Unless associated with direct trauma there usually is no swelling or inflammation. The affected hand may be painful to move and its range of movement may be limited. There may be accompanying aching pain in the forearm and may occasionally extend to the arm and shoulder. Other symptoms include pain and tingling only at night, increased sweating of the affected limb, clumsiness and changes in hand and grip strength.

Carpal tunnel syndrome is caused by activities that involve excessive wrist movements, arthritis, tendonitis, trauma and swelling and edema of the wrist and hand. Repetitive wrist and hand movements such as in knitting, crocheting, hooking rugs, playing a musical instrument, woodworking, gardening and lifting weights can cause median nerve entrapment. Exposure to low frequency vibration such as in the operation of power tools can also cause nerve irritation. Other less common causes of this disorder include use of oral contraceptives, pregnancy, menopause, diabetes mellitus, hypothyroidism, mumps, leprosy, heavy metal toxicity, blood dyscrasias, sarcoidosis, amyloidosis and cancer. C6 nerve root compression must be distinguished from carpal tunnel syndrome for proper diagnosis and appropriate treatment.

Conventional medical treatment of carpal tunnel syndrome is usually conservative and consists of splinting the wrist to immobilize it for several weeks until irritation of the median nerve has healed. Pain killers such as aspirin and Tylenol (acetaminophen) are frequently prescribed. In severe cases that don't respond to conservative therapy surgical resection of the carpal tunnel ligament is helpful.

Lifestyle

Avoid activities that involve repetitive motion to the wrist. Decrease activities such as knitting, crocheting, hooking rugs, playing musical instruments, typing, woodworking, hammering, operation of power tools, gardening, lifting weights and other activities that contribute to the development of this disorder. These activities should be decreased or avoided altogether to allow the median nerve to heal from the irritation.

Splinting with an arm or hand brace may be necessary for several weeks to immobilize the wrist and forearm and prevent further repetitive motion.

Physical therapies such as massage, ultrasound and acupuncture may be very beneficial.

Vitamins and Minerals
(Daily unless otherwise stated)

Vitamin B-complex - 50-100 mg. May be deficient. Helps the body respond to stress and aids in proper nerve function.
Vitamin B6 (Pyridoxine) - 50-200 gm. May be deficient. Important for proper nerve function. Supplementation is very beneficial. Consume for 6 to 12 weeks for best results. Large dose of vitamin B6 may be toxic to the nervous system and should consumed with proper medical consent.
Pyridoxine-5-Phosphate (PAK) - 50-100 mg. Active form of vitamin B6. Supplementation may be beneficial.

Calcium - 800-1200 mg. Important for proper nerve function and supplementation helps to prevent muscle spasms of the wrist.

Magnesium - 600-800 mg. Important for proper nerve function and supplementation helps to prevent muscle spasms of the wrist.

Highly Recommended

Avoid repetitive hand motions that aggravate CTS / physical therapy / vitamin B-complex / vitamin B6 / calcium / magnesium.

CHAPTER 10

Cataracts

Cataracts are opacities of the lens of the eye and can lead to painless and progressive loss of vision.

Cataracts are the most common cause of impaired vision and blindness in North America. Cataracts affects 0.5% of the population and affects males and females equally. They are particularly prevalent in the over 65 years of age population. Over four million people suffer from varying degrees of cataracts.

Blurred and dimmed vision are often the first symptoms of cataracts. Double vision, frequent change in eye glass prescription and need for brighter reading light are other symptoms. As the disease progresses vision may become progressively worse until blindness sets in. Appropriate therapy may be necessary.

The exact cause of cataracts is unknown. Many different factors can contribute to the development of cataracts. Cataracts may be due to eye injuries, trauma, surgery, diabetes and other diseases. Excessive consumption of sugar in the diet can lead to the development of cataracts. The great majority of cataracts, however, are senile cataracts, which are apparently a part of the aging process of the human body and tend to affect adults over the age of 65 years.

Conventional medical treatment of cataracts focuses on surgical removal of the opacities. Surgical treatment is effective in restoring visual acuity in individuals with fully developed cataracts. However, it does not identify the cause or prevent the development of cataracts. Avoid antihistamines because these drugs can increase cataract formation.

Diet

Avoid white sugar and refined carbohydrates, chocolate, coffee, tea and alcohol. Excessive consumption of white sugar and refined carbohydrates is strongly associated with the development of cataracts. Increase consumption of whole, unprocessed foods, vegetables and fiber.

Vitamins and Minerals
(Daily unless otherwise stated)

Vitamin A - 10,000-25,000 IU. Deficiency may cause cataracts. Important in the development of vision. Also acts as a potent antioxidant.
Vitamin B2 (Riboflavin) - 10-25 mg. Deficiency associated with the development of cataracts.
Vitamin C - 500-2000 mg. Concentrated 30-50 times more in the eye than elsewhere in the body. Acts as a powerful antioxidant that prevents free radical damage, important in connective tissue stabilization and reduces intraocular pressure.
Vitamin E - 400-800 IU. A potent antioxidant that helps to prevent free radical damage to the lens of the eye.

Selenium - 200-400 mcg. A potent antioxidant that prevents growth of cataracts.
Zinc - 25-50 mg. Deficiency may cause cataracts. Supplementation improves sugar metabolism and prevents further growth of opacities.

Food Supplements
(Daily unless otherwise stated)

Glutathione - 250-500 mg. A powerful naturally occuring antioxidant that helps to prevent free radical damage to the lens of the eye.
Bioflavonoids - 1-2 gm. Helps to increase connective tissue integrity in the retina. Works synergistically with vitamin C.
Quercitin - 25-50 mg. Inhibits an enzyme in the eye that leads to the development of cataracts.

Herbal Medicines

Specific plants and plant derivatives may be useful in treating early stages of cataract development. External application of the fresh juice of **Silver ragwort (Cineraria maritima)** to the lens of the eye is effective in the early stages of cataract development. Two drops twice per day in the affected eye is sufficient to retard further cataract development. **Bilberry (Vaccinium myrtillus)** contains a high amount of bioflavonoids that help to stabilize connective tissue of the lens and eye. One or more of these herbal medicines may be consumed as a tea, tincture, fluid extract, solid extract or supplement.

Highly Recommended

Avoid white sugar and refined carbohydrates / vitamin A / vitamin B2 / vitamin C / vitamin E / selenium / zinc / bioflavonoids / quercitin / Silver ragwort.

CHAPTER 11

Celiac Disease

Celiac disease is a chronic intestinal malabsorption disorder caused by intolerance to the protein, gluten, commonly found in wheat, rye, oats and barley. Celiac disease is also known as Non-tropical Sprue and Gluten Enteropathy.

Celiac disease occurs in 1 in 2500 individuals in North America and occurs in 1 in 300 individuals in southwest Ireland. Celiac disease is slightly more common in females than in males. The average age of onset of this disease is between 10 and 15 years, although the disease probably begins much earlier in childhood. Celiac disease occurs commonly in infants from 1 to 3 years and in adults between 30 and 40 years old. Until recently it was thought that the infant form and the adult form were separate entities, but it is now believed that they are the same. Remissions and exacerbations following the ingestion of gluten containing foods is common.

Gluten is a protein of wheat, rye, oats, barley and other grains that gives dough its elastic character. Gliaden a protein derivative of gluten also contributes to Celiac disease. In addition to being found in grains and cereals gluten is found in soup, beer, wine, vodka, whiskey, malt, ice creams, hot dogs, sauces, commercial soaps and is a hidden additive in many other processed foods.

Celiac disease is caused by either a hypersensitivity reaction or a local toxic reaction to gluten. A hereditary factor is implicated, because the disease occurs more frequently when another family member is affected. A high consumption of cow's milk is associated with an increased prevalence of celiac disease. Breastfeeding is believed to prevent the development of celiac disease in infants and children. Celiac disease also occurs at a higher incidence in individuals with thyroid dysfunction, diabetes, psychiatric disturbances, dermatitis herpetiformis and hives. There is evidence that Celiac disease is associated with the development of lymphoma and cancer of the small intestine. This is especially true of individuals who have not been treated with a gluten free diet.

Symptoms of Celiac disease include anemia, weight loss, abnormal sensation such as tingling or burning in the arms or legs, muscle weakness, skin disorders, abdominal bloating, abdominal pain, diarrhea, occasional constipation, pale, malodorous stools, and swelling and edema. Vitamin deficiencies, folic acid and iron deficiency anemia, decreased protein absorption, abnormal blood protein levels and abnormal blood electrolyte levels can also occur.

Diagnosis of Celiac disease is based upon intestinal biopsy and the demonstration of structural changes in the intestinal wall. An abnormally flattened lining of the small intestine, particularly the section of the small intestine called the jejunum, is the hallmark of this disease. Abnormal absorption of nutrients occurs. A Xylose test may be used to determine whether malabsorption occurs. In many cases, the elimination of gluten from the diet provides a dramatic improvement of symptoms and restoration of the normal function of the intestines.

Conventional medical treatment includes the use of corticosteroids that may be used in individuals that do not respond to a gluten free diet.

Lifestyle

Stress can aggravate Celiac disease. Stressors should be identified and reduced. Exercise, meditation, hypnotherapy and biofeedback are excellent ways to reduce stress.

Diet

A gluten free diet is a strongly recommended. Eliminate all grains containing gluten including wheat, rye, oats and barley. All other foods containing gluten including alcoholic beverages, canned soups, hot dogs, salad dressings, ice cream and many packaged and processed foods should also be eliminated. Individuals with Celiac disease should read the labels of all packaged and processed foods that they consume. Avoid sugar and refined carbohydrates, because a high consumption of these products is associated with impared digestion and absorption. Grains such as rice, millet and corn are gluten free and may be consumed. Increase consumption of whole, unprocessed foods, vegetables and fruits. Individuals placed on a gluten free diet can experience a complete remission of symptoms within days of following the diet. Most individuals are symptom free after several months of a gluten free diet.

Vitamins and Minerals
(Daily unless otherwise stated)

Multi-vitamin - 1-2 capsules/tablets. Can supply many of the vitamins and minerals that may be deficient.
Vitamin A - 5000-10000 IU. May be deficient due to impaired absorption of fats.
Vitamin B-complex - 100 mg. May be deficient. Helps the body respond to stress.
Vitamin B6 (Pyridoxine) - 25-50 mg. Absorption may be impaired and deficiency is associated with the development of depression.
Vitamin B12 - 50-100 mcg. May be deficient and can cause anemia.
Folic acid - 200-400 mcg. May be deficient and can cause anemia.
Vitamin D - 200-400 IU. May be deficient due to impaired absorption of fats.
Vitamin E - 200-400 IU. May be deficient due to impaired absorption of fats.
Vitamin K - 2-5 mg. May be deficient due to impaired absorption of fats.

Copper - 2-3 mg. May be deficient.
Iron - 10-25 mg. May be deficient and can cause anemia.
Selenium - 200-400 mcg. May be deficient.
Zinc - 10-25 mg. May be deficient.

Food Supplements
(Daily unless otherwise stated)

Adrenal glandular extract - 500-1000 mg. Helps to support and stimulate adrenal gland function and helps the body respond to stress.

Highly Recommended

Gluten free diet / Avoid gluten found in wheat, rye, oats, barley and other gluten containing foods / multiple vitamin and mineral complex / vitamin B-complex.

CHAPTER 12

Cervical Dysplasia

Cervical dysplasia is a precancerous condition that occurs in the cervix of the female uterus and is characterized by the presence of abnormal cells.

Cervical dysplasia occurs in approximately 2% of the adult female population in North America. It occurs in females between the ages of 20 and 45 years. Cervical cancer is second only to breast cancer as the leading cause of cancer deaths in females over the age of forty years.

One of first warning signs of cervical dysplasia is vaginal bleeding between menstrual periods, after sexual intercourse or after menopause has ceased. There may also be increased vaginal discharge.

Risk factors for the development of cervical dysplasia include early age of sexual intercourse before 18 years of age, multiple sex partners, herpes simplex II infection, human papilloma virus (HPV) infection, oral contraceptive use, diethyl stilbestrol (DES) use, smoking, poor diet and nutritional deficiencies. Cervical dysplasia most commonly occurs in females in the late twenties and early thirties and can occur well above the age of forty years.

The Papinocolau (PAP) smear is most effective in diagnosing cervical dysplasia. A PAP smear involves a sampling of the cells of the cervix. The cells are then analyzed and the presence of abnormal cells is indicative of cervical dysplasia or cervical cancer. PAP smears are analyzed and graded from I to V depending on the degree of abnormal cells. Class I is normal and indicates no abnormal cells present. Class II indicates the presence of slightly abnormal cells. Class III indicates active cervical dysplasia. Class IV strongly suggests cancer. Class V is positive for cancer. PAP smears should be started in females between the ages of 18 to 21 and should be repeated every one to three years. The presence of an abnormal PAP should alert the patient and doctor of cervical dysplasia and the possibility of the development of cancer. Appropriate treatment for cervical dysplasia is necessary to prevent the development of cervical cancer and possible malignancy. The PAP test can detect 90% of cervical dysplasia and cancer. Its use has reduced deaths from cervical cancer by greater than 50% through recognization and treatment of cervical dysplasia. Cervical cancer could be eliminated as a cause of death if all women had an annual PAP test. However less than 40% of women do have an annual PAP test.

Conventional medical treatment of cervical dysplasia focuses on a positive identification and removal of the abnormal cells present. A cervical or cone biopsy may be necessary. A biopsy involves the removal of a wedge-like piece of the cervix. Conization, cauterization, cryotherapy and laser therapy are effective medical treatments. Surgery, radiation and chemotherapy are reserved for those individuals in which cervical dysplasia progresses to cervical cancer and malignancy.

Lifestyle

Avoid any of the risk factors associated with the development of cervical dysplasia. Smoking is strongly discouraged.

Diet

Decrease consumption of fats including saturated fats from meat, butter, margarine and oils. Avoid white sugar and refined carbohydrates. Increase consumption of fiber and whole, unprocessed foods.

Vitamins and Minerals
(Daily unless otherwise stated)

Vitamin A - 25,000-50,000 IU. May be deficient. Involved in the development and maintenance of cervical cells. Please note that dosages of vitamin A beyond 25,000 IU should be administered under the advice and supervision of a qualified health professional.
Beta-carotene - 100,000-300,000. Provitamin A. Involved in the development and maintenance of cervical cells.
Vitamin B-complex - 100 mg. May be deficient. Helps the body respond to stress.
Vitamin B6 (Pyridoxine) - 25-50 mg. Involved in the development the reproductive system.
Vitamin B12 - 100-200 mcg. Works synergistically with folic acid.
Folic acid - 5-10 mg. Necessary for the development and maintenance of cervical cells. Oral contraceptive use diminishes folic acid levels in the body.

Vitamin C - 1000-3000 mg. Supplementation may be beneficial.

Selenium - 200-400 mcg. A potent antioxidant.
Zinc - 25-50 mg. May be deficient and is required for proper development of the reproductive organs.

Herbal Medicines

Specific plants and plant derivatives may be useful in treating cervical dysplasia. Escarotic treatment consists of a combination of vitamins, minerals and herbal medicines applied topically to the cervix. Escarotic treatment is effective in the treatment of class II and III cervical dysplasia. Escarotic treatment consists of a **zinc chloride / bloodroot (Sanguinaria canadensis) mixtures, Bromelain, Calendula (Calendula officinalis), vitamin A suppositories and a mixture of bitter orange oil, vitamin A, ferric sulphate, thuja oil, tea tree oil, goldenseal (Hydrastis canadensis) and magnesium sulphate.** Escarotic treatment promotes abnormal cervical cells to slough off and die, while encourages the development of normal, healthy cervical cells. This treatment should be conducted under the supervision of a qualified health professional.

Highly Recommended

Vitamin A / beta-carotene / folic acid / zinc / bromelain / Calendula / Goldenseal / bitter orange oil / thuja oil / Escarotic treatment.

48

CHAPTER 13

Chronic Fatigue Syndrome

Chronic fatigue syndrome is the term used to describe the complex of symptoms that include fatigue, malaise, depression, persistent "flu-like" illness, muscle weakness and sore throat. This disease is also known as post-viral fatigue syndrome, chronic mononucleosis, chronic Epstein-barr (EBV) syndrome and "yuppie flu."

The exact prevalence of chronic fatigue syndrome is not known. A conservative estimate suggests that it may affect 2 to 4% of the population. The onset of this disease is usually in late adolescence or young adulthood, although it can occur both earlier or later in life. It is believed to affect two to three times more females than males.

Symptoms of chronic fatigue syndrome include persistent or relapsing fatigue or fatigability that does not resolve with bedrest. It is severe enough to impair average daily activity below 50% of normal for a period of at least 6 months. Other symptoms include muscle weakness or pain, muscle numbness or tingling, difficult movement or coordination, depression or other emotional disturbance, loss of concentration, sleep disturbance (insomnia or excessive sleep), digestive upset, sore throat, low grade fever, tender lymph node enlargement of the head and neck region, arthritis and joint pain, skin rash, weight change (weight loss or gain), liver enlargement and spleen enlargement.

The exact cause of chronic fatigue syndrome is unknown. Leading theories of the cause of this diseases include viral infection, immune system dysfunction, neuromuscular dysfunction involving muscles and nerves, nutritional deficiencies and psychological and stress related factors. Viral infection has long been presumed to be the cause of this disease. Epstein-barr virus, a herpes virus, is the prime supect in causing chronic fatigue syndrome. Epstein-barr virus is responsible for the cause of infectious mononucleosis, otherwise known as "kissing disease" in teenagers and young adults. Many individuals with chronic fatigue syndrome test positive for the Epstein-barr virus. However, a number of other viruses are believed to cause this disease.

Chronic fatigue syndrome is a recurrent disorder that typically lasts from 6 months to two years. However, it may persist for four to six years, or longer, in some individuals. Some individuals feel tired all the time, whereas other individuals experience periods of relatively good health between periods of fatigue. Exacerbations of this disease can occur one to six times per year and are typically superimposed on a somewhat more tolerable, but chronic fatigue that remains relatively constant.

The diagnosis of chronic fatigue syndrome is complicated by the fact that no one specific organism is responsible for causing this illness. Diagnosis should be made from a thorough history, signs and symptoms and labwork.

Conventional medical treatment of chronic fatigue syndrome is still controversial. The medical establishment fails to recognize chronic fatigue syndrome as a real disease and offers little therapy in treating this disease. Doctors are often less than sympathetic and suggest that the disease is strictly psychological in origin. Pain killers and antidepressants are frequently prescribed with little consideration to the patient's welfare.

Lifestyle

Stressors should be identified and reduced. Stress is strongly associated with impairment of immune function and increases susceptibility to infection. Stress reduction techniques such as relaxation, deep breathing exercises, meditation, visualization and hypnotherapy may be effective in reducing stress. Supportive therapy in the form of counselling may be strongly beneficial. Regular exercise, at least three to four times per week, is an important means of stress reduction, increases blood circulation and makes the body feel better. Although individuals with chronic fatigue syndrome may often be too tired to exercise, a conscious effort should be made to walk outdoors on a regular basis. A brisk walk, swimming, cycling or other aerobic exercises are strongly recommended. There is also mounting evidence that moderate exercise can stimulate the immune system and fight infection.

Diet

A diet high in sugar and refined carbohydrates, fats and processed foods is associated with decreased energy levels. Sugar and refined carbohydrates impairs all aspects of immune function and should be strictly avoided. Avoid coffee, tea, colas, chocolate and other caffeine containing beverages and foods. Caffeine is a nervous system stimulant that can result in alterations in energy levels. A well balanced diet emphasizing whole and unprocessed foods, whole grains and cereals, fresh fruits and vegetables is strongly recommended. Increase consumption of complex carbohydrates and fiber. A liberal consumption of water is neccessary to ensure proper hydration and helps the body function efficiently.

Vitamins and Minerals
(Daily unless otherwise stated)

Vitamin A - 10,000-25,000 IU. Supplementation helps to stimulate immune function.

Vitamin B-complex - 50-100 mg. Helps the body respond to stress and supplemention can help to improve endurance and stamina.

Vitamin B5 (Pantothenic Acid) - 500-1500 mg. May be deficient and deficiency is associated with tiredness, insomnia, sullenness and depression. Helps to support the function of the adrenal glands.

Vitamin B6 (Pyridoxine) - 25-100 mg. Is required as a cofactor in many enzymatic processes in the body and is necessary for proper muscle contraction.

Vitamin B12 - 100-1000 mcg. Is required for maturation of red blood cells, DNA production and proper nerve function. Supplementation helps to decrease fatigue and improve general well being.

Folic acid - 400-800 mcg. May be deficient and deficiency can cause fatigue.

Vitamin C - 500-3000 mg. May be required in higher amounts in individuals with this disease. It is widely used for its immune supporting and antiviral activity.

Iron - 10-25 mg. May be deficient resulting in anemia and fatigue. Is required for the production of red blood cells and the oxygen carrying capacity of blood.

Magnesium - 600-1200 mg. Is required for energy production and for proper muscle contraction. Magnesium deficiency results in irritability of the nervous system, fatigue, muscle spasms, convulsions, tremors, depression and psychotic behavior, Stress, anxiety and nervousness alone can lead to magnesium deficiency. Individuals with this disease have low red blood cell magnesium levels. Supplementation may be beneficial in improving the symptoms associated with this disease.

Potassium - 500-3000 mg. Potassium deficiency is associated with chronic muscle weakness and fatigue. Supplementation may be beneficial.

Zinc - 25-50 mg. Supplementation can help to improve muscle strength and endurance and can stimulate parts of the immune system.

Food Supplements
(Daily unless otherwise stated)

Adrenal glandular extract - 500-1000 mg. Helps to support and nourish the adrenal gland. Supplementation aids adrenal gland function and the body's response to stress.

Liver glandular extract - 500-1000 mg. Helps to support and stimulate liver function. It is a rich source of B-complex vitamins, iron and proteins that aid immune function and increase energy level.

Omega-6 oils (evening primrose, borage oil) - 1000-3000 mg. Supplementation may be beneficial in activating the immune system.

Thymus glandular extract - 100-250 mg. Helps to support and stimulate the thymus gland function. The thymus gland plays an important role in activation of the immune system and the development of T-cells.

Herbal Medicines

Specific plants and plant derivatives may be useful in treating chronic fatigue syndrome. **Astragalus (Astragalus membraneceous), Baptisia (Baptisia tinctoria), Chinese ginseng (Panax ginseng), Garlic (Allium sativum), Licorice (Glycyrrhiza glabra), Lomatium (Lomatium dissectum and Ligusticum porteri), Pokeweed (Phytolacca decandra), Purple coneflower (Echinacea angustifolia), Shitake mushroom (Lentinus edodes), Siberian ginseng (Eleutherococcus senticosus) and Yarrow (Achillea millefolium)** may be useful plants in treating this disease. One or more of these herbal medicines may be consumed as a tea, tincture, fluid extract, solid extract or supplement.

Highly Recommended

Avoid white sugar and refined carbohydrates / Vitamin A / Vitamin B-complex / Vitamin B-5 / vitamin C / iron / magnesium / zinc / adrenal glandular extract / liver glandular extract / omega-6 oils / thymus glandular extract / Chinese ginseng / Garlic / Purple coneflower.

CHAPTER 14

Common Cold

The common cold is an acute and highly contagious viral infection of the upper respiratory system. The illness is commonly characterized by nasal congestion, sore throat, watery discharge and low grade fever.

The common cold occurs in 50 to 80% of the entire population and is one of the most common infections in the world. The average individual gets two to five colds per year. It is interesting to note that 10 to 20% of all individuals do not get colds.

Usually the common cold starts with a runny nose, nasal congestion, sneezing, thin, watery discharge, sore throat, scratchy throat, productive or non-productive cough, a stuffy feeling in the head, slight headache, watering of the eyes, tender and enlarged lymph nodes, fatigue and tiredness, inability to concentrate and perhaps a slight fever. A fever as high as 39.0 degrees Celcius (102 degrees Fahrenheit) can occur, especially in children. Inflammation of the upper respiratory system including the nose, paranasal sinuses, throat, larynx and often the trachea and bronchi occurs. Inflammation and swelling of the membranes of nose occur and block passageways. The senses of taste and smell are blunted. Appetite is usually decreased and all the individual wants is to lie down and rest.

Influenza or the flu, is also an acute and highly contagious upper respiratory condition that is often similar to the common cold. Unlike a cold, severe muscle aches and pains and a fever up to 39.4 degrees celcius (103 degrees Fahrenheit) commonly occur.

The common cold is caused by over one hundred different viruses including rhinoviruses, coranoviruses, respiratory syncitial viruses and adenoviruses. Colds are more common in young children with developing immune systems, elderly individuals with ill health and individuals with poor immune systems. Factors that contribute to the development of the cold include poor nutrition, stress, excessive alcohol and tobacco use, allergies, chemical sensitivities and lack of proper rest. It takes one to three days after exposure to the cold virus to develop symptoms. Colds are highly contagious and are spread by sneezing and close person to person contact. The average cold lasts from four to ten days and the intensity and duration of the illness can vary from person to person. Colds that last longer than two weeks suggest a poor immune response and underlying causes should be explored.

Conventional medical treatment of the common cold focuses on drug therapy to provide symptomatic relief. Antihistamines, decongestants, cough suppressants and pain killers are frequently prescribed. Aspirin should be used with discretion, especially in young children. Reye's disease, a severe and occasionally fatal disease, is caused by aspirin use. A vaccine to the common cold is highly unlikely because so many different and highly mutating viruses can cause the disease. Alpha interferon and Amantadine are new drugs that help to stimulate immune function and prevent viral spread. However, they are experimental drugs and their effectiveness is yet to be proven. Antibiotics are ineffective against cold viruses and should not be used.

Lifestyle

Rest and sleep as needed. If you are tired and fatigued it is your body's way of telling you that you should rest and relax. Rest is needed to fight the viral infection and build a healthy immune response.

Stress can lower the immune system function and lead to the development of a cold. Stressors should be identified and reduced if possible.

Avoid tobacco smoking. Smoking can irritate and damage the throat and lungs. It can also impair the immune system and decrease immune response.

A vaporizer that is capable of moistening the membranes of the upper respiratory system may be beneficial.

Conscientious handwashing and clean personal hygiene can help to decrease person to person spreading of the cold virus.

Diet

Avoid white sugar and all refined carbohydrates. Sugar competes with vitamin C for uptake and absorption into white blood cells of the immune system. Avoid mucous forming foods including all dairy and cheese including goat's milk and yogurt, eggs, grains rich in mucous including wheat and oats, starchy vegetables including potatoes, yams, turnips and squash. Mucous forming foods increase mucous and sputum production in the nose, mouth and throat. Decrease alcohol consumption. Increase fluid consumption. Drink copious amounts of water, broth, vegetable juice and unsweetened fruit juice. Dilute fruit juice with water. Increase consumption of whole and unprocessed foods, vegetables and fruits. Increase consumption of garlic and onions. Garlic is one of the most potent antiviral and antibiotic substances available.

Vitamins and Minerals
(Daily unless otherwise stated)

Vitamin A - 10,000-20,000 IU. Helps to stimulate immune function and is important for the membranes of the upper respiratory system.
Beta-carotene - 50,000-100,000 IU. Pro-vitamin A. Helps to stimulate the immune system and is important for the membranes of the upper respiratory system. Does not produce the toxic side effects of vitamin A in large doses.
Vitamin C - 500-3000 mg. Increases immune function and has antiviral and antibacterial effects. 500-1000 mg of vitamin C can be consumed every two hours. Best effects at the onset of a cold and less effective once a cold has developed.

Zinc - 25-50 mg. Increases immune function and has antiviral effects. Decreases viral replication. Best effects at the onset of a cold and less effective once a cold has developed. Supplementation helps to reduce the course and severity of the common cold.

Food Supplements
(Daily unless otherwise stated)

Bioflavonoids - 500-1000 mg. Helps to enhance immune function. Works synergistically with vitamin C.
Thymus glandular extract - 500-1000 mg. The thymus gland is an important gland that regulates immune function. The glandular extract provides the raw materials to enhance and support the thymus gland.

Herbal Medicines

Specific plants and plant derivatives may be useful in treating the common cold. Many plants and plant derivatives have been used to stimulate immune function, fight viral infection and provide symptomatic relief for individuals suffering from the common cold. **Astragalus (Astragalus membranaceous), Boneset (Eupatorium perfoliatum), Garlic (Allium sativum), Goldenseal (Hydrastis canadensis), Licorice (Glycyrrhiza glabra), Ligusticum (Ligusticum lucidum), Myrrh (Commiphora molmol) and Purple coneflower (Echinacea** angustifolia) help to enhance immune function and have antiviral effects. **Aniseed (Pimpinella anisum), Bloodroot (Sanguinaria canadensis), Coltsfoot (Tussilago farfara), Cowslip (Primula vera), Grindelia (Grindelia camporum), Hyssop (Hyssopus officinalis), Mullein (Verbascum thapsus), White horehound (Marrubium vulgare) and Wild cherry bark (Prunus serotina)** are expectorants that help to expel and breakup mucous discharge. **Cleavers (Galium aparine) and Poke root (Phytolacca americanum)** help to clear up lymphatic congestion. **Elder blossum (Sambucus nigra), Catnip (Nepeta cataria), Cayenne (Capsicum frutescens), Ginger (Zingiber officinalis) Peppermint (Mentha piperita) and Yarrow (Achillea millefolium)** increase sweating and help warm the body and aid in the removal of waste material. An old fashioned steam bath consisting of a bowl of boiling water and the aromatic oil of a plant such as **Eucalyptus (Eucalyptus globulus), Peppermint (Mentha piperita) and Wintergreen (Galutheria procumbens)** is beneficial for clearing nasal congestion. **Slippery Elm (ulmus fulva)** is a demulcent that helps to soothe sore and inflammed membranes of the mouth and throat. **Ma Huang (Ephedra sinica)** is a natural decongestant that helps to dry inflammed wet membranes and dilate the bronchi to make breathing easier. One or more of these herbal medicines may be consumed as a tea, tincture, fluid extract, solid extract or supplement.

Highly Recommended

Avoid mucous forming foods / Avoid white sugar and refined carbohydrates / beta-carotene / vitamin C / zinc / bioflavonoids / thymus glandular extract / Coltsfoot / Echinacea / Ephedra / Garlic / Goldenseal / White horehound.

CHAPTER 15

Constipation

Constipation is defined as the infrequent, difficult passage of stool. However, it may mean different things to different people, including stools that are infrequent, difficult to expel, hard stool, small stool or the sense of incomplete evacuation.

Constipation is believed to affect between 10 and 20% of the North American population. 25 to 50% of the population over the age of 60 years are affected. The frequency of constipation increases with age. Constipation affects males and females equally. Between 250 and 350 million dollars a year are spent on laxatives in North America. The widespread use of laxatives indicates how common constipation actually is.

There is a wide variation in the frequency of normal bowel movements. The frequency of bowel movements varies according to individual body make-up, type of intestine, eating habits, physical activity and cultural habits. Normal bowel movements may mean three movements per day for one person and three movements per week for another person. Therefore, an individual that has less than three bowel movements per week is constipated. On the other hand, a change in frequency of movements from three per day to three per week may indicate constipation. Almost always constipation is due to a delay in the transit time within the large intestine or colon.

A wide variety of factors including dietary, structural, endocrine, metabolic, neurological, connective tissue disorders and drugs may affect colon transit time. Evaluation of individuals suffering with chronic constipation must include consideration of a wide variety of possible causes. Chronic constipation of one month or longer is due to a motility disorder. Factors that decrease movement of material through the colon include advanced age, sedentary lifestyle, low fiber diet, irritable bowel syndrome, hypothyroidism, inflammatory bowel disease, Hirschsprung's disease (Toxic megacolon), use of constipating drugs such as iron supplements, pain killers and certain antidepressants and local rectal problems such as hemorrhoids, fissures and tumors. Intestinal obstruction can also cause constipation and the use of laxatives can make this condition worse. Continued use of laxatives can lead to chronic constipation. Constipation also occurs during pregnancy.

Chronic constipation can cause uncomfortable symptoms such as nausea, heartburn, indigestion, headache, depression, insomnia, bad breath, diverticulitis, appendicitis, abdominal pain, low back pain, distress to the rectum, flatulence, hemorrhoids, fissures and hernias.

Conventional medical treatment of constipation focuses on the use of laxatives to promote bowel movements. Laxatives such as mineral oils, bulking agents such as metamucil, Milk of Magnesia (Magnesium sulphate) and lactose are often recommended.

Lifestyle

Lack of exercise and a sedentary lifestyle impairs normal colon function and can lead to constipation. Daily exercise, such as walking, cycling and swimming is strongly encouraged. Stress can decrease colon motility. Stressors should be identified and reduced. Deep breathing exercises, meditation, biofeedback and yoga are excellent ways to reduce stress.

Diet

Increase consumption of fiber. Vegetable fiber, largely undigestible and unabsorbable, increases stool bulk and increases motility through the colon. Certain components of fiber absorb water, making stool softer and making passage easier. Fruits and vegetables are recommended. Whole, unprocessed foods are recommended. Avoid white sugar, refined carbohydrates, processed and refined foods. Increase consumption of prunes and prune juice. Prunes are an excellent laxative.

Vitamin and Minerals
(Daily unless otherwise stated)

Multi-vitamin - 1-2 tablets/capsules. Provides all necessary vitamins and minerals needed for proper function.
B-complex - 100 mg. Supplementation helps the body respond to stress.
Folic acid - 1-2 mg. May be deficient and supplementation may be beneficial.

Vitamin D - 200-400 IU. May be deficient and supplementation helps to prevent colon cancer.

Vitamin E - 400-800 IU. May be deficient and supplementation helps to heal the lining of the colon.

Food Supplements
(Daily unless otherwise stated)

Digestive enzymes and/or Hydrochloric acid - 1-2 capsules with each meal. May be deficient and causes impaired digestion and absorption of nutrients. Supplementation may be beneficial.

Fiber - 10-30 gm. Use bulking agents such as bran, psyllium and flaxseed. Vegetable fiber is undigestible and unabsorbable. Increases stool bulk and increases colon motility. Produces natural effects by stimulating the colon to eliminate stool and is not habit forming.

Lactobacillus acidophilus - 1-2 capsules. Supplementation helps to repopulate the colon with "friendly" bacteria. Helps to decrease flatulence and improve motility through the colon.

Milk of Magnesia (Magnesium sulphate) - 1-2 tbsp. Draws water into the colon creating softer stool and promoting movement through the colon. Also relaxes the colon wall.

Herbal Medicines

Specific plants and plant derivatives may be useful in treating constipation. **Anise (Pimpinella anisum), Balm (Melissa officinalis), Chamomile (Matricaria chamomilla), Fennel (Foeniculum vulgare), Ginger (Zingiber officinale) and Peppermint (Mentha piperita)** contain aromatic oils that help to relax the colon wall and promote the movement of stool. **Aloe (Aloe vera), Flaxseed (Linum usitatissimum), Licorice (Glycyrrhiza glabra), Olive oil (Olea europa), Psyllium (Plantago psyllium), Rhubarb (Rheum palmatum) and** are laxatives that encourage bowel movements. Strong laxatives, called cathartics, encourage strong and rapid bowel movements. **Cascara (Cascara sagrada), Castor oil plant (Ricinus communis) and Senna (Cassia angustifolia)** are cathartics. There use should be recommended by a qualified health professional. One or more of these herbal medicines may be consumed as a tea, tincture, fluid extract, solid extract or supplement.

Highly Recommended

Increase consumption of whole and unprocessed foods / multiple vitamin and mineral supplement / digestive enzymes and/or hydrochloric acid / fiber / Lactobacillus acidophilus / Aloe vera / Cascara / Ginger / Peppermint / Psyllium / Senna.

CHAPTER 16

Depression

Depression is a common psychological disorder that is character-ized by loss of pleasure in life, lack of joy and happiness, melancholic outlook, dejection and generalized ill health.

Depression is the most common psychological disturbance in the general population. 10 to 20% of the population, 20 to 50% of patients seen in general practice settings, to 30 to 60% of general hospital inpatients suffer from depression.

Depression is characterized by poor appetite with weight loss or increased appetite with weight gain, insomnia or hypersomnia, agitation or depression of movement and muscle coordination, loss of interest or pleasure in usual activities, loss or decrease in sexual drive, feelings of worthlessness, self reproach or inappropriate guilt, diminished ability to think and concentrate and recurrent thoughts of suicide or death.

There are two major categories of depression. Unipolar depression is characterized by one or more episodes of depression alone. Bipolar depression is characterized by episodes of depression alternating with episodes of mania.

Undiagnosed medical illness often presents as depression and should be considered in the evaluation of any depressed patient. Hormone dysfunction, infectious disease, cancer, most notable pancreatic cancer, present with the symptom of depression. 5% of depressed individuals have a specific psychological disorder that is known to respond to medication.

Conventional medical treatment of depression focuses on drug therapy to alleviate depression and alter moods. Tricyclic antidepres-sants, monoamine oxidase inhibitors and alkali metals are groups of drugs that are routinely prescribed. Commonly prescribed medication include Elavil (amitryptiline), propranolol, lithium, methyl dopa, prozac, and Tofranil (imipramine). Side effects of these medications include seizures and drastically altered moods and behavior. Unusual excitation, confusion, hallucinations and oversedation may occur. Muscle relaxants such as Valium (diazepam) and Xanax (lorazepam) are also commonly prescribed.

Lifestyle

Stress can aggravate depression. Stressors should be identified and reduced. Daily exercise such as walking, cycling, hiking, swimming is strongly encouraged. Being outdoors and breathing fresh air is stimulating and rejuvenating to the body. Deep breathing exercises, meditation, biofeedback and yoga are other useful techniques in reducing stress.

Diet

Food sensitivities can cause mental and behavioral changes by a variety of ways including cerebral allergy, food addiction, hypoglycemia, caffeine addiction, hypersensitivity to chemical food additives, reactions to chemicals and proteins in certain foods. A food sensitivity or allergy test may be necessary to identify offending foods. Avoid white sugar and refined carbohydrates and caffeine containing beverages and foods. Increase consumption of whole and unprocessed foods, fresh fruits and vegetables.

Vitamins and Minerals
(Daily unless otherwise stated)

Vitamin B-complex - 50-100 mg. May be deficient. Helps the body respond to stress.
Biotin - 200-400 mcg. May be deficient. Deficiency can cause headaches, nausea, insomnia, lethargy and muscle weakness.
Folic acid - 200-400 mcg. May be deficient and can cause depression.
Vitamin B6 (Pyridoxine) - 50-100 mg. Use of MAO inhibitor drugs and oral contraceptives can cause vitamin B6 deficiency. It is necessary for conversion of the amino acid, tryptophan into the brain neurotransmitter, serotonin. Disturbances of tryptophan metabolism can cause depression.
Vitamin B1 (Thiamine) - 5-10 mg. May be deficient and can cause depression.
Vitamin B2 (Riboflavin) - 5-10 mg. May be deficient and can cause depression.
Vitamin B12 - 50-100 mcg. May cause depression at low levels.

Vitamin C - 500-2000 mg. Low levels may cause depression, tiredness, irritability and general ill-health

Calcium - 600-1200 mg. Supplementation is especially effective for post-menopausal and post-delivery depression and depression among the elderly.

Iron - 10-25 mg. Chronic deficiency, most commonly associated in women with menstrual problems, is associated with marked depression in monamine oxidase activity in the brain and the development of depression.

Magnesium - 400-800 mg. Magnesium deficiency is associated with depression and it helps to maintain proper serotonin levels in the brain.

Potassium - 1000-2000 mg. Low levels can cause depression, weakness, fatigue and tearfulness.

Food Supplements
(Daily unless otherwise stated)

Adrenal glandular extract - 500-1000 mg. Helps to support and stimulate adrenal gland function. It is the major gland responsible for helping the body respond to stress.

Digestive enzymes and/or hydrochloric acid - 1-2 capsules before each meal. May be deficient and can impair digestion and absorption of essential nutrients.

Omega-3 oils (flaxseed, fish oil) - 1500-3000 mg. May be deficient. Helps to supply essential fatty acids.

Omega-6 oils (evening primrose, borage oil) - 1500-3000 mg. May be deficient. Helps to supply essential fatty acids.

Phenylalanine - 500-1000 mg. An amino acid that is used to make the brain neurotransmitter, dopamine. Supplementation may help to elevate moods and decrease depression.

Tryptophan - 1000-3000 mg. An amino acid that is used to make the brain neurotransmitter, serotonin.

Tyrosine - 3000-6000 mg. An amino acid that is used to make the brain neurotransmitter, dopamine. Supplementation may help to elevate moods and help to alleviate depression.

Herbal Medicines

Specific plants and plant derivatives may be useful in treating mild to moderate depression. **Green tea (Camellia nitida), Cola nut (Kola** nitida), and Ma Huang (Epehdra sinensis) contain caffeine and other natural stimulants that help to stimulate the nervous system and increase arousal. **Hops (Humulus lupulus), Passion flower (Passiflora incarnata), Skullcap (Scutellaria lateriflora) and Valerian (Valerian officinalis)** are natural muscle relaxants that help to relax muscles, improve sleep quality and induce relaxation. **St. John's wort (Hypericum perforatum)** has mood elevating effects and is useful in treating mild to moderate depression. A standardized extract of Hypericum perforatum (4:1) is recommended at a dosage of 1500-3000 mg per day. One or more these herbal medicines may be consumed as a tea, tincture, fluid extract, solid extract or supplement.

Highly Recommended

Avoid food and environmental sensitivities and allergies / avoid white sugar and refined carbohydrates / eat whole and unprocessed foods / multi vitamin and mineral complex / vitamin B-complex / vitamin B-6 / vitamin B12 / phenylalanine / tyrosine / St. John's wort / Valerian.

CHAPTER 17

Diabetes

Diabetes is a condition characterized by an abnormality in sugar utilization and is associated with increased blood sugar levels.

Approximately 5 to 10% of the population are diabetics by this definition. The most common form of diabetes is non-insulin dependent diabetes mellitus (NIDDM) or adult onset diabetes. Approximately 90% of individuals with blood sugar abnormalities are non-insulin dependent diabetics. Insulin dependent diabetes mellitus (IDDM) or juvenile onset diabetes has its onset in childhood or early adulthood. Approximately 10% of individuals with blood sugar abnormalities are insulin dependent diabetics.

Diabetes is due to a problem with the hormone insulin. Insulin is a small hormone produced in the pancreas. Insulin is passed into the blood in response to a rise in blood sugar levels. Insulin promotes the storage and uptake of sugar and amino acids, increases protein and fat production and inhibits fat and sugar breakdown. Non-insulin dependent diabetes is associated with an abnormality in insulin production, release and sensitivity of the body to insulin. Insulin dependent diabetes is strictly due to an abnormality in the production of insulin. The pancreas does not produce enough insulin to meet the body's needs.

Individuals with NIDDM are not dependent on insulin and are not prone to acidosis. Although most individuals are over the age of 40 years, onset can occur in younger individuals. Behavior and environmental factors appear to be involved in the development of NIDDM. Especially prominent is the role of excessive food intake and the development of obesity in 60 to 90% of diabetics. Insulin levels may be normal or variable and abnormal response to insulin by the body is common.

Individuals with IDDM are dependent on insulin and are prone to acidosis in the blood. Insulin therapy is required. Without insulin the body partially breaks down fat in a process called ketoacidosis. Toxic byproducts called ketones are produced that result in acidic blood. Viral infection and autoimmune disorders have been linked to the development of IDDM. There is a strong genetic predisposition in developing IDDM.

Diabetics are at increased risk for the development of atherosclerosis (hardening of the arteries), stroke, heart disease, high blood pressure, kidney failure, retinopathy (disorders of the retina of the eye), skin infections and ulcers and other serious complications.

Three classic signs of diabetes include increased frequency of urination, increased thirst with increased fluid intake and increased appetite with increased consumption of food. Other symptoms of diabetes include blurred vision, yeast infection and persistent skin infection. The diagnosis of diabetes is based upon the finding of persistently elevated blood sugar levels. Fasting blood sugar should be within the normal limits of 80 to 120 mg/dl. A reading above the upper limit is suggestive of diabetes. A glucose tolerance test (GTT) measures blood sugar levels for several hours after an individual consumes a quantity of sugar. Persistently elevated blood sugar levels is diagnostic of diabetes.

Conventional medical treatment of diabetes focuses on the replacement of insulin. IDDM are dependent on insulin supplementation. NIDDM generally do not require insulin supplementation. NIDDM are frequently prescribed oral hypoglycemic drugs that reduce blood sugar levels. Commonly prescribed oral hypoglycemic drugs include Diabeta (glyburide), Diabinese (chlorpropamide), Dymelor (acetohexamide), Orinase (tolbutamide) and Tolinase (tolazamide).

Lifestyle

Stress can aggravate diabetes and raise blood sugar levels. Stressors should be identified and eliminated. Exercise should be a part of daily routine and is a great way to reduce stress, lose weight and build self esteem. A conscious effort to exercise every day, such as walking, swimming, cycling, hiking or other activity for at least 30 minutes, should be made.

Diet

Avoid white sugar, refined carbohydrates, chocolate, coffee, tea, alcohol, colas, fats and oils, white flour, processed foods. Increase consumption of whole, unprocessed foods, grains, legumes and vegetables. 70 to 75% of calories should come from complex carbohydrates, 15 to 20% from protein and the remaining 5 to 10% from fat. Additionally total fiber intake should be increased up to 100 grams per day.

Vitamins and Minerals
(Daily unless otherwise stated)

Vitamin B1 (Thiamine) - 10-25 mg. Required for proper sugar utilization in the body.
Vitamin B3 (Niacin) - 25-50 mg. May be deficient and is required for the production of glucose tolerance factor (GTF) which works in concert with insulin in regulating blood sugar levels.
Vitamin B6 (Pyridoxine) - 25-50 mg. May be low especially with individuals prone to developing neurological disorders.
Vitamin B12 - 10-50 mcg. Supplementation may benefit individuals with diabetic neuropathy.
Vitamin C - 250-500 mg. May be deficient and is required for proper crosslinking of connective tissue and immune function. Helps to prevent atherosclerosis and improve glucose tolerance.
Vitamin E - 400-800 IU. A powerful antioxidant. Diabetics may have increased requirements.

Chromium - 200-400 mcg. A necessary component of glucose tolerance factor (GTF) that is important in regulating blood sugar levels. Supplementation has been shown to improve glucose tolerance.
Copper - 2-3 mg. Deficiency associated with low glucose tolerance.
Magnesium - 400-800 mg. Involved in sugar breakdown and utilization. May be low especially in individuals prone to diabetic retinopathy.
Manganese - 2-3 mg. Involved in sugar breakdown and utilization.
Phosphorus - 2-5 gm. Deficiency can cause impaired glucose response.
Potassium - 1000-2000 mg. Deficiency is associated with decreased insulin levels.
Zinc - 10-25 mg. Helps to breakdown and utilize sugar. Depleted at a higher rate in diabetics.

Food Supplements
(Daily unless otherwise stated)

Bioflavonoids - 500-1000 mg. Works synergistically with vitamin C in promoting healthy connective tissue. Important in preventing blood vessel disorders associated with diabetes including diabetic retinopathy.
Brewer's Yeast - 5-10 gm. High in chromium and one of the richest sources of glucose tolerance factor. Supplementation has been shown to improve glucose tolerance and fat metabolism.
Co-enzyme Q10 - 30-60 mg. May deficient in some diabetics and supplementation may be beneficial.

Fiber - 20-50 gm. Helps to increase stool transit time through the digestive system, increase feeling of fullness, decrease appetite and decrease absorption of sugar into the body.

Glutathione - 500-1000 mg. A powerful antioxidant. Levels are frequently low in diabetics.

Omega-3 oils (flaxseed, fish oil) - 1000-3000 mg. Involved in fat metabolism and supplementation may increase insulin sensitivity and improve response to increased sugar levels.

Omega-6 oils (evening primrose, borage oil) - 1000-3000 mg. Involved in fat metabolism and supplementation may increase insulin sensitivity and improve response to increased sugar levels.

Herbal Medicines

Specific plants and plant derivatives may be useful in treating diabetes and controlling blood sugar levels. **Garlic (Allium sativum) and Onions** significantly reduce blood sugar levels, decrease total cholesterol, decrease triglycerides and increase HDL cholesterol. Garlic lowers blood sugar levels by increasing insulin release from the pancreas and by sparing insulin degradation in the liver. This method of action is similar to sulfonylurea drugs used to treat NIDDM. **Bitter melon (Momordica charantia)** is a fruit that has been traditionally used to treat diabetes throughout Asia. Consumption of this fruit consistently decreases blood sugar levels. Bitter melon lowers blood sugar levels by inhibiting sugar uptake from the digestive system. This method of action is similar to phlorizin, a drug used to treat NIDDM. **Fenugreek (Trigonella foenum graecum)** is an aromatic herb cultivated in the Mediterranean and Asia. Fenugreek seeds reduce blood sugar levels by increasing insulin production in the pancreas. **Bilberry (Vaccinium Myrtillus)** is a cousin to the huckleberry and blueberry. These plants have been traditionally used to treat diabetes and are effective in stabilizing connective tissue. One or more of these herbal medicines may be consumed as a tea, tincture, fluid extract, solid extract or supplement.

Highly Recommended

Begin a daily exercise program / avoid white sugar, refined carbohydrates, fats and oils / increase consumption of whole and unprocessed foods / multiple vitamin and mineral supplement / vitamin B3 / vitamin C / chromium / brewer's yeast / fiber / omega-3 oils / Garlic / Bitter melon.

CHAPTER 18

Diarrhea

Diarrhea is the condition of rapid movement of fecal matter through the intestines resulting in abnormally frequent evacuations of watery stools. Poor absorption of water, nutrients and electrolytes occurs.

Diarrhea can occur to anyone at any age. Acute attacks of diarrhea can last one to two weeks in duration. Chronic diarrhea can last for several months in duration. Foreign travel and drinking water is a frequent cause of diarrhea.

Symptoms of diarrhea include frequent and watery bowel movements, abdominal cramps and generalized weakness. Other symptoms vary depending on the cause, duration and severity of the illness and the part of the intestines affected. Fever, nausea, vomiting, lack of hunger, inability to eat and weight loss can occur with infectious diarrhea. The stools often contain mucous and may contain blood. Complications of diarrhea include electrolyte (sodium, potassium, magnesium, chloride) loss, dehydration and metabolic acidosis. In severe cases loss of consciousness, coma and fatal heart arrhythmias can occur. Proper diagnosis of the cause of diarrhea and appropriate treatment is necessary.

Stool is the normal end product of digestion and is stored in the colon and rectum. Stool is composed of 60 to 90% water and the remaining solid matter consisting of inorganic matter, undigested roughage, fat, protein, dried constituents of digestive juices and dead bacteria. Diarrhea occurs when there is increased fluid content of the stool and increased frequency of bowel movements.

Diarrhea may be caused by many different factors including local irritation to the intestines, malabsorption of certain foods, damage to the intestinal wall and emotional disorders. Local irritation to the intestines can be caused by bacterial or viral infection and chemical agents including a variety of different drugs. Damage to the intestinal wall can be caused by Crohn's disease, ulcerative colitis, tuberculosis, lymphoma and cancer. Malabsorption of fats, bile salts, lactose, mannitol, sorbitol and other sugars and carbohydrates can result in diarrhea. Altered intestinal transit time resulting in rapid movement of material can be caused by surgery including bowel or small intestine resection, stomach surgery and use of certain drugs including the antibiotic tetracycline. Emotional factors such as stress and anxiety can cause increased movement of material through the intestines and increased secretion of mucous in the colon. Irritable bowel syndrome is one of the most common causes of chronic diarrhea. Other less common causes of diarrhea include pancreatic disease, liver disease, hyperthyroidism, pelvic inflammatory diseases, diabetes mellitus, heavy metal toxicity, food allergies, malnutrition, increase consumption of low calorie sweetners and laxative abuse. Since diarrhea is a symptom and not a disease, further laboratory and diagnostic procedures may be necessary to determine the exact cause of the condition.

Conventional medical treatment of diarrhea focuses on drug therapy to alleviate the symptoms. Mild cases of diarrhea of short duration can be treated conservatively with a bland diet, increased intake of liquids and the administration of kaolin-pectin compounds to relieve the symptoms. Imodium (loperamide), Lomotil (diphenoxylate), paregoric (camphorated opium tincture) and codeine phosphate are frequently prescribed to decrease movement of material through the intestines and relieve muscle cramps. Antibiotics are prescribed to inhibit the growth of bacteria that may be causing diarrhea. Intravenous electrolyte replacement may be necessary in severe forms of diarrhea.

Lifestyle

Stress can aggravate diarrhea. Stressors should be identified and reduced. Exercise, yoga, meditation, biofeedback and other techniques may be useful in reducing stress and aiding digestion.

Rest may be necessary if the the diarrhea is caused by an infectious agent. Rest and sleep as needed.

Diet

Avoid white sugar and refined carbohydrates, coffee, tea and other stimulants, spicy foods, fatty foods, wheat, milk and other dairy products. Foods such as rice, rolled oats, yogurt, vegetable soups and steamed vegetables may be beneficial. Increase liquid consumption including water, broth, vegetable juice and diluted, unsweetened fruit juice. Yogurt and kefir and apple sauce may be beneficial in replacing electrolytes and

70

bacteria in children. A fluid drink consisting of 5 ml (1 tsp) salt, 5 ml (1 tsp) sodium bicarbonate, 20 ml (4 tsp) sugar in 1 liter of water is beneficial in replacing lost electrolytes. Another electrolyte replacement drink consisting of tomato juice, sauerkraut and carrot juice may be beneficial.

Vitamins and Minerals
(Daily unless otherwise stated)

Vitamin A - 10,000-20,000 IU. May be deficient.
B-complex - 50-100 mg. May be deficient. Intramuscular or intravenous injections may be beneficial.
Folic acid - 5-20 mg. May be deficient.
Vitamin C - 500-3000 mg. Helps to stimulate the immune system and has antibacterial and antiviral effects. Do not consume in large doses because the acid can be irritating and can cause diarrhea.
Vitamin D - 200-400 IU. May be deficient and is necessary for proper calcium absorption.
Vitamin E - 400-800 IU. May be deficient. Helps to decrease inflammation in the intestines.

Calcium - 800-1200 mg. May be deficient and supplementation helps to relieve abdominal cramps.
Magnesium - 400-800 mg. May be deficient and supplementation helps to relieve abdominal cramps.
Potassium - 75-150 mg. May be deficient and deficiency can cause heart arrhythmias.

Food Supplements
(Daily unless otherwise stated)

Charcoal tablets - 4-8 tablets. Helps to bind bacterial and viral toxins produced in the intestines. Do not consume with vitamins, minerals or other supplements.
Digestive enzymes and/or Hydrochloric acid - 1-2 capsules with each meal. May be deficient. Necessary for proper digestion and absorption of nutrients.
Fiber (psyllium, guar gum, oat bran) - 10-30 gm. Helps to increase stool mass and absorb water lost with diarrhea.
Lactobacillus acidophilus - 2-4 capsules between meals. Important for repopulating the intestines and colon of friendly bacteria that do not produce disease.

Herbal Medicines

Specific plants and plant derivatives may be useful in treating diarrhea. **Garlic (Allium sativum) and Goldenseal (Hydrastis canadensis)** are potent antibiotics that are effective in treating infectious diarrhea caused by bacteria and viruses. Robert's formula consisting of **Comfrey (Symphytum officinalis), Geranium (Geranium maculatum), Goldenseal (Hydrastis canadensis), Marshmallow (Althea officinalis), Pokeroot (Phytolacca americana), Purple coneflower (Echinacea angustifolia)** and **Slippery Elm (Ulmus fulva)** helps to soothe the irritated intestinal lining. **Balm (Melissa officinalis), Chamomile (Matricaria chamomilla), Fennel (Foeniculm vulgare), Ginger (Zingiber officinalis)** and **Peppermint (Mentha piperita)** are carminative herbs that help to relieve flatulence, abdominal cramps and soothe inflammed intestines. One or more of these herbal medicines may be consumed as a tea, tincture, fluid extract, solid extract or supplement.

Highly Recommended

Fluid and electrolyte re-hydration / multiple vitamin and mineral complex / folic acid / charcoal tablets / fiber / Lactobacillus acidophilus / Chamomile / Comfrey / Garlic / Goldenseal / Marshmallow / Peppermint / Slippery elm.

CHAPTER 19

Ear Infection

An ear infection is a viral or bacterial infection of the middle ear, usually following an upper respiratory infection. Ear infection is also called otitis media. An ear infection of the outer ear called otitis externa can also occur.

An ear infection can occur at any time at any age. It is most common in children from three months to three years and occurs in 20 to 40% of children under the age of 6 years. Recurrent ear infections may occur.

Ear infections may be acute or chronic depending on the duration of the infection. An acute ear infection lasts one to two weeks and usually follows an acute cold or sore throat. Symptoms include irritability, earache, throbbing pain, dizziness, nausea, vomiting, diarrhea, chills and fever as high as 39.0 degrees celcius (103 degrees fahrenheit). The eardrum is usually red, inflammed and bulging. Complications of an acute ear infection can include a ruptured ear drum, fluid discharge from the ear, hearing loss, mastoiditis, brain infection, meningitis and facial paralysis. An acute ear infection requires proper diagnosis and appropriate treatment. A chronic ear infection generally lasts longer than two weeks and can last several months. Chronic ear infection is also called fluid ear or serous otitis media. It is usually caused by incomplete resolution of an acute ear infection. A history of allergies is common. Symptoms include decreased hearing, dullness and a feeling of fullness or fluid in the ear. Chronic ear infections are usually painless. The eardrum is usually dull, retracted and transluscent.

Ear infections may be caused by a virus or bacteria that invades the middle ear. 40% of acute ear infections are caused by the bacteria Streptococcus pneumoniae and 20% are caused by Hemophilus influenza. Food and inhalant allergies are common in children with recurrent ear infections. 85 to 95% of children with recurrent ear infections have food allergies and sensitivities. Food allergies to milk and dairy products, eggs, wheat, chicken, corn, citrus fruits and peanuts are common. 10 to 20% of children of these children have inhalant allergies to dust, molds, pollens and other airborne substances. Early bottle feeding of children is associated with the development of recurrent ear infections. A cow's milk intolerance or allergy most likely develops. Breast feeding a minimum of six months is recommended. Mother's milk contains natural antibiotic and immune fortifying substances that help to develop the child's immune system. Also avoid feeding on the child's back because this may cause regurgitation of fluid into the eustachian tube.

The eustachian tube is a narrow tube that connects the middle ear to the mouth and nose. The function of this tube is to equalize pressure on either side of the eardrum. In children the tube is shorter, wider and more horizontal than in adults. This makes children especially prone to infections of the middle ear that originate in the nose and mouth and travel through the tube. The eustachian tube normally opens three to four times per minute as a result of swallowing. This allows for the equalization of pressure between either side of the eardrum and the clearing of fluid from the middle ear. Abnormal patency of the eustachian tube leads to ear infections. Allergies can cause the swelling and blockage of the eustachian tube. This leads to the accumulation of fluid in the middle ear. Fluid builds up and provides a good growth medium for bacteria.

Conventional medical treatment of ear infection focuses on drug therapy. Antibiotics including penicillin, ampicillin, amoxicillin, erythromycin and tetracycline are frequently prescribed. Non-prescription ear drops, decongestants and antihistamines may be effective in relieving the symptoms associated ear infection. Myringotomy is a surgical treatment in which tubes are placed in the eardrum to allow drainage of fluid from the middle ear. This surgical treatment is reserved for children with recurrent ear infections that don't respond to drug therapy. Surgical treatment may be necessary in some cases.

Lifestyle

Local application of heat to the affected ear is beneficial in reducing the symptoms of the infection. Warming the ear with warm packs or blowing warm air into the canal may be beneficial.

Recurrent ear infections are more common in homes where cigarette smoking is more prevalent. Avoid secondary cigarette smoke.

Don't swim or get water in the ear while you have an infection. Keep the ear dry. Cotton placed in the ear may help to keep the ear dry and warm.

Diet

Food allergies and sensitivities are associated with ear infections. Avoid all milk and dairy products, eggs, wheat, corn, citrus fruits and peanuts. Milk and dairy products are also mucous forming and can promote the blockage of the eustachian tube. Decrease consumption of white sugar and refined carbohydrates including honey, fructose, molasses, brown sugar, dried fruit and concentrated fruit juices. A food allergy or sensitivity test may be necessary to determine specific foods. Increase consumption of whole, unprocessed foods. Also increase consumption of garlic and onions for their antibiotic effects.

Vitamins and Minerals
(Daily unless otherwise stated)

Vitamin A - 10,000-20,000 IU. Helps to increase immune function.
B-complex - 25-50 mg. Helps the body respond to stress and infection.
Beta-carotene - 20,000-120,000 IU. Dose should be age dependent. 20,000 IU times age. Precursor of vitamin A. Helps to increase immune function. Does not produce toxicity like vitamin A.
Vitamin C - 500-3000 mg. Helps to increase immune function and has antiviral properties. Dose age dependent. 500 mg times age of child.

Manganese - 5-10 mg. May be deficient. Deficiency has been associated with the development of ear infections.
Selenium - 50-100 mg. May be deficient.
Zinc - 5-30 mg. Dose should be age dependent. 5 mg times age of child. Helps to increase immune function and fight infection. Also important in wound healing.

Food Supplements
(Daily unless otherwise stated)

Bioflavonoids - 250-500 mg. Helps to increase immune function. Works synergistically with vitamin C.
Omega-6 oils (evening primrose, borage oil) - 1000-3000 mg. Helps to decrease pain and inflammation in the middle ear. Also helps to dissolve chronically hardened ear wax.
Thymus glandular extract - 50-300 mg. Important for proper immune function. Dose should be age dependent. 50 mg times age of child.

Herbal Medicines

Specific plants and plant derivatives may be useful in treating common ear infections. **Garlic (Allium sativum), Goldenseal (Hydrastis canadensis), Licorice (Glycyrrhiza glabra), Mullein (Verbascum thapsus), Purple coneflower (Echinacea angustifolia) and White oak bark (Quercus alba)** contain antibiotic properties that are effective against ear infections. A few drops of warm **mullein oil** or **garlic and olive oil** into the affected ear three times daily is effective. Warm **glycerin oil** also helps to moisten and soothe the inflammed ear drum. A popular ear oil combination containing 1 part **Indian tobacco (Lobelia inflata),** 1 part **Myrrh (Commiphora molmol),** 1 part **Sassafras (Sassafras officinalis),** 1 part **Wintergreen oil (Gaultheria procumbens)** and 4 parts **olive oil** may be used. Place 4 drops in the affected ear three times daily. Put cotton in the ears after placing the oil there. One or more of these herbal medicines may be consumed as a tea, tincture, fluid extract, solid extract or supplement.

Highly Recommended

Avoid food sensitivities and allergies / Avoid white sugar and refined carbohydrates / Decrease consumption of milk, cheese and dairy / vitamin A / beta-carotene / vitamin C / zinc / thymus glandular extract / Echinacea / Garlic / Goldenseal / Mullein oil.

CHAPTER 20

Eczema

Eczema or atopic dermatitis is a general term for any inflammatory process involving the skin. Early signs of eczema include redness, itching, minute blisters, weeping, oozing and crusting of affected skin areas. Later signs of eczema include scaling, hardening and often pigmentation.

Eczema is a common allergic reaction in children, but it also occurs in adults, usually in a more severe form. Eczema is estimated to affect 2 to 5% of the population and affects males and females equally. Childhood eczema often begins in infancy, the rash appearing on the face, neck and folds on the elbows and knees. The rash may disappear by itself when the offending allergy is removed. However, in severe forms of the disease the rash may become more extensive and in some instances cover the entire surface of the body.

The cause of this disease is not entirely known. Allergies to food and environment are known to aggravate eczema. Genetics plays a strong role in the development and the severity of eczema. An individual with eczema usually has another family member with the same condition. Eczema can be aggravated by stress, illness, food allergies, environmental allergies, infection, surgery and certain drugs.

Conventional medical treatment of eczema focuses on the use of non-steroidal anti-inflammatory drugs and cortisone to decrease inflammation of the skin.

Lifestyle

Stress can aggravate eczema. Stressors should be identified and decreased. Exercise should be a part of daily routine and is a great way to reduce stress. Other forms of stress reduction including deep breathing exercises, meditation, biofeedback and yoga should also be explored.

Environmental allergens should be identified and decreased. Allergies to pollen, dust, molds, animals and sensitivities to pesticides, insecticides and other chemicals in the environment can also aggravate eczema. A conscious effort to limit exposure to these allergens should be made.

Diet

Food sensitivities and allergies can aggravate eczema. Avoid white sugar, refined carbohydrates, fats, coffee tea, chocolate, alcohol, citrus fruits, nuts, corn, tomato, soy, potato, wheat and any other foods that can aggravate eczema. Increase consumption of whole, unprocessed foods, fresh vegetables and fruits. A food sensitivity or allergy test may required to determine offending foods.

Vitamins and Minerals
(Daily unless otherwise stated)

Vitamin A - 10,000-50,000 IU. Required for the development and maintenance of healthy skin. Inhibits the production of toxins that can aggravate eczema.
Vitamin B-complex - 50-100 mg. Helps the body respond to stress.
Vitamin C - 500-2000 mg. Used to make connective tissue and skin strong. Supplementation may be beneficial.
Vitamin E - 400-800 IU. A powerful antioxidant that prevents free radical damage to the skin and is necessary for proper skin nutrition.

Food Supplements
(Daily unless otherwise stated)

Digestive enzymes and/or Hydrochloric acid - 1-2 capsules with each meal. May be deficient and supplementation may help to improve digestion and absorption of food and vitamins and minerals.
Omega-3 oils (flaxseed, fish oil) - 1000-3000 mg. A rich source of essential oils that are utalized by the skin. Involved in fat metabolism and decreases inflammation of the skin.
Omega-6 oils (evening primrose, borage oil) - 1000-3000 mg. A rich source of essential oils that are utalized by the skin. Involved in fat metabolism and decreases inflammation of the skin.

Herbal Medicines

Specific plants and plant derivatives may be useful in treating eczema and relieving symptoms associated with this disease. Plants that have been traditionally used to treat eczema include **Burdock (Arctium lappa), Chaparral (Larrea tridentata), Dandelion (Taraxacum officinale), Sarsaparilla (Smilax officinale) and Yellow dock (Rumex crispus).** Although the constituents of these plants differ, they are collectively known as alteratives or blood cleansers. They help to increase elimination of toxins through the skin. One or more of these herbal medicines may be consumed as a tea, tincture, solid extract, fluid extract or supplement.

Topical application of **Aloe (Aloe vera), Comfrey root (Symphytum officinale), Licorice root (Glycyrrhiza glabra) and Marshmallow (Althea officinalis)** may be beneficial. These herbal medicines are soothing and healing and help to decrease inflammation of the skin.

Highly Recommended

Eliminate all food sensitivities and allergies / vitamin A / vitamin E / omega-3 oils / omega-6 oils / Burdock / Comfrey / Dandelion / Licorice / Yellow dock.

CHAPTER 21

Endometriosis

Endometriosis is the condition of having uterine tissue in abnormal locations. Another term used to describe abnormal uterine growth is fibroids. The most common location of uterine tissue is in the uterine musculature itself and around the ovaries and fallopian tubes, but can also occur in and around the urinary bladder, rectum, pelvic cavity floor and peritoneum. Location of uterine tissue beyond the pelvic area is rare, but does occur in some instances.

Approximately 10% of the adult female population have endometriosis of varying degrees and severity. Endometriosis is cross-cultural and affects women of many different races and nationalities. Endometriosis most commonly occurs in women during their reproductive years. Age of onset of women suffering from endometriosis is between the late 20's to the early 40's. Most women who have endometriosis never have been pregnant. Endometriosis occurs in between 25 to 50% of infertile females.

The exact cause of endometriosis is unknown. Genetics is known to play an important role and endometriosis tends to occur at a higher rate when another family member has the disease. Retrograde menstrual flow is the most likely cause of endometriosis. During the normal female menstrual cycle, uterine tissue is built up and prepared in anticipation of fertilization of the female egg. If fertilization does not occur the uterus sheds its lining and menstruation occurs. It is currently believed that retrograde menstruation of uterine tissue into the fallopian tubes, ovary and pelvic area occurs. The deposition of tissue in these areas leads to the symptoms associated with endometriosis. Other theories suggest that uterine tissue is spread by blood and lymph. A high fat diet has also been associated with the development of endometriosis. A retroflexed uterus and the development of adhesions between pelvic organs and tissues is often a complication of endometriosis.

Intermenstrual and menstrual pelvic pain is the most common symptom of endometriosis. Pain in the lower abdomen, the low back, the uterus and other pelvic organs is common. Difficult and painful menstruation, pain between menstrual cycles, abdominal cramping, painful intercourse, the passage of large clots and shreds of tissue during menses, constipation, nausea, vomiting and infertility are other signs of endometriosis. Anemia often occurs. The only definitive way to diagnose endometriosis is by pelvic exam and laparoscopy. A laparoscopy is a surgical procedure by which the pelvic area is examined.

Conventional medical treatment of endometriosis includes the use of birth control pills and the steroid hormone, danazol, to suppress the pain and inflammation. Unpleasant side effects of hormone therapy include weight gain, bloating, fluid retention, breast tenderness, oily skin and acne. Surgical excision of the abnormal uterine tissue and total uterine hysterectomy are often recommended. Surgery is only moderately effective in many cases. It is often very difficult to excise all abnormal uterine tissue. Following surgery many women have recurrent pain and discomfort.

Lifestyle

Visualization techniques should be used in conjunction with diet and supplementation. Stressors should be identified and reduced. Exercise should by a part of daily routine and is a great way to reduce stress and get in shape if overweight. Other stress reduction techniques such as deep breathing exercises, meditation, biofeedback and yoga should be utalized.

Diet

Avoid white sugar, refined carbohydrates, salt, fats and oils, nuts, chocolate, coffee, tea, alcohol and red meat. A high fat diet is associated with the development of endometriosis and fat should be less than 20% of total caloric intake. Increase consumption of complex carbohydrates, whole, unprocessed foods, vegetables and fruits.

Vitamins and Minerals
(Daily unless otherwise stated)

Vitamin A - 10,000-25,000 IU. Helps to maintain the lining of the vagina and uterus. Also acts as a potent antioxidant and improves immune function.

Beta-carotene - 50,000-100,000 IU. Helps to maintain the lining of the vagina and uterus. Also acts as a potent antioxidant and improves immune function. Does not have the toxic side effects that vitamin A does in high doses.

Vitamin B-complex - 50-100 mg. May be deficient and supplementation helps the body respond to stress.

Vitamin B-6 - 25-50 mg. Used by the liver activate and inactivate hormones such as estrogen and detoxify toxins.

Vitamin C - 500-2000 mg. Important in the development and maintenance of connective tissue.

Vitamin E - 400-1,200 IU. Has anti-inflammatory activity and helps to regulate estrogen levels.

Calcium - 800-1200 mg. Needed for proper development of tissues such as the uterus. Helps to prevent pain and cramping.

Magnesium - 400-800 mg. Needed for proper development of tissues such as the uterus. Helps to prevent pain and cramping.

Food Supplements
(Daily unless otherwise stated)

Omega-3 oils (flaxseed, fish oil) - 1000-3000 mg. Involved in fat metabolism and decreases inflammation and cramping in the uterus.

Omega-6 oils (evening primrose, borage oil) - 1000-3000 mg. Involved in fat metabolism and decreases inflammation and cramping in the uterus.

Herbal Medicines

Specific plants and plant derivatives may be useful in treating endometriosis. Many plants contain natural estrogens and estrogen precursors. Plant estrogens, though less active than synthetic estrogens due exert biological activity. When there are high levels of circulating estrogens in the body, this can lead to increased uterine growth and the development of fibroids. Plant estrogens can decrease the body's estrogens by competively inhibiting the activity of estrogen. Plant estrogens can be a natural source of estrogen that can help to minimize the symptoms of endometriosis. Many of these plants have been used traditionally to minimize uterine pain and discomfort. Extracts of **Dong quai (Angelica sinensis), Peony root (Paeonia lactiflora), Black haw bark (Viburnum prunifolium), Cramp bark (Viburnum opulus) Blue cohosh (Caulophyllum thalictroides), Black cohosh (Cimicifuga racemosa),**

Unicorn root (Aletris farinosa), Chaste tree (Vitex agnus castus), Red raspberry (Rubus strigosus) have been used. One or more of these herbal medicines can be consumed as a tea, tincture, fluid extract, solid extract or a supplement.

Highly Recommended

Avoid white sugar, refined carbohydrates, caffeine containing beverages, fats and oils / vitamin A / beta-carotene / vitamin E / calcium / magnesium / omega-3 oils / omega-6 oils / Dong quai.

CHAPTER 22

Epilepsy

Epilepsy is a recurrent nervous system disorder resulting from abnormal electrical activity of the brain. It is characterized by sudden, brief attacks of altered consciousness, convulsive motor activity, sensory phenomenom or inappropriate behavior.

Epilepsy is believed to occur in 0.5 to 2.0% of the population. Over 70% of those having epilepsy experience their first attack during childhood or after the age of 50 years. The type of seizure varies with age of onset.

Epilepsy is not a specific disease, but rather a group of symptoms that are manifestations of any number of conditions that overstimulate the nerve cells of the brain. The symptoms of epilepsy vary depending on the area of the brain where the abnormal discharge occurs. Seizures are classified according to where they occur and the physical symptoms that are displayed.

Grand mal or tonic clonic seizures last approximately 2 to 5 minutes in duration and are characterized by bilateral jerks of the arms and legs. There may be an aura before the seizure with apprehension, mood changes and visual disturbances occurring hours to days before the seizure begins. During the seizure there is loss of consciousness, rapid eye fluttering and rapid muscle spasms. The individual may be incontinent and in danger of biting his tongue. These seizures may appear at any age. After the seizure the individual may be confused, sleepy, have headaches and muscle soreness.

Petit mal seizures last approximately 10 to 30 seconds with transient loss of consciousness, eye fluttering, and with or without muscle spasms. They are genetic in origin, commonly occur in children between the ages of 5 and 12 years and disappear during puberty.

Infantile spasm seizures commonly occur in young children less than two years old. They are characterized by sudden flexion of the arms, forward flexion of the trunk and extension of the legs.

Partial or focal seizures are isolated seizures that occur in only one part of the brain. They are characterized by abnormalities in taste, smell, vision, hearing and a general dream-like or feeling of unreality. The most common site of this seizure is the temporal lobe in the brain. A jacksonian seizure is a specific type of partial seizure that is starts in the hand or feet and marches up the arm or leg.

Atonic or akinetic seizures are characterized by sudden, brief loss of body tone that can produce nodding of the head, weakness of the knees or total collapse and falling. The individual usually remains conscious during the attack. This type usually occurs in children.

Status epilepticus is a serious medical emergency when the seizures lasts for hours or days.

The exact cause of epilepsy is not known in 75% of individuals with this disorder. Any physical trauma including childbirth and a hit to the head can cause scarring of brain tissue and can cause epilepsy. A small area of scar tissue within the brain can act as a focus capable of generating abnormal electrical activity. This abnormal electrical activity can spread to other areas and given sufficient stimuli can cause a seizure. Other potential causes of seizures include acute infection, fever, heat stroke, central nervous system infections including meningitis, encephalitis, rabies, toxoplasmosis; metabolic disturbances including hypoglycemia, hypoparathyroidism and ketosis; heavy metal toxicity including lead, mercury and cadmium; excessive use of alcohol, lack of oxygen to the brain, hemorrhage and stroke. Seizures can also occur as withdrawal symptoms from chronic alcohol use, sedative-hypnotic drugs, tranquilizers and other drugs. Seizures can be precipitated by hyperventilation, physical stress from trauma, lack of sleep, poor nutrition, fever and illnesses, emotional stress, bright light, hormonal changes such as those occuring during menstruation and pregnancy, fluid and electrolyte imbalances, alcohol and other drugs. Another common trigger is inadequate dosage of an anti-epileptic drug or use of an ineffective drug.

Diagnosis of epilepsy is based upon history and the presence of physical signs including trauma, infection and fever. A family history, blood glucose and calcium abnormalities predispose to the development of epilepsy. It is confirmed by electroencephalogram (EEG), magnetic resonance imaging (MRI) and computerized tomography (CT) scan of the brain to identify abnormalities.

85

Conventional medical treatment of epilepsy focuses on drug therapy to inhibit seizures. Commonly prescribed anti-seizure medication include Phenytoin (dilantin), Amytal (phenobarbital), Nembutal (pentobarbital), Depakene (valproic acid), Tegretol (carbamazepine), Mysolim (primidone) and Zarontin (ethosuximide). Side effects of these drugs include nausea, vomiting, skin rash, digestive upset, lymph node enlargement, abnormal function of the liver and kidneys, suppression of bone marrow activity, blood cell dyscrasias, confusion, delerium and psychosis. Valium (diazepam) and other muscle relaxants are occasionally used.

Lifestyle

A normal lifestyle should be encouraged. Stress can initiate seizure activity. Stressors whould be identified and reduced. Moderate exercise, yoga, meditation and biofeedback are excellent ways to reduce stress. Driving of automobile is usually restricted until seizure free for at least one year.

Diet

A low carbohydrate and high fat diet may be beneficial. Overuse of stimulants such as coffee, tea and other caffeine containing beverages can stimulate attacks. Avoid white sugar and refined carbohydrates. Increase consumption of whole and unprocessed foods, vegetables and fruits. Food senstivities and allergies may be associated with the development of epileptic attacks. A food sensitivity test may be necessary to identify specific sensitivities. Food additives and perservatives may be associated with the development of seizures.

Vitamins and Minerals
(Daily unless otherwise stated)

Vitamin B-complex - 50-100 mg. May be deficient. Required by the brain and nervous system for many different functions.
Vitamin B6 (Pyridoxine) - 25-50 mg. Involved in many enzymatic processes of the brain and nervous system. Supplementation may be beneficial.
Folic acid - 400-800 mcg. May be deficient. Deficiency is commonly caused by use of anti-seizure drugs. Should be taken with vitamin B12.

Calcium - 800-1200 mg. Helps to exert a calming effect on the nervous system. Take together with magnesium.

Magnesium - 400-800 mg. May be deficient. Suppresses epileptic outbursts and helps to prevent muscle spasms. Exerts a calming effect on the nervous system.

Manganese - 5-10 mg. May be deficient.

Zinc - 10-25 mg. May be deficient. Deficiency is commonly caused by use of anti-seizure drugs. Poor absorption and diarrhea contribute to deficiency.

Food Supplements
(Daily unless otherwise stated)

Choline - 2-4 gm. Used for electrical conduction in the brain and nervous system. Supplementation may be beneficial.

Dimethyl glycine - 100-200 mg. Used as a precursor to calming neurotransmitters in the brain that helps to prevent epileptic outbursts. Also used in methionine metabolism in the liver.

Taurine - 500-1500 mg. Used as a calming neurotransmitter in the brain that helps to prevent epileptic outbursts. Helps to stablize the blood-brain barrier and prevent hypoglycemia.

Herbal Medicines

Specific plants and plant derivatives may useful in treating epilepsy and supplement drug therapy. **Catnip (Nepeta cataria), Chamomile (Matricaria chamomilla), Hops (Humulus lupulus), Passionflower (Passiflora incarnata), Skullcap (Scutellaria lateriflora) and Valerian (Valerian officinalis)** are beneficial. A Chinese patent herbal medicine formula called **Saiko-reishi** helps to decrease epileptic outbursts and is available as a tea. One or more of these herbal medicines may be consumed as a tea, tincture, fluid extract, solid extract or supplement.

Highly Recommended

Avoid white sugar, refined carbohydrates and caffeine containing beverages / vitamin B6 / calcium / magnesium / choline / taurine / Valerian / Saiko-reishi.

CHAPTER 23

Gallstones

Gallstones or cholelithiasis are stone-like masses that form in the gall bladder and lead to pain and inflammation. Acute inflammation of the gall bladder results in severe pain in the right upper abdominal region, fever, nausea, prostration and occasionally, jaundice. Chronic inflammation of the gall bladder results in habitual indigestion accompanied by flatulence and nausea. The indigestion is most evident after a heavy meal or a meal high in fat.

Gallstones affect 20% of all women and 8% of all men over the age of forty years. Over one million cases of gall stones are diagnosed annually in North America and 500,000 gall bladder operations are performed each year. Females, especially overweight females over the age of forty years are more likely to be affected than men.

Bile is a clear yellow, green or orange fluid produced in the liver. It is concentrated and stored in the gall bladder and is poured into the small intestine when it is needed for digestion. Bile helps to alkalinize the contents of the stomach and intestines and aids in the digestion and absorption of fats. Bile is composed of bile salts, cholesterol, phospholipids, bilirubin and electrolytes. Gallstones are formed in the gall bladder when there is too much cholesterol in bile. Cholesterol and protein in bile precipitate out of solution and form stones. The stones grow larger till they are large enough to cause pain and inflammation. Approximately 90% of gallstones are cholesterol stones.

Gallstone formation is the result of many years of a high fat diet and lifestyle. Gallstones may be asymptomatic and produce no symptoms for many years. Transient colicky pain in the upper right and mid-abdominal areas is usually the first symptom of stones. The pain may be dull to excruciating and may last for several hours and may radiate to the back and right shoulder blade. Nausea, vomiting, fever, and chills indicate an acute attack. Stones may block the outlet from the gall bladder and may pass though the duct into the small intestine. If they obstruct the outlet or duct then the pain may be excruciating and can lead to jaundice, pancreatitis and infection.

The exact cause of gallstone formation is not entirely known. High fat diet, obesity, and family history are strongly associated with the development of stones. Additional risk factors include use of estrogen and birth control pills, use of cholesterol reducing medication such as Lovastatin and Cholestyramine, diabetes, liver disease, pancreatic disease and pregnancy. Diagnosis of gallstones is usually based on history and location of pain. X-ray and ultrasound usually confirm the presumption of gall stones.

Conventional medical treatment of gallstones focuses on surgical operations to remove the gall bladder. Drugs such as Chenodeoxycholic acid (CDCA) and Chenodiol are occasionally used to dissolve the stones, but there use is limited. It is interesting to note that gall bladder surgeries are performed three times more commonly in North America than in Europe.

Lifestyle

Make exercise a part of daily routine. Regular exercise is a great way to lose weight and keep in shape. Exercise also helps to build self esteem and helps to lower cholesterol.

Diet

Decrease fats, especially saturated fat. Avoid sugar, refined carbohydrates, chocolate, alcohol, fats and oils, nuts, spicy foods, butter and margarine, cheese, milk and other dairy products. Avoid fried foods. Bake, broil, boil or steam foods. Food sensitivities, especially, onion, egg and pork, may also be associated with the development of gallstones. Increase consumption of whole, unprocessed foods, vegetables and fruits. Specifically increase consumption of beets, carrots, artichokes, radish and citrus fruits including lemon, orange and grapefruit. These foods may be consumed as fresh juices. These foods help to increase flow of bile and help to expel gallstones. Eat small meals and don't overeat.

Vitamins and Minerals
(Daily unless otherwise stated)

Vitamin B12 - 100-200 mcg. Deficiency contributes to gallstone formation.

Folic acid - 400-800 mcg. Deficiency contributes to gallstone formation.
Vitamin C - 500-1000 mg. Deficiency leads to gallstone formation.
Vitamin E - 400-800 IU. Deficiency leads to gallstone formation.

Food Supplements
(Daily unless otherwise stated)

Bile Salts - 3-6 capsules. Important for digestion and absorption of fat. Supplementation helps to increase solubility of bile.
Choline - 400-800 mg. Important for proper cholesterol metabolism and aids in fat digestion and absorption.
Digestive Enzymes and/or Hydrochloric acid - 1-2 capsules with each meal. May be deficient and supplementation helps to improve digestion and absorption of food.
Inositol - 400-800 mg. Important for proper cholesterol metabolism and aids in fat digestion and absorption.
Lecithin (Phophatidyl choline) - 5-10 gm. Helps to normalize the constituents of bile and aids in fat digestion and absorption.
Methionine - 500-1000 mg. Important for proper cholesterol and fat metabolism and aids in fat digestion and removal.
Omega-3 oils (flaxseed, fish oil) - 1000-3000 mg. Involved in fat metabolism and decreases inflammation in the gall bladder.
Omega-6 oils (evening primrose, borage oil) - 1000-3000 mg. Involved in fat metabolism and decreases inflammation in the gall bladder.
Taurine - 500-1500 mg. Increases the solubility of bile and helps to decrease stone formation.
Unsaturated Oils (olive, sunflower, flaxseed oil) - 5-10 gm. Aids in fat digestion and absorption. Also stimulates the gall bladder to contract to expel its contents into the intestines. A gall bladder flush consisting of 1 ounce of unsaturated oil to 4 ounces of lemon or grapefruit or apple cider vinegar is used to aid the gall bladder in passing gall stones. It is dangerous to try this flush without proper medical consent. A stone may become lodged in the neck of the gall baldder or the bile duct and can cause a medical emergency.

Herbal Medicines

Specific plants and plant derivatives may be useful in treating gall stones. Many plants have been used traditionally to treat gall bladder and liver disorders. **Artichoke (Cynara scolymus), Boldo (Peomus boldo), Dandelion (Taraxacum officinale), Fringe tree (Chionanthus** virginicus), Milk thistle (Silybum marianum), and Oregon grape root (Berberis aquifolium) stimulate flow of bile from the gall bladder. Celandine (Chelidonium majus), Chamomile (Matricaria chamomilla), Fennel (Foeniculum vulgare), Ginger (Zingiber officinale) and Peppermint (Mentha piperita) relax the bile duct and intestines and promote the passage of stones. One of more of these herbal medicines may be consumed as a tea, tincture, fluid extract, solid extract or supplement.

Highly Recommended

Avoid white sugar, refined carbohydrates, fats and oils / increase fiber intake / multiple vitamin and mineral complex / bile salts / choline / digestive enzymes and/or hydrochloric acid / lecithin / taurine / unsaturated oils / Artichoke / Celandine / Dandelion / Fringe tree / Milk thistle.

CHAPTER 24

Gout

Gout is a disease characterized by recurrent attacks of arthritis in which uric acid appears in excessive amounts in the blood and may be deposited in joints, tendons and other tissues.

Excessive levels of uric acid occur in the blood of 10 to 20% of the adult population. Gout occurs in 3 out of 1000 people. 95% of individuals with gout are males over the age of 30 years. Gout occurs infrequently in females.

The exact cause of gout is not fully understood. It is a disorder of the metabolism of purines. Purines are nitrogenous substances that are found in high concentrations in protein foods and the net product of their metabolism is uric acid. The uric acid, normally expelled by the kidneys in urine, is retained in the blood in excess amounts. Uric acid crystals are deposited in joints and tendons, where they form lumps called tophi. The uric acid crystals also predispose to the development of kidney stones and could permanently damage the kidney. Other factors associated with the development of gout include obesity, hereditary diseases such as Down's syndrome, glycogen storage disease, decreased kidney dysfunction, hyperthyroidism, hypothyroidism, hypertension, heart attack and excess exercise.

Gout may be precipitated by overindulgence in food and alcohol, fatigue, emotional stress, minor trauma, surgery, infection and administration of penicillin, insulin or diuretic drugs.

The acute form of gout usually begins suddenly, without warning. 70% of attacks involve the big toe of the foot, although other joints including the foot, ankle, knee, wrist and elbow may be involved. Throbbing, crushing and excruciating pain of affected joints occurs. Individuals suffering with gout may be bedridden or have difficulty walking due to the pain. Swelling, tenderness and inflammation of the overlying skin results. The skin may be a hot, shiny dusky red or purplish color. Slight fever, rapid heart beat, headache, chills and malaise can also be associated with gout.

The first attack of gout lasts a few days to several weeks. The symptoms usually disappear until the next attack. As the disease progresses, attacks tend to last longer and the interval between attacks becomes shorter. If left untreated a chronic form of gout can develop and persist for many years. Decreased range of motion and joint deformation can result. In 10 to 20% of those individuals with chronic gout, damage to the kidneys occurs as a result of kidney stone formation.

Conventional medical treatment of gout focuses on the use of drugs and surgery to alleviate symptoms associated with this disease. Drugs used include colchicine, allopurinol (Probenecid, Colbenemid), indomethacin, phenylbutazone and occasionally corticosteroids. Surgery to affected joints is occasionally performed when conservative therapy fails.

Lifestyle

Stress can aggravate attacks of gout. Stressors should be identified and reduced. Exercise, meditation, yoga and biofeedback are excellent ways to reduce stress.

Avoid aspirin and other salicylate pain killing drugs. They antagonize the excretion of uric acid from the kidneys.

Diet

A diet low in purines is strongly recommended. Avoid foods high in purines including all meats, especially organ meats and seafood, beans, legumes and peas. Decrease consumption of alcohol, especially beer. Decrease all sugar and refined carbohydrates including fructose, a fruit sugar. Decrease fats and proteins and increase consumption of complex carbohydrates. Avoid coffee and other stimulant beverages. Increase consumption of fruit and vegetables and whole, unprocessed foods. Increase daily fluid intake to at least 6 to 8 glasses of water. Alkalinizing the urine with water and sodium bicarbonate aids in increasing elimination of uric acid from the kidneys. Increase intake of cherries, blueberries, huckleberries and other dark berries. They contain natural bioflavonoids that help to decrease inflammation.

Vitamins and Minerals
(Daily unless otherwise stated)

Vitamin B-complex - 50-100 mg. Helps to decrease the body's susceptibility to stress.
Folic acid - 10-40 mg. Supplementation helps to decrease the production of uric acid.
Vitamin C - 500-3000 mg. Aids in the removal of uric acid by increasing the rate of excretion by the kidneys.
Vitamin E - 400-800 IU. Helps to decrease inflammation.

Food Supplements
(Daily unless otherwise stated)

Amino Acids (Alanine, aspartic acid, glutamic acid and glycine) - 2-4 gm. Decreases reabsorption of uric acid in the kidneys.
Bromelain - 500-1000 mg. Supplementation helps to decrease the production of uric acid. Also helps to reduce inflammation. Take between meals.
Omega-3 oils (flaxseed, fish oil) - 1000-3000 mg. A rich source of essential oils that is important for fat metabolism and helps to decrease inflammation.
Quercitin - 250-500 mg. A naturally occuring bioflavonoid that helps to decrease inflammation.

Herbal Medicines

Specific plants and plant derivatives may be useful in treating gout. Herbal diuretics increase excretion from the kidneys and aid in the removal of uric acid. **Bearberry (Arctostaphylos uva-ursi), Buchu (Barosma betulina), Burdock (Arctium lappa), Cleavers (Galium aparine), Couch grass (Agropyrens repens), Juniper (Juniperis communis) and Parsley (Petroselinum sativum)** are effective urinary diuretics. One or more of these herbal medicines may be consumed as a tea, tincture, fluid extract, solid extract or supplement. **Devil's claw (Harpagophytum procumbens)** has been used to reduce the pain and inflammation associated with gout. **Meadow saffron (Colchicum autumnale)** is the source of colchicine, the drug of choice in the treatment of gout. Colchicine is very effective in reducing pain and inflammation and terminating an attack of acute gout. Meadow saffron is poisonous. Side effects include indigestion, diarrhea, hair loss, seizures, low blood pressure and bone marrow depression. Meadow saffrom extracts should only be administered under the care of a licensed health care professional.

Highly Recommended

Low purine diet / avoid white sugar and refined carbohydrates / Increase fluid intake / vitamin B-complex / vitamin C / bromelain / omega-3 oils / Bearberry / Buchu / Cleavers / Couch grass / Juniper / Meadow saffron.

CHAPTER 25

Hayfever

Hayfever or rhinitis is an acute, seasonal allergy generally induced by wind borne allergens.

Hayfever affects 10 to 20% of the entire population. Individuals of all ages and ethnic backgrounds and males and females are affected equally.

Symptoms of hayfever include excessive tearing and crying, clear, watery nasal discharge from the nose and itching of the nose, roof of mouth, pharynx and eyes. Itching may begin gradually or abruptly following onset of the pollen season. Frontal headaches, irritability, anorexia, depression and insomnia may also occur. The delicate lining of the eye, called the conjunctiva, becomes red and itchy. The nasal mucous membranes became pale, swollen and bluish and nasal congestion almost always occurs. Coughing and asthmatic wheezing may develop as the pollen season progresses.

Hayfever is caused by an acute reaction to specific allergens. Histamine is released when the body comes in contact with certain substances to which it is sensitive. Histamine dilates the small blood vessels to the extent that reddening and swelling as seen with inflammation occurs. Nasal congestion, clear, watery discharge, itchy and watery eyes and the other characteristic symptoms of hayfever occur. Hayfever is caused by an acute allergic reaction to airborne allergens usually including the pollens, grasses, molds and other allergens. Spring type allergens include the tree pollens including oak, elm, maple, alder, birch, cottonwood. Summer type allergens include grasses including bermuda, timothy, sweet vernal, orchard, johnson and weed allergens including sheep sorral, english plantain. Fall type allergens include weed allergens including ragweed. House dust, mites, animal dander and occasionally airborne fungus and molds can cause hayfever. Dry homes and hot air ventilation systems, especially in winter, can aggravate hayfever. Allergies to molds are worse in damp, rainy weather and worse in damp, musty surroundings. Chronic use of decongestants can aggravate hayfever and their excessive use is discouraged. Geographical variation exist as to the type of pollen and the duration and severity of the pollen season.

Diagnosis of hayfever is based upon symptoms and history. An environmental sensitivity or allergy test may be necessary to identify specific allergens. A skin scratch or patch test may be effective in identifying specific allergens.

Conventional medical treatment of hayfever focuses on drug therapy to provide symptomatic relief. Commonly prescribed antihistamines include Actifed (triprolidine), Benadryl (diphenhydramine), Chlor-Trimeton (chlorpheniramine), Dimetane (bropheniramine), and Triaminicin (phenylpopanolamine). Drowsiness is the main side effect associated with antihistamine use. Commonly prescribed decongestants include Allerest (phenylephrine), Dristan (xylometazoline) and Sudafed (pseudoephedrine HCl). Decongestants are stimulants that increase alertness and wakefulness. Do not take before bedtime. Steroids are occasionally prescribed, but their use is limited to their detrimental side effects.

Lifestyle

Stress can aggravate hayfever. Stressors should be identified and reduced. Daily exercise, meditation, deep breathing exercises, yoga and biofeedback are useful techniques in reducing stress. Effort should be made to avoid specific allergens that cause hayfever where possible. Smoking can also aggravate hayfever and should be eliminated.

Diet

Avoid white sugar, refined carbohydrates, excess use of coffee, tea and other stimulants. Use of caffeine containing beverages may be beneficial for short term symptomatic relief. Avoid specific food sensitivities that can cause allergies and complicate hayfever. Avoid milk, cheese and other dairy products. They are mucous forming foods that only increase nasal congestion. Increase consumption of whole, unprocessed foods, vegetables and fruits.

Vitamin and Minerals
(Daily unless otherwise stated)

Vitamin B-complex - 50-100 mg. Helps the body respond to stress and may help to improve energy level.

97

Vitamin C - 2000-5000 mg. Has a natural antihistamine effect at higher doses that stabilizes cells and prevent release of histamine.

Zinc - 25-50 mg. May be deficient. Helps to stimulate the immune system.

Food Supplements
(Daily unless otherwise stated)

Adrenal glandular extract - 500-1000 mg. Has antihistamine effects and supplementation may help to improve energy level.
Bioflavonoids - 1000-2000 mg. Helps to stabilize cells and prevent histamine release. Works synergistically with vitamin C.
Digestive enzymes and/or Hydrochloric acid - 1-2 capsules before each meal. May be deficient and supplementation helps to improve digestion and absorption of foods.
Thymus glandular extract - 500-1000 mg. Helps to support and stimulate the function of the thymus gland. This gland plays and important role in the immune system.

Herbal Medicines

Specific plants and plant derivatives may help to reduce the allergic response and the symptoms associated with hayfever. **American pokeroot (Phytolacca decandra), Cayenne (Capsicum frutescens), Chaparral (Larrea divericata), Cleavers (Galium aparine), Eyebright (Euphrasia officinalis), Kola nut (Cola nitida), Goldenseal (Hydrastis canadensis), Green tea (Camellia sinensis), Indian tobacco (Lobelia inflata), Licorice (Glycyrrhiza glabra), Ma Huang (Ephedra sinica), Nettles (Urtica dioca)** and **Purple coneflower (Echinacea angustifolia)** may be beneficial in treating hayfever. One or more of these herbal medicines may be consumed as a tea, tincture, fluid extract, solid extract or supplement.

Highly Recommended

Avoid food and environmental sensitivities and allergies / Avoid milk, cheese and dairy / vitamin B-complex / vitamin C / adrenal glandular extract / bioflavonoids / Cayenne / Ephedra / Green tea / Kola nut / Nettles.

CHAPTER 26

Heart Disease

Heart disease refers to a variety of diseases that affect the heart including mitral valve prolapse, angina pectoris, heart attack, congestive heart failure and heart arrhythmias.

Heart disease is the most common cause of death in North America. It is estimated to affect 10 to 20% of the entire population. One in three men and one in ten women can expect to develop some form of heart disease before the age of 60 years. It is responsible for an estimated one million deaths per year.

The heart is a hollow muscular organ lying slightly to the left of the midline of the chest. The heart serves as a pump controlling the blood flow in the arteries and veins throughout the body.

Mitral valve prolapse is a condition in which the mitral valve separating the left atrium and left ventricle is pushed back too far during heart contraction. The prolapsed portion of the valve causes a clicking sound that may be heard with a stethoscope. Mitral valve prolapse is a fairly common condition found in persons of all ages and usually has no serious consequences.

Angina pectoris is a condition in which the coronary arteries are unable to transport adequate blood and oxygen supply to the heart muscle. It is usually a consequence of atherosclerosis or hardening of the arteries due to excess accumulation of cholesterol. It may cause acute pain or discomfort in the chest that comes on with exertion. It usually lasts less than fifteen minutes and is relieved with rest or medication.

Heart attack is the common description for the condition in which the formation of a blood clot within a coronary artery may shut off, or occlude blood flow to a section of heart muscle. This occlusion may cause permanent damage to a section of heart muscle and can lead to heart failure. It is usually a consequence of atherosclerosis or hardening of the arteries due to excess accumulation of cholesterol. It may cause acute pain or discomfort that lasts longer than fifteen minutes and is not relieved by rest or medication. Immediate medical treatment is necessary.

Heart failure is the inability of the heart to perform its function of pumping sufficient blood to assure a normal flow through the circulatory system. The heart is unable to pump the blood out returning from the veins. In the condition known as congestive heart failure, one or more chambers of the heart do not empty adequately during contraction of heart muscle. This results in shortness of breath, swelling, edema and the abnormal retention of sodium and water throughout the body.

Heart arrhythmias are disturbances in the normal rate and rhythm of the heart beat. Electrical impulses that affect the heart beat are generated in the heart's pacemaker and travel throughout the heart to initiate muscle contraction. Disturbances to the heart rate can occur anywhere along the electrical pathways in the heart and cause irregular rate and rhythm. Heart rate may speed up or slow down or become totally irregular.

Conventional medical treatment of heart disease focuses on drug therapy and surgery. Commonly prescribed anti-anginal medication includes nitroglycerin and nitroglycerin derivatives. Commonly prescribed heart failure medication includes Lanoxin (digoxin) and other cardiac glycosides. Commonly prescribed anti-arrhythmiac medication include Calan (verapamil), Inderal (propranolol) and Procan (procainamide). Coronary bypass surgery is commonly performed on individuals with blocked arteries around the heart who would otherwise develop heart attacks and heart failure.

Lifestyle

Cigarette smoking is detrimental to health and is strongly associated with the development of heart disease. A conscious effort to quit smoking should be done as soon as possible. Stressors can aggravate heart disease and precipitate heart attacks. Stressors should be identified and reduced as much as possible. Aerobic exercise such as walking, cycling, hiking, swimming, jogging and many other sports are strongly recommended. Exercise is a vital and necessary part of heart health and fitness and should be a part of daily routine. Meditation, deep breathing, biofeedback, yoga and hypnotherapy are other excellent ways to reduce stress and control heart rate and rhythm.

Diet

Total fat intake should be less than 30% of calories and should preferably be approximately 20% of calories. Saturated fats should be less than 10% of calories. Complex carbohydrates should constitute 50% or more of calories. Sugar and refined carbohydrates should be limited. Protein intake should provide the remainder of the calories. Sodium intake should not exceed 3 grams per day. Alcohol consumption should not exceed 2 ounces of ethanol per day. Coffee, tea, colas and chocolate and other caffeine containing beverages and foods should be limited. Caffeine is a nervous system stimulant that can increase heart rate, blood pressure and can cause irregular heart beats. Total calories should be sufficient to maintain a person's recommended weight. Refined and processed foods should be avoided. A wide variety of foods should be consumed emphasizing whole and unprocessed foods, whole grains and cereals, fresh fruits and vegetables.

Vitamins and Minerals
(Daily unless otherwise stated)

Vitamin A - 10,000-25,000 IU. A potent antioxidant that helps to prevent free radical damage to heart muscle.
Vitamin B-complex - 50-100 mg. Helps the body respond to stress that is associated with heart disease.
Vitamin C - 500-2000 mg. An antioxidant that helps to prevent free radical damage to heart muscle.
Vitamin E - 400-800 IU. A potent antioxidant that helps to prevent free radical damage and decrease inflammation to the heart.

Calcium - 600-1200 mg. Is necessary for heart muscle contraction. Supplementation helps to increase the contractile force of the heart, dilate blood vessels and decrease blood pressure. Works synergistically with magnesium and potassium.
Copper - 2-3 mg. May be deficient and deficiency is associated with the development of premature heart contraction and sudden heart failure.
Magnesium - 500-1000 mg. Is necessary for heart muscle contraction. Supplementation helps to increase the contractile force of the heart, dilate blood vessels and decrease blood pressure. Works synergistically with calcium and potassium. Supplementation may be beneficial in treating angina pectoris, heart attack, mitral valve prolapse, irregular heart beat and congestive heart failure.

Potassium - 1000-3000 mg. May be deficient in heart tissue despite normal blood levels. Supplementation helps to regulate heart rate and is useful in treating irregular heart beats. Many drugs cause depletion of potassium and supplementation is often necessary. Works synergistically with calcium and magnesium.

Selenium - 200-400 mcg. A potent antioxidant that helps to prevent free radical damage to heart muscle. May be deficient and deficiency is associated with the development of alcoholic heart disease.

Food Supplements
(Daily unless otherwise stated)

Carnitine - 500-1500 mg. May be deficient. Is necessary for transport of fats into heart muscle cells for breakdown and production of energy.

Coenzyme Q10 - 30-60 mg. Used in energy production within heart muscle cells. Supplementation is indicated in heart disease including angina, mitral valve prolapse, congestive heart failure and hypertensive heart disease.

Taurine - 500-1000 mg. Stabilizes heart cell walls by normalizing the movement of potassium in and out of heart cells.

Herbal Medicines

Specific plants and plant derivatives may be useful in treating heart disease and improving heart function. **Broom tops (Sarothamnus scoparius), Cactus (Cactus grandifloris), Hawthorn (Crataegus oxycantha), Lily of the Valley (Convallaria majus) and Motherwort (Leonurus cardiaca)** may be beneficial in treating heart disease. One or more of these herbal medicines may be consumed as a tea, tincture, fluid extract, solid extract or supplement. These herbal medicines should be used under the recommendation of an appropriate health care practitioner.

Highly Recommended

Daily exercise / Stop cigarette smoking / low fat diet / avoid caffeine containing beverages / vitamin A / vitamin B-complex / vitamin C / vitamin E / calcium / magnesium / potassium / selenium / carnitine / coenzyme Q10 / taurine / Hawthorn.

CHAPTER 27

Hemorrhoids

Hemorrhoids are enlarged and dilated superficial veins that occur in the tissue inside or just outside the rectum. They are also called piles.

Hemorrhoids occur in 35% of the population. They may begin to form at 20 years of age, but generally produce symptoms in individuals over the age of 30 years. 50% of people over the age of 50 years suffer with hemorrhoids. Their prevalence increases with age and they affect males and females equally.

The exact cause of hemorrhoids is not entirely understood. Genetics and family history plays a role in the development of the disease. Hemorrhoids appear to be caused by increased pressure in the veins of the anus and rectum. Prolonged sitting or standing, heavy lifting, vigorous exercise, constant straining, constipation, hard, dry stools that are difficult to pass and attempting to pass stool for long periods of time increases pressure in the veins of the anus and rectum. Failure to follow through on the urge to defecate can lead to the development of dilated veins. They can also be caused by increased abdominal pressure from coughing, sneezing, pregnancy, liver cirrhosis and cancer of the colon rectum and abdomen. Pregnancy is the most common cause of hemorrhoids in females.

Rectal bleeding before, during or after a bowel movement is the most common sign of hemorrhoids. Frank, red blood that appears in the toilet bowel after defecation may indicate hemorrhoids. It is important to realize that this is not the only cause of rectal bleeding. More serious diseases including inflammatory bowel disease and colon cancer can cause bleeding. Anemia due to blood loss may occur. A proper diagnosis is important in assessing the exact cause of rectal bleeding. Other symptoms include rectal irritation, local swelling and inflammation, a sense of incomplete defecation, difficulty in cleaning the anus, occasional mucous discharge, the development of anal fissures, ulcerations or strangulation. Pain is not usually a symptom associated with hemorrhoids. Anal itching is not directly associated with hemorrhoids. Anal itching may be caused by abrasive use of toilet paper, bacterial, viral or parasitic infection and allergies.

Conventional medical treatment of hemorrhoids focuses on sclerosing therapy, cryotherapy (liquid nitrogen), rubber band ligation, hemorrhoidectomy and electric current therapy.

Lifestyle

Exercise may be beneficial. Daily exercise such as walking, cycling, jogging and swimming improves overall cardiovascular fitness. A hot sitz bath with epsom salts may help to improve this condition.

One effective remedy is to place a warm, moist tea bag directly on the hemorrhoid. Tea contains a high amount of tannic acid that causes shrinking and contraction of the blood vessel. This may repeated several times.

Diet

Increase consumption of fiber. Increase consumption of fresh vegetables and fruits, legumes and whole grains. Increase consumption of water and natural juices. This helps to prevent constipation and to improve digestion. Increase consumption of bilberries, blue berries and other dark berries. They contain bioflavonoids that help to improve the strength of connective tissue that surrounds veins. Decrease consumption of sugar and refined carbohydrates and refined and processed foods.

Vitamins and Minerals
(Daily unless otherwise stated)

Vitamin A - 10,000-25,000 IU. Important in the development and maintenance of the lining of the veins, arteries and capillaries.
Vitamin B-complex - 50-100 mg. May be deficient. Helps the body and the colon respond to stress.
Vitamin C - 500-3000 mg. Important in the development of strong connective tissue that surrounds veins and enhances immune function.
Vitamin E - 400-600 IU. Helps to decrease inflammation, important in wound healing and improves blood viscosity.

Zinc - 10-25 mg. Necessary in wound healing and helps to increase the strength of the blood vessel wall. The topical application of zinc oxide ointment may be effective.

104

Food Supplements
(Daily unless otherwise stated)

Bioflavonoids - 1000-2000 mg. Important in the development of strong connective tissue that surrounds veins. Works synergistically with vitamin C.

Herbal Medicines

Specific plants and plant derivatives may be useful in treating hemorrhoids. Astringent herbs contain high amounts of tannic acid and cause shrinking and contraction of blood vessels. They stop bleeding and other discharges, prevent bacterial infection and help to alleviate diarrhea. **Calendula (Calendula officinalis), Cranesbill (Geranium maculatum), Goldenseal (Hydrastis canadensis), Lesser Celandine (Ranunculus ficaria), Meadowsweet (Filipendula ulmaria), Myrrh (Commiphora molmol), Stone root (Collinsonia canadensis) and Witch hazel (Hamamelis virginia)** are effective astringents. Witch hazel is one of the most common and effective astringents and is widely available in most pharmacies. Demulcent herbs help to soothe swollen inflammed tissue. **Chickweed (Stellaria media), Comfrey (Symphytum officinalis), Marshmallow (Althea officinalis) and Slippery Elm (Ulmus fulva)** are effective demulcents. The topical application of one or more of these astringent and demulcents herbs may be effective in reducing the inflammation and bleeding associated with hemorrhoids. **Butcher's broom (Ruscus aculeatus), Gotu kola (Centella asiatica), Hawthorn (Crataegus oxyacantha) and Horse chestnut (Aesculus hippocastanum)** contain plant derivatives that help to improve the strength and permeability of blood vessel walls. Both oral consumption and topical applications of these herbal medicines may help to improve the strength and integrity of the blood vessel wall. One or more of these herbal medicines may be consumed as a tea, tincture, fluid extract, solid extract or supplement.

Highly Recommended

Dietary fiber / vitamin A / vitamin C / bioflavonoids / Stone root / Witch hazel / Chickweed / Butcher's broom / Gotu kola / Horse chestnut.

CHAPTER 28

Herpes

Herpes infection is a common viral infection that cause cold sores and genital sores.

Herpes infection is almost universal in western cultures and is estimated to affect in 40 to 100% of the population. The majority of individuals infected for the first time have no symptoms and the disease often goes undiagnosed. The initial infection is almost always a self-limited disease, but recurrent reactivation of the infection can present severe symptoms that are often difficult to treat. After the initial infection the virus remains in the body and the disease enters a quiescent stage in which no active sores are apparent. During reactivation of the infection, local sores reappear at the site of the primary infection. It is estimated that 20 to 40% of the population have recurrent herpes infection.

Herpes infection is caused by a group of 70 related viruses found in many animal species. The various strains of herpes viruses affecting humans fall into two major categories. Herpes simplex virus type I is primarily non-genital herpes infection that cause red, inflammed sores on the face, neck, lips, eyes, trunk, buttocks and legs. Cold sores of the lips are the most common manifestation of HSV type I. Herpes simplex virus type II is primarily genital herpes, affecting the genitalia of both males and females equally. Exceptions are the newborn infant with ocular herpes contracted during childbirth. Other herpes infection include chickenpox (Varicella) and shingles (Herpes zoster).

Cold sores and fever blisters are the most common cause of ulcers on the lips, gums and mouth. The sores begin as small vesicles that break, enlarge and coalesce, producing large ulcers with irregular borders. The ulcers are associated with tingling and slight pain and usually last from 1 to 2 weeks in duration. The ulcers tend to recur in the same location, because the virus resides in the nerves that supply that particular area. Factors that contribute and exacerbate herpes infection include sunburn, menstruation, minor infections, food allergies and stress.

Conventional medical treatment of recurrent herpes infection focuses on drug therapy. At present, there is no cure for herpes infection.

Antiviral agents such as Zovirax (acyclovir) and vidarabine are used topically and orally to reduce the symptoms associated with infection.

Lifestyle

Stress can precipitate and exacerbate herpes infection. Stressors should be identified and reduced. Exercise and meditation, deep breathing exercises, biofeedback and yoga are excellent ways to reduce stress. Epsom salt and sodium bicarbonate baths may soothing to inflammed areas of the skin. A mouthwash containing 3-5 ml (1/2-1 tsp) sodium bicarbonate in water is soothing and cleansing to the mouth.

Diet

Avoid foods high in the amino acid arginine, including chocolate, peanuts, peanut butter, almonds, brazil nuts, filberts, cashews, walnuts, pecans and all other nuts, sugar and refined carbohydrates, cakes and sweets, alcohol, coffee and tea. Herbal teas are fine. Foods that must be eaten with discretion include whole grain products (cereals, breads, pasta, pancakes), lentils, barley and other grains, oats, corn, rice, soybeans and soy products, chick peas, sprouts, peas and beans, carob, fruits and berries that contain seeds and citrus fruits. Foods to emphasize, especially during active outbreaks include dairy products (cheese, yogurt, kefir, cottage cheese, sour cream, milk), all fish and seafood, chicken, turkey, eggs, organ meats, potatoes and brewer's yeast.

Vitamins and Minerals
(Daily unless otherwise stated)

Vitamin A - 25,000-50,000 IU. Important for the development and maintenance of mucous membranes such as the mouth, lips and external genitalia. Helps to improve healing of these tissues.
Vitamin B-complex - 100 mg. May be deficient and helps the body deal with stress.
Vitamin B12 - 100-1000 mcg. Supplementation helps to improve symptoms of herpes infection. Intramuscular injections may be beneficial.
Vitamin C - 1000-3000 mg. Helps to increase immune function and decreases the duration of the disease, especially those with recurrent herpes infection.

Vitamin E - 400-1200 IU. Reduces pain and inflammation caused by herpes infection. Topical application of vitamin E oil may be effective.

Zinc - 25-50 mg. Enhances immune function and inhibits viral reproduction. Topical application of zinc sulphate ointment (0.05%) greatly reduces ulcer size and recurrence.

Food Supplements
(Daily unless otherwise stated)

Bioflavonoids - 500-1000 mg. Helps to decrease inflammation and the duration of active ulcers. Works synergistically with vitamin C.
Lactobacillus acidophilus - 1-2 capsules. Supplementation improves the symptoms of herpes infection and provides effective relief.
Lithium succinate - 5-10% ointment. Topical application of lithium succinate ointment reduces the symptoms associated with recurrent herpes infection.
Lysine - 500-1000 mg. A naturally occuring amino acid that inhibits viral reproduction. Supplementation significantly decreases the symptoms associated with herpes infection and decreases the rate of recurrence.

Herbal Medicines

Specific plants and plant derivatives may be useful in treating recurrent herpes infection. **Barberry (Berberis vulgaris), Calendula (Calendula officinalis), Garlic (Allium sativum), Goldenseal (Hydrastis canadensis), Licorice (Glycyrrhiza glabra), Myrrh (Commiphora molmol) and Saint John's wort (Hypericum perforatum)** have been used to treat herpes infection. Licorice extract s have been used successfully to reduce the symptoms associated with infection. One or more of these herbal medicines may be consumed as a tea, tincture, fluid extract, solid extract or supplement. Topical applications of one or more of these herbal medicines is also recommended.

Highly Recommended

Decrease stress / avoid food sensitivities and allergies / avoid foods high in arginine / vitamin A / vitamin B-complex / vitamin C / zinc / Lactobacillus acidophilus / lysine / Calendula / Garlic / Goldenseal / Licorice / Myrrh.

CHAPTER 29

Hyperactivity

Hyperactivity or Attention Deficit Disorder, is a disorder of children characterized by hyperactive behavior. Inappropriate attention and impulsivity are commonly associated with hyperactivity.

Hyperactivity is defined as difficulty staying seated and sitting still and running and climbing on things excessively. Inattention is defined as a failure to finish tasks started, easy distractibility, seeming lack of attention, difficulty concentrating on tasks requiring sustained attention. Impulsivity is defined as acting before thinking, difficulty taking turns, problems organizing work and constant shifting from one activity to another. Other characteristics of this disorder include poor school performance, emotional lability, depression, opposition, anxiety, aggressiveness, low frustration tolerance and poor peer relationships. Learning difficulty is often associated with hyperactivity due to the child's inability to focus their attention on school work. Children with hyperactivity have normal and above average IQ's and intelligence.

Hyperactivity occurs in 5 to 10% of school age children and is ten times more common in boys than in girls. Onset is typically before the age of 3 years and invariably before the age of 7 years. The average age of children with this disorder is between the ages of 8 and 10 years. Intensity and severity of this disorder vary considerably. Hyperactive children may experience symptom free periods lasting for weeks or months. Exacerbations and remissions are common. Hyperactivity is not limited to children and can occur in adolescents and adults. Adolescents and adults who displayed hyperactive behavior as children often retain residual effects. Fidgetiness, restlessness, difficulty completing assigned tasks and difficulty focusing attention for extended periods of times are common traits.

The exact cause of hyperactivity is unknown. Biochemical, physiological and behavioral causes have been suggested. Food sensitivities and allergies have been associated with the development of hyperactive behavior. Diagnosis of hyperactivity is based on the exclusion of other disorders. A proper medical and social history is required to rule out other possible causes of hyperactive behavior.

Conventional medical treatment of hyperactivity focuses on drug therapy and behavioral modification. Stimulant drugs such as Ritalin (methylphenidate), Cylert and Dexedrine are widely used to treat this disorder. Side effects of these drugs include sleep disturbance and insomnia, depression or sadness, headaches, stomach aches, decreased appetite, increased blood pressure and with large doses stunted growth. It is important to emphasize that no single approach is entirely effective and a holistic approach is recommended.

Lifestyle

Counselling may be beneficial to both parents and child. Consistent parenting techniques, establishing boundaries and limits, token rewards and a structured daily environment and routine should be incorporated into the treatment approach.

Drug use and inhalant allergies can contribute to the development if hyperactive behavior. Aluminum and lead toxicity can also contribute to hyperactivity.

Diet

Food sensitivities and allergies are strongly associated with the development of hyperactive behavior. Avoid sugar and refined carbohydrates, artificial sweeteners, chocolate, coffee, tea, soft drinks and other refined and processed foods. Common sensitivities include white flour, wheat, corn, strawberries, citrus fruits including lemon, grapefruit and oranges, peanuts and other nuts, pork and lunch meats and dairy including milk and cheese. An elimination diet should be used where the offending allergens or sensitizing foods are eliminated from the diet. Food additives and preservatives including colorings, dyes and artificial flavorings are other common sensitivities. Avoid foods that contain natural salicylates including all berries, plums, apricots, apples, pears and oranges. Increase consumption of whole, unprocessed foods, vegetables and fruits.

Vitamins and Minerals
(Daily unless otherwise stated)

Multi-vitamin - 1-2 tablets/capsules. Supplies all necessary vitamin and minerals that may be deficient.

Vitamin B-complex - 25-50 mg. Aids in the development of a healthy nervous system and supplementation may be benficial.
Vitamin B3 (Niacin, Niacinamide) - 100-500 mg. Helps to regulate the nervous system and supplementation is beneficial in reducing the symptoms of hyperactivity.
Vitamin B6 (Pyridoxine) - 50-200 mg. Effective in regulating the function of the nervous system.

Calcium - 500-1000 mg. Supplementation exerts a calming effect and may be beneficial.
Magnesium - 300-600 mg. Supplementation exerts a calming effect and may be beneficial.
Zinc - 10-25 mg. Required for the use of essential fatty acids.

Food Supplements
(Daily unless otherwise stated)

Omega-3 oils (flaxseed, fish oil) - 500-2000 mg. A rich source of essential oils that are utalized by the nervous system. May be deficient and supplementation helps to correct the deficiency.
Omega-6 oils (evening primrose, borage oil) - 500-2000 mg. A rich source of essential oils that are utalized by the nervous system. May be deficient and supplementation helps to correct the deficieny.

Herbal Medicines

Specific plants and plant derivatives may be useful in treating hyperactivity and attention deficit disorder. **Chamomile (Matricaria chamomilla), Green oats (Avena sativa), Hops (Humulus lupulus), Passion flower (Passiflora incarnata), and Skullcap (Scutellaria lateriflora) and Valerian (Valerian officinalis)** have been used. One or more of these herbal medicines may be consumed as a tea, tincture, fluid extract, solid extract or supplement.

Highly Recommended

Establish boundaries and limits / avoid food sensitivities and allergies / multiple vitamin and mineral complex / vitamin B-complex / vitamin B3 / vitamin B6 / calcium / magnesium / omega-6 oils / Chamomile.

CHAPTER 30

Hypertension

Hypertension or high blood pressure is defined as blood pressure greater than 140/90 millimeters of mercury on three or more different readings.

Hypertension is estimated to affect 20 to 40% of the North American population. Hypertension is twice as common in blacks as it is in whites. It occurs equally among males and females.

Hypertension is an asymptomatic disease and most individuals are not aware that they have it. Approximately 25% of individuals are not aware that they have high blood pressure and take no steps to reduce it. Symptoms including dizziness, flushed face, headaches, frequent nose bleeds, anxiety, stress, and nervousness are not due to hypertension.

Direct consequences of hypertension include congestive heart failure, aneurysm, cerebral hemorrhage and blood vessel rupture. Indirect consequences of hypertension resulting from decreased blood flow and lack of oxygen include heart attack, kidney sclerosis and stroke. Atherosclerosis, hardening of the arteries, contributes to elevated blood pressure by increasing blood vessel resistance.

Risk factors that contribute to an elevation of blood pressure include hyperlipidemia or high fat level in circulating blood, high blood cholesterol, diabetes mellitus, cigarette smoking, atherosclerosis, high salt intake, poor nutrition and advanced age.

Essential hypertension is estimated to affect 90 to 95% of all hypertensives and has no known cause. Current evidence suggests that genetic factors may increase the predisposition to high blood pressure. Over-activation of the central nervous system may occur causing chronic blood vessels constriction, elevated heart rate and elevated blood pressure. Imbalance between sodium, potassium, calcium and magnesium may occur. High sodium levels and low potassium, calcium and magnesium levels are associated with elevations in blood pressure. Over activation of kidney enzymes causing fluid retention is also believed to be associated with the development of high blood pressure.

Diagnosis of hypertension should be made a licensed health professional. At least two blood pressure readings on three different occasions are necessary to make the diagnosis of high blood pressure.

Conventional medical treatment of high blood pressure focuses at drug therapy to control elevated levels. Commonly prescribed medication include beta blockers, peripheral vasodilators, diuretics, central nervous system agonists, calcium channel blockers and ACE inhibitors. Common beta blockers include Corgard (nadolol), Inderal (propranolol), Lopressor (metoprolol), Sectal (acebutolol) and Tenormin (atenolol). Common peripheral vasodilators include Apresoline (hydrazaline), Loniten (minoxidil) and Minipress (prozosin). Common diuretics include Lasix (furosemide), Spironolactone and thiazide diuretics. Common central nervous system agonists include Aldomet (methyl dopa) and Catapress (clonidine). Common calcium channel blockers include Calan (verapamil) and Isoptin (verapamil). Common ACE inhibitors include Capoten (captopril) and Vasotec (enalapril).

Lifestyle

Avoid cigarette smoking. Cigarette smoking is strongly associated with high blood pressure, atherosclerosis and stroke. Nicotine is a nervous system stimulant that raises blood pressure.

Stressors should be identified and reduced. Exercise, meditation, biofeedback, yoga and other relaxation techniques are beneficial in reducing stress and learning to control blood pressure. Daily exercise in the form of walking, bicycling, swimming, jogging or any other aerobic sport is strongly encouraged. Relaxation, meditation and reflection should also be a part of daily routine.

Diet

Limiting salt intake to less than 2 grams per day may be beneficial in reducing high blood pressure in some hypertensives who are sodium sensitive. Decrease consumption of sugar and refined carbohydrates. Decrease consumption of coffee, tea, chocolate and other caffeine containing foods and beverages. Fat intake should be limited as obesity can contribute to a sedentary lifestyle and can increase blood pressure. Increase consumption of whole and unprocessed foods, whole grains and cereals, fresh fruits and vegetables. A high fiber intake is strongly recommended and is associated with a decrease in blood pressure. A vegetarian diet high in fiber, vegetable protein, unsaturated fats, potassium and magnesium shows a significant decrease in blood pressure.

Vitamins and Minerals
(Daily unless otherwise stated)

Vitamin A - 10,000-25,000 IU. Low levels of vitamin A are associated with a elevated blood pressure levels.
Vitamin B-complex - 50-100 mg. Helps the body respond to stress and supplementation may be beneficial in association with dietary factors in reducing high blood pressure.
Vitamin C - 500-2000 mg. A low intake of vitamin C is associated with high blood pressure levels.
Vitamin D - 200-400 IU. Supplementation may beneficial in reducing high blood pressure in some individuals.

Calcium - 800-1200 mg. A low intake of dietary calcium is associated with high blood pressure levels. Supplementation may be more effective in reducing high blood pressure that salt restriction.
Magnesium - 600-1000 mg. Magnesium is a potent dilator of blood vessels because of its ability to displace calcium from smooth muscle around blood vessels. Supplementation is effective in reducing high blood pressure, especially when combined with calcium.
Potassium - 1500-5000 mg. A low intake of dietary potassium is associated with high blood pressure levels. Supplementation may be beneficial, especially in conjunction with calcium and magnesium.

Food Supplements
(Daily unless otherwise stated)

Coenzyme Q10 - 30-60 mg. May be deficient in hypertensives and supplementation may be beneficial.
Omega-3 oils (flaxseed, fish oil) - 1500-3000 mg. A rich source of essential oils that may be beneficial in reducing elevated blood pressure levels.
Omega-6 oils (evening primrose, borage oil) - 1500-3000 mg. A rich source of essential oils that may be beneficial in reducing elevated blood pressure levels.
Zinc - 25-50 mg. Supplementation appears to reverse cadmium and lead toxicities that may cause high blood pressure.

Herbal Medicines

Specific plants and plant derivatives may be useful in helping to control high blood pressure. **Garlic (Allium sativum), Ginkgo (Ginkgo biloba), Hawthorn (Crataegus oxycantha), Khella (Ammi visnaga), Mistletoe (Viscum album)** may be useful in treating hypertension. One or more of these herbal medicines may be consumed as a tea, tincture, fluid extract, solid extract or supplement.

Highly Recommended

Quit cigarette smoking / reduce stress / exercise daily / avoid salt, fats, white sugar and refined carbohydrates / vitamin B-complex / calcium / magnesium / potassium / omega-3 oils / omega-6 oils / Garlic / Ginkgo / Hawthorn.

CHAPTER 31

Hypoglycemia

Hypoglycemia is an abnormally low level of sugar or glucose in the blood.

The exact prevalence of hypoglycemia is not known. It is estimated that 10 to 25% of the adult population may be hypoglycemic. It occurs equally in males and females and occurs at all ages. It is estimated that 50% of the individuals with hypoglycemia are over the age of 50 years and suffer from thyroid gland dysfunction.

Hypoglycemia may result from an excessive rate of removal of sugar from the blood or from decreased release of sugar into the blood. Insulin is a hormone produced in the pancreas in response to high blood sugar levels. Insulin increases removal of sugar from the blood into cells of the body. Overproduction of insulin or an overdose of insulin used by diabetics can lead to increased utilization of sugar, so that sugar is removed from the blood at an accelerated rate. Reactive hypoglycemia occurs approximately 2 to 4 hours after a meal. It typically occurs after a high carbohydrate meal and is a results of excess insulin increase. Low blood sugar levels result and the characteristic symptoms of hypoglycemia occur.

Symptoms of hypoglycemia include nervousness, irritability, faintness, weakness, muscle weakness, tremors and shakes, heart palpitations, rapid heart rate, increased blood pressure, tingling in the skin, hunger, sweating, dizziness, lack of balance, blurred vision, headaches, cold hands and feets, anxiety, depression, mood swings and inability to concentrate. Mid-morning or mid to late afternoon fatigue and craving for sweets and binge eating are common. Symptoms are episodic and occur only when an individual is hypoglycemic. Hypoglycemia may be tolerated for brief periods of time without symptoms. However, if the blood sugar level remains very low for a prolonged period of time, serious complications can occur. Hypoglycemic shock is a severe form of hypoglycemia that can occur in response to excess insulin. Mental confusion, hallucinations, convulsions and deep coma eventually occur as the brain and nervous system is deprived of glucose. This is an acute emergency that demands immediate medical attention.

Hypoglycemia may be caused by many different factors. Heredity may play a role in its development. Poor diet and diet high in sugar and refined carbohydrates is probably the most common cause of hypoglycemia. Coffee, tea, smoking and other stimulants can lead to the blood sugar abnormalities. Chronic stress, adrenal gland exhaustion and hypothyroidism can contribute to the development of low blood sugar levels. Other causes include pregnancy induced hypoglycemia, neonatal hypoglycemia, kidney disease, liver disease, hereditary enzyme deficiency, epilepsy and seizures, non-pancreatic tumors and hypothyroidism. Drug sensitivities and allergies including alcohol, aspirin and other common drugs can cause blood sugar abnormalities. Related disorders include food and inhalant sensitivities and allergies, asthma, hayfever, eczema, indigestion, malabsorption, constipation or diarrhea.

Diagnosis of hypoglycemia is based upon symptoms and blood tests to detect abnormally low blood sugar levels. A four to five hour glucose tolerance test (GTT) is frequently done to detect the body's response to a large quantity of sugar. A blood sugar level less than 50 mg/dl is diagnostic of hypoglycemia.

Conventional medical treatment often disregards the significance of hypoglycemia. Hospital dieticians recommend a high protein, low carbohydrate diet. Acute and severe hypoglycemic shock requires immediate medical attention. Intravenous injections of glucose may be necessary. If the hypoglycemic individual is conscious and can swallow then sugar, candy, sweetened fruit juice or honey may be given by mouth.

Lifestyle

Stress can contribute to the development of hypoglycemia. Stressors should be identified and reduced. Exercise is a great way to reduce stress. Moderate exercise such as walking, jogging, cycling, swimming and other aerobic exercises are strongly encouraged. Meditation, deep breathing exercises, biofeedback and yoga are excellent ways to reduce stress.

Diet

Strictly avoid sugar and all refined carbohydrates including white sugar, honey, molasses, fructose, turbinado sugar, raw cane sugar, brown sugar, maple syrup and dried fruit. Avoid foods that have sugar as an

117

ingredient including chocolate, candy bars, alcohol, carbonated soda beverages and sweentened fruit juices. Also avoid foods where sugar is used as a hidden ingredient such as sauces and dressings. Avoid stimulants including coffee, tea, carbonated soda beverages and diet aids. Also avoid white flour and other refined and processed foods. Increase consumption of vegetables, complex carbohydrates and protein foods. Increase consumption of complex carbohydrates including whole grains, beans, legumes and brown rice. Increase foods high in fiber. Increase consumption of protein foods including beef chicken, fish, lamb, turkey, yogurt, cottage cheese, raw cheese, nuts and tofu. Small, frequent meals should be consumed throughout the day. Having snacks between meals helps to maintain proper blood sugar levels and prevent hypoglycemia. Food sensitivies and allergies are associated with the development of hypoglycemia. A food sensitivity or allergy test is recommended.

Vitamins and Minerals
(Daily unless otherwise stated)

Vitamin B-complex - 50-100 mg. May be deficient. Important in maintaining proper blood sugar levels. Intramuscular injections may be beneficial.

Vitamin B3 (Niacin) - 25-50 mg. Required for the production of glucose tolerance factor (GTF) which works with insulin in maintaining proper blood sugar levels.

Vitamin B5 (Pantothenic acid) - 250-500 mg. Important in adrenal gland function and is used in the metabolism of sugar.

Vitamin B6 (Pyridoxine) - 25-100 mg. May be deficient. Used as a co-enzyme in many chemicals processes including the breakdown of sugar.

Vitamin B12 - 100-1000 mcg. Supplementation may be beneficial especially with individuals that have nervous system problems.

Vitamin C - 500-3000 mg. Supplementation may help to improve adrenal gland function and improve glucose tolerance.

Chromium - 200-400 mcg. A necessary component of glucose tolerance factor (GTF) that is important in regulating blood sugar levels along with insulin. Supplementation has been shown to improve glucose tolerance.

Copper - 2-3 mg. Deficiency associated with low glucose tolerance.

Magnesium - 400-800 mg. Involved in sugar breakdown and utilization. May be low especially in individuals prone to nervous system problems.

Manganese - 2-4 mg. May be deficient. Involved in sugar breakdown and utilization.

Phosphorus - 2-5 gms. Deficiency can cause impaired glucose response.

Potassium - 50-100 mg. Deficiency is associated with increased insulin levels and can cause hypoglycemia.

Zinc - 10-25 mg. May be deficient. Helps to breakdown and utilize sugar in the body.

Food Supplements
(Daily unless otherwise stated)

Adrenal glandular extract - 500-1000 mg. Supplementation helps to support and stimulate adrenal gland function. Helps to maintain blood sugar levels and prevent abnormalities.

Bee pollen - 1-2 tbsp or as directed. A rich source of B-complex vitamins and vitamin C. Supplementation may be beneficial for individuals with hypoglycemia.

Bioflavonoids - 500-1000 mg. Works together with vitamin C in promoting healthy connective tissue. Important in preventing blood vessels disorders associated with hypoglycemia and diabetes.

Brewer's Yeast - 5-10 gm. High in chromium and one of the richest natural sources of glucose tolerance factor (GTF). Supplementation has been shown to improve glucose tolerance and fat metabolism.

Digestive enzymes and/or Hydrochloric acid - 1-2 capsules before each meal. May be deficient and is associated with poor digestion and absorption and the development of food sensitivities and allergies.

Liver glandular extract 500-1000 mg. Supplementation helps to support and stimulate liver gland function. Important in maintaining proper blood sugar levels and preventing hypoglycemia. Also a rich, natural source of B-complex vitamins and vitamins A, D, E and K. Intramuscular injections may be beneficial.

Omega-3 oils (flaxseed, fish oil) - 1000-3000 mg. Involved in fat metabolism and supplementation may increase insulin sensitivity and help to stabilize blood sugar levels.

Omega-6 oils (evening primrose, borage oil) - 1000-3000 mg. Involved in fat metabolism and supplementation may increase insulin sensitivity and help to stabilize blood sugar levels.

Highly Recommended

Decrease stress / Avoid white sugar and refined carbohydrates / avoid all caffeine containing beverages and foods / vitamin B-complex / vitamin B-5 / vitamin B12 / vitamin C / chromium / magnesium / potassium / adrenal glandular extract / brewer's yeast / liver glandular extract / omega-6 oils.

CHAPTER 32

Hypothyroidism

Hypothyroidism is a deficiency of thyroid gland function and is marked by underproduction of the hormone, thyroxine.

Hypothyroidism occurs in approximately 10 to 15% of the adult population. Mild to severe hypothyroidism occurs in 10 to 12% of the population, while moderate to severe hypothyroidism occurs in 1 to 4% of the population. Hypothyroidism occurs slightly more in females than in males. Hypothyroidism that occurs in children results in delayed physical growth and decreased mental development.

The thyroid gland is one of the largest endocrine glands in the body and is located in the front and sides of the neck just below the adam's apple. It serves as a storehouse for iodine. Thyroxine is the chief hormone produced in the thyroid gland. The main function of the thyroid gland is to maintain normal growth and metabolism. Metabolism is a general term used to describe the sum of all physical and chemical processes that occur in the human body. It includes the digestion and absorption of food particles into amino acids, carbohydrates and fats that are used to build and maintain the body structure and function. Body temperature is a reliable indicator of thyroid gland function. The normal oral human body temperature is 36.4 to 37.6 degrees Celcius (97.6 to 99.2 degrees Fahrenheit). Low oral body temperature below 36.4 degrees Celcius (97.6 degrees Fahrenheit) suggests hypothyroidism.

Symptoms of hypothyroidism include physical and mental sluggishness, fatigue, malaise, depression, muscle weakness, forgetfulness and memory impairment, moderate weight gain, obesity, cold intolerance, cold hands and feet, decreased sexual desire, slowed digestion and constipation. Other symptoms include swelling and edema throughout the body, enlargement of the tongue, brittle and cracked fingernails and dry, thin hair. With females symptoms include menstrual cycle irregularities including a shorter cycle, prolonged heavy bleeding, infertility, premature birth and miscarriages. With men symptoms include impotence and baldness. High cholesterol and triglycerides, low body temperature, decreased heart rate, enlarged heart, high blood pressure, impaired kidney function, anemia and delayed tendon reflexes can occur.

The exact cause of hypothyroidism is not known. Underactive thyroid function is believed to be a normal part of aging. Heredity can play an important role its development. Other causes include pituitary gland disorders, radioactive iodine therapy, thyroid surgery, congenital enzyme deficiency, nerve damage and nutritional deficiencies including iodine, vitamin A, vitamin E and zinc. Excessive use of stimulants drugs and diet pills can decrease thyroid gland function.

Diagnosis of hypothyroidism is based upon history and symptoms and blood tests to determine thyroxine (T4) levels. Additional tests may be required to determine if the problem occurs in the thyroid gland itself or as a result of pituitary gland dysfunction.

Conventional medical treatment of hypothyroidism focuses on drug therapy to replace thyroid hormone. Synthetic L-thyroxine is a commonly prescribed and effective medication. A consequence of long term use of L-thyroxine is bone loss and the development of osteoporosis.

Lifestyle

Exercise stimulates thyroid function. Regular, daily exercise such as walking, cycling, jogging, swimming and other forms of aerobic exercise are great ways to stimulate the thyroid gland.

Stress can contribute to thyroid dysfunction. Stressors should be identified and reduced. Exercise, meditation, deep breathing exercises, biofeedback and yoga are excellent techniques to reduce stress.

Diet

Avoid cruciferous vegetables that contain substances that inhibit thyroid function. These foods include turnips, cabbage, broccoli, cauliflower, brussel sprouts, spinach, kale, mustard, cassava root, soybean, peanuts, walnuts, pine nuts and millet. Cooking of these foods inactivates the substances that interfere with proper thyroid function. Increase consumption of foods high in iodine including seaweeds, kelps, clams, lobsters, oysters sardines and other salt water fish. Use iodized salt. Avoid white sugar and refined carbohydrates. Avoid coffee, tea, colas, chocolate and other caffeine containing beverages and foods. Avoid heavy chlorinated and fluorinated waters. These chemicals inhibit iodine uptake in the thyroid. Avoid chronic use of diet pills. They decrease thyroid function and can cause hypothyroidism. Increase consumption of whole and unprocessed foods, fresh fruits and vegetables.

Vitamins and Minerals
(Daily unless otherwise stated)

Vitamin A - 10,000-25,000 IU. Required for production of thyroxine and other thyroid hormones. Avoid in excess doses.
Vitamin B-complex - 50-100 mg. Necessary for proper metabolism and helps the body respond to stress.   Intramuscular injections may be beneficial.
Vitamin B2 (Ribolfavin) - 10-25 mg. Necessary for proper thyroid function.
Vitamin B3 (Niacin) - 25-50 mg. Necessary for proper thyroid function.
Vitamin B6 (Pyridoxine) - 25-50 mg. Necessary for proper thyroid function.
Vitamin C - 500-3000 mg. Necessary for proper thyroid function. Avoid in excess doses.
Vitamin E - 400-800 IU. Required for proper production of thyroxine and other thyroid hormones. Increases iodine uptake in the thyroid. Avoid in excess doses.

Iodine - 150-300 mcg. An important part of thyroid hormone. Required for the production of thyroxine and other thyroid hormones.
Zinc - 25-50 mg. Required for production of thyroxine and other thyroid hormones.

Food Supplements
(Daily unless otherwise stated)

Liver glandular extract - 500-1000 mg. A rich source of B-complex vitamins and vitamins A, D, E and K. Important for proper metabolism and supplementation may be beneficial in stimulating metabolism.
Pituitary glandular extract - 250-500 mg. Helps to stimulate pituitary gland function that stimulates thyroid gland function. Responsible for producing thyroid stimulating hormone (TSH).
Thyroid glandular extract - 500-1000 mg. Supplies the raw materials for thyroxine and other thyroid hormones and helps to stimulate thyroid gland function. Dessicated thyroid glandular is available by prescription only while thyroxine free glandular extracts are available as over-the-counter medicine.

Tyrosine - 250-500 mg. An amino acid that is used specifically to make thyroxine and other thyroid hormones.

Herbal Medicines

Specific plants and plant derivatives may be useful in treating hypothyroidism and stimulating thyroid gland function. **Kelp (Fucus resiculosis), Irish moss (Chondrus crispus) and Parsley (Petroselinum sativum)** are specifically used to stimulate thyroid function. One or more of these herbal medicines may be consumed as a tea, tincture, fluid extract, solid extract or supplement.

Highly Recommended

Exercise / avoid cruciferous vegetables / multiple vitamin and mineral complex / iodine / liver glandular extract / thyroid glandular extract / tyrosine / Kelp / Irish moss.

CHAPTER 33

Inflammation

Inflammation is a normal response to injury or trauma and usually involves swelling, edema, redness, heat amd loss of function.

Inflammation literally means "to set on fire" and is the body's reaction to injury or trauma. The inflammatory response can be provoked by physical, chemical and biological agents including trauma, exposure to excessive amounts of sunlight, x-rays and radioactive materials, corrosive chemicals, extremes of heat and cold and infectious agents such as bacteria, viruses and other microrganisms.

The classic signs of inflammation are heat, redness, swelling, pain and loss of function. These signs are manifestations of the changes that occur during the inflammatory process. The major components of this process are changes in blood flow through blood vessels, increased capillary permeability and the presence of white blood cells. Large quantities of chemicals such as histamine are released in response to local trauma. This causes an increase in local blood flow and increase in capillary permeability. As a result, large quantities of fluid and protein leak out into the surrounding tissue. Localized swelling and edema results. The fluid begins to clot around the blood vessels. A clot will usually form within 5 minutes after a blood vessel wall has been damaged. White blood cells migrate to the area of tissue damage and prevent infection. The inflamed tissue is separated from normal tissue which delays the spread of bacteria and other toxic products.

Conventional medical treatment of inflammation focuses on drug therapy. Commonly prescribed anti-inflammatory medication include aspirin (ASA), Motrin (ibuprofen), Tylenol (acetaminophen), Indocid (indomethacin), Fenopron (fenoprofen), Naprosyn (naproxen), Tolectin (tolmetin), and Clinoril (sulindac). Side effects of these commonly prescribed non-steroidal anti-inflammatories include nausea, vomiting, headaches, dizziness, tinnitus (ringing in ears) and digestive upset. In addition, the use of these NSAID's should be reserved for short periods of treatment since their prolonged use can inhibit tissue repair and wound healing. Steroids are occasionally prescribed, but their use is limited due to toxic side effects.

124

Lifestyle

Rest, ice, compression and elevation (RICE) is the important first aid response to trauma and inflammation. Ice packs should be applied to the damaged tissue for 24 to 72 hours following injury. Ice and cold applications cause blood vessel constriction and reduce inflammation. The injured tissue should be immobilized from further movement to prevent further damage and inflammation. The injured part should be elevated to decrease inflammation and swelling. After 72 hours warm hot packs should be applied to the damaged tissue. This helps to increase blood supply to the injured tissue and increases wound healing.

Physical Therapy

Physical therapy modalities such as cold packs, hot packs, ultrasound, low voltage muscle stimulation and TENS (transcutaneous electroneural stimulation) may be beneficial in reducing inflammation and promote tissue healing.

Vitamins and Minerals
(Daily unless otherwise stated)

Vitamin B-complex - 50-100 mg. Helps the body respond to stress and supplementation may be beneficial.
Vitamin C - 2000-5000 mg. Has demonstrated anti-inflammatory, antihistamine and membrane stabilizing activity. Inflammation may increase vitamin C excretion and supplementation may be beneficial.
Vitamin E - 400-1200 mg. Has demonstrated anti-inflammatory and membrane stabilizing effects.

Magnesium - 500-1000 mg. Helps to relieve muscle spasm that usually accompanies inflammation.
Zinc - 50-100 mg. Helps to inhibit histamine release and decrease inflammation.

Food Supplements
(Daily unless otherwise stated)

Adrenal glandular extract - 500-1000 mg. Helps to stimulate and support adrenal gland function. Promotes cortisol release from the adrenal gland which has potent anti-inflammatory activity.

Bioflavonoids - 1000-2000 mg. Helps to stabilize connective tissue around blood vessels and reduce inflammation. Works synergistically with vitamin C.

Bromelain (1800-2200 m.c.u.) - 500-1000 mg. A sulfur containing proteolytic enzyme obtained from the pineapple plant. Activates anti-inflammatory prostaglandins in the body and promotes removal of fluid that causes inflammation and swelling. Take without food and between meals for best results.

Chondroitin sulphate - 3-6 capsules. Necessary for proper growth and repair of damaged blood vessels and damaged connective tissue.

Glycosaminoglycans - 2-6 gm. Necessary for proper growth and repair of damaged blood vessels and damaged connective tissue. Supplement for one month.

Green lipped mussel (Perma canaliculus) - 3-6 capsules. Rich source of glycosaminoglycans and chondroitin sulphate, that is necessary for blood vessel and connective tissue repair and maintenance.

Omega-3 oils (flaxseed, fish oil) - 1500-3000 mg. Decreases inflammation by increasing natural anti-inflammatory prostaglandins in the body.

Omega-6 oils (evening primrose, borage oil) - 1500-3000 mg. Decreases inflammation by increasing natural anti-inflammatory prostaglandins in the body.

Herbal Medicines

Specific plants and plant derivatives may be beneficial in reducing inflammation. **Black cohosh (Cimicifuga racemosa), Blue cohosh (Caulophyllum thalictroides), Devil's claw (Harpagophytum procumbens), Licorice (Glycyrrhiza glabra), Passionflower (Passiflora officinalis), Pineapple (Ananas comosus), Pipsissewa (Chimaphila umbellata), Tumeric (Curcuma longa), Valerian (Valerian officinalis), White willow bark (Salix alba), Wild yam (Dioscorea villosa), and Wintergreen (Gaultheria procumbens)** may be beneficial. One or more of these herbal medicines may be consumed as a tea, tincture, fluid extract, solid extract or supplement.

Highly Recommended

Rest, ice, compression, immobilization and elevation / physical therapy / vitamin C / magnesium / bioflavonoids / bromelain / chondroitin sulphate / omega-3 oils / omega-6 oils / Devil's claw / Valerian / White willow bark.

CHAPTER 34

Inflammatory Bowel Syndrome

Inflammatory bowel disease (IBD) refers to an inflammation of the small and large intestines. Crohn's disease, also known as regional enteritis, is an inflammation of the terminal portion of the small intestine. Ulcerative colitis is an inflammation of the large intestine or colon. Both Crohn's disease and Ulcerative colitis are characterized by extensive inflammation and ulceration of the intestines.

Inflammatory bowel disease is slightly more prevalent in females than in males and often between the ages of 20 and 60 years. It occurs more often between the age groups of 20 to 30 years and 50 to 60 years.

Individuals with inflammatory bowel disease suffer from recurrent attacks of diarrhea, cramping of the abdomen, weight loss and fever. Bloody diarrhea is not typically present in Crohn's disease, but abscesses, fistulas, peri-anal ulcerations and narrowing of the intestinal opening are a common sequelae. Individuals with Ulcerative colitis suffer from attacks of bloody, mucoid diarrhea that are usually precipitated by physical or emotional stress. These attacks can last for days, weeks or months and are followed by periods of remission that can extend from weeks to several decades. Some individuals experience relatively few attacks throughout their lifetime, while others have frequent, prolonged and potentially serious attacks that predispose to cancer of the colon. Both acute and chronic diarrhea can lead to electrolyte imbalance, poor nutrient absorption and weight loss. Complications of a severe attack of diarrhea include a sudden cessation of bowel function, anemia, infection, toxemia and the development of toxic megacolon. Toxic megacolon refers to a dilation of the colon by accumulating feces, fluid and toxic substances.

The exact cause of inflammatory bowel disease is unknown. Genetic predisposition to IBD is a strong possibility because there is a higher incidence of Crohn's disease and Ulcerative colitis among close relatives. Definitive diagnosis of inflammatory bowel disease is made after a proper stool analysis, barium enema and sigmoidoscopy. A sigmoidoscopy is a procedure used to directly visualize and examine the large and small intestines.

Conventional medical treatment of inflammatory bowel disease includes the use of drugs to suppress the symptoms associated with the disease and the use of surgery to remove parts of the affected intestines. Anti-inflammatory drugs used include cortisone and sulfasalazine. Anti-diarrhea drugs include Imodium and Lomotil. Surgical removal of the affected intestines of individuals with inflammatory bowel disease is restricted to severe conditions that don't respond to other forms of treatment. Surgery may be the only treatment available to some individuals, but caution should be exercised before the surgery is done. Nearly half of those individuals treated by surgery experience a recurrence of the disease in another area of the intestines.

Lifestyle

Physical and emotional stress can aggravate and exacerbate inflammatory bowel disease. Stressors should be identified and reduced. Exercise is a great way to reduce stress and should be encouraged. Meditation, hypnotherapy and biofeedback may be beneficial in reducing stress and promoting relaxation.

Diet

Avoid sugar and refined carbohydrates, fats and oils, fried and greasy foods, butter, margarine, coffee, tea, chocolate, carbonated beverages, spicy foods, milk and dairy products, animal products, meat, alcohol, tobacco and refined, processed foods. A food sensitivity or allergy test is encouraged to identify offending foods. Increase consumption of whole, unprocessed foods, vegetables and fruits. Steam, broil, boil and bake your foods. Limit intake of grains, especially wheat. Drink plenty of fluids including water, herb teas, fresh fruit and vegetable juices. Fruit juics should be unsweetened and diluted. Vegetable juices such as cabbage, aloe, carrot and beet juice are encouraged.

Vitamins and Minerals
(Daily unless otherwise stated)

Vitamin A - 25,000-50,000 IU. Diarrhea may lead to decreased absorption and supplementation may help to heal the lining of the intestines. **Folic Acid - 400-800 mcg.** May be deficient. Use of Sulfasalazine may increase deficiency. Supplementation may decrease diarrhea.

128

Vitamin B-complex - 50-100 mg. May be deficient. Intramuscular injections may be used.
Vitamin B5 (Pantothenic Acid) - 250-500 mg. May be deficient.
Vitamin C - 500-1000 mg. May be deficient. Required for the normal development and maintenance of connective tissue lining the intestines.
Vitamin D - 400 IU. May be deficient.
Vitamin E - 400-800 IU. May be deficient and supplementation helps to heal the intestines.
Vitamin K - 15-30 mg. May be deficient.

Calcium - 800-1200 mg. May be deficient.
Iron - 10-25 mg. Diarrhea may lead to blood loss and anemia.
Magnesium - 500-1000 mg. May be deficient. Helps to relieve intestinal spasms and relax muscles around the intestines.
Selenium - 400-800 mcg. May be deficient.
Zinc - 10-25 mg. May be deficient.

Food Supplements
(Daily unless otherwise stated)

Bromelain - 600-1200 mg (1800-2400 m.c.u.). Has anti-inflammatory activity and protein digesting ability.
Digestive Enzymes and/or Hydrochloric Acid - 1-2 capsules with each meal. Needed for proper digestion and absorption of nutrients and amino acids. Supplementation may help to heal the lining of the intestines.
Fiber - 5-10 gm. Increases intestinal bulk and improves transit time through the colon. Avoid water soluble fibers such as wheat bran and increase consumption of water insoluble fibers such as oat bran and apple pectin.
Lactobacillus acidophilus - 2-4 capsules. Friendly bacteria that normally inhabit the digestive system. May be deficient and supplementation may help to normalize the microflora of the intestines and help diarrhea.
N-acetyl glucosamine - 1500-3000 mg. A naturally occuring sugar that helps to prevent diarrhea and heal the damaged lining of the digestive tract.
Omega-3 oils (flaxseed, fish oil) - 1000-3000 mg. Involved in fat metabolism and decreases inflammation in the digestive system.
Omega-6 oils (evening primrose, borage oil) - 1000-3000 mg. Involved in fat metabolism and decreases inflammation in the digestive system.
Protein Supplement (Free form Amino Acids) - 5-20 gm. Protein is needed to repair the damaged lining of the digestive system and free form amino acids are readily absorbed.

Thymus glandular extract - 500-1000 mg. Helps to stimulate the immune system and supplementation may enhance the repair process of the intestines.

Herbal Medicines

Specific plants and plant derivatives may be useful in treating inflammatory bowel disease. Many plants have been used traditionally used to treat inflammatory bowel syndrome. **Aloe (Aloe vera) juice** is soothing and healing to the damaged lining of the intestines. **Licorice (Glycyrrhiza glabra)** heals ulcerations in the stomach and intestines. **Garlic (Allium sativum)** is a natural antibiotic that eliminates any infection and has a healing effect on the colon. **Chamomile (Matricaria chamomilla), Lemon balm (Melissa officinalis), Ginger (Zingiber officinalis), Rosemary (Rosemarinus officinalis), Peppermint (Mentha piperita), Valerian (Valerian officinalis)** and **Blessed thistle (Cnictus bendictus)** relax intestinal spasm and soothe the inflammed lining of digestive system. Robert's Formula is a popular combination of herbal medicines that have been used to treat inflammatory bowel syndrome. Constituents of this formula include **Marshmallow (Althea officinalis), Geranium (Geranium maculatum), Goldenseal (Hydrastis canadensis), Purple coneflower (Echinacea angustifolia), Slippery Elm (Ulmus fulva), Bromelain (1800-2400 m.cu.)** and **Cabbage powder.** One or more of these herbal medicines may be consumed as a tea, tincture, fluid extract, solid extract or supplement.

Highly Recommended

Avoid food sensitivities and allergies / avoid white sugar and refined carbohydrates / fresh vegetable juices / multiple vitamin and mineral complex / bromelain / digestive enzymes and/or hydrochloric acid / fiber / Lactobacillus acidophilus / N-acetyl glucosamine / omega-3 oils / omega-6 oils / Aloe vera juice / Garlic / Goldenseal / Marshmallow / Purple coneflower / Slippery elm.

CHAPTER 35

Insomnia

Insomnia is a relatively common disorder that results in abnormal wakefulness, an inability to fall asleep or to remain asleep throughout the night.

Insomnia is estimated to affect 15 to 25% of the entire population. Males and females are equally affected. Approximately 10% of the population, six to ten million people, resort to the use of sedative-hypnotic medication or sleeping pills.

The causes of insomnia may be physical or psychological or, more often, a combination of both. Some individuals are more sensitive to conditions around them than others and may be kept awake by slight noises, light or sharing their bed. Beverages that contain caffeine, such as coffee and tea, may cause insomnia in many people. A heavy meal before bedtime may prevent sleep. Drinking large quantities of fluids before bedtime may cause an uncomfortable feeling of distention in the bladder and cause awakenings during the night.

The type of bedding may be a cause of insomnia. Changing to a firmer mattress, doing without a pillow or making other changes in bedding may help. Those who are bothered by the weight of blankets may sleep better under light weight blankets or with a device that supports the bedclothes at the foot of the bed.

Elderly persons are particularly prone to sleep disturbances and insomnia. Chronic sleep induced respiratory problems and painful muscle cramping during the night may contribute to insomnia.

Stress is the among the most common causes of sleep disturbance and insomnia. Financial problems, marital problems, traumatic life events, death of a family member, personal problems, job problems and many other personal and family events are associated with sleep disturbances. Frequently insomnia persists long after the traumatic event has passed and the condition becomes chronic and self-perpetuating as the person becomes more anxious and worried about being not able to sleep.

Conventional medical treatment focuses on drug therapy to relieve insomnia. Muscle relaxants and sedative-hypnotics are frequently prescribed. Commonly prescribed medication includes Ativan (lorazepam), Librium (chlordiasepoxide), Halcion (triazolam), Valium (diazepam), Serax (oxezepam), Restoril (temazepam). Side effects of over-the-counter anti-histamines includes drowsiness and lethargy and these drugs are occasionally used to treat insomnia. Gravol (dimenhydrinate) an over-the-counter drug used to treat motion sickness is also used to treat insomnia. Most experts agree that sleeping pills do not help and may cause dependence and addiction problems. If prescribed, sleeping pills should only be used to treat insomnia for short duration.

Lifestyle

Stress can cause and aggravate insomnia. Stressors should be identified and reduced. Deep breathing exercises, meditation, biofeedback and yoga are excellent techniques to help decrease stress. Exercise is also strongly encouraged. Daily aerobic exercise helps to reduce stress.

Diet

All caffeine sources should be reduced including coffee, tea, chocolate, colas and other caffeine containing beverages and foods. A small alcohol consumption may be beneficial in helping to induce sleep, while high levels may disrupt normal sleeping patterns. Decrease consumption of sugar and refined carbohydrates. Increase consumption of whole and unprocessed foods, grains and cereals, fresh fruits and vegetables. A glass of milk before bedtime is very useful in relieving insomnia. Milk is high in the amino acid, tryptophan, that helps to induce sleep.

Vitamins and Minerals
(Daily unless otherwise stated)

Vitamin B-complex - 50-100 mg. Helps the body respond to stress and supplementation may be beneficial.
Vitamin B3 (Niacinamide) - 500-1000 mg before bedtime. A dose of niacinamide before bedtime helps decrease anxiety and aggression and has muscle relaxant and hypnotic action comparable to the action of minor tranquilizers.

Calcium - 800-1200 mg. Helps to relax tight and spasmed muscles and supplementation may be beneficial in the evening.
Magnesium - 600-1000 mg. Helps to relax tight and spasmed muscles and supplementation may be beneficial in the evening.

Food Supplements
(Daily unless otherwise stated)

Inositol - 250-500 mg. Supplementation helps to produce a calming effect. May be beneficial before bedtime in producing relaxation and promoting sleep.
Tryptophan - 500-1000 mg. The amino acid L-tryptophan is a precursor to the brain neurotransmitter, serotonin, that plays an important role in the induction and maintenance of sleep. Supplementation before bedtime increases the onset, duration and quality of sleep.

Herbal Medicines

Specific plants and plant derivatives are useful in treating insomnia and promoting both the quality and duration of sleep. **Hops (Humulus lupulus), Jamaican dogwood (Piscidia erythrina), Passion flower (Passiflora incarnata), Skullcap (Scutellaria laterifolia) and Valerian (Valerian officinalis)** are useful in treating insomnia. One or more of these herbal medicines may be consumed prior to bedtime as a tea, tincture, fluid extract, solid extract or supplement.

Highly Recommended

Decrease stress / avoid all caffeine sources / Decrease consumption of white sugar and refined carbohydrates / vitamin B-complex / vitamin B3 / calcium / magnesium / Hops / Passionflower / Valerian.

CHAPTER 36

Irritable Bowel Syndrome

Irritable bowel syndrome or IBS is the most common cause of chronic diarrhea and lower abdominal discomfort. It is a common benign disorder of colon or large intestine function and is typically characterized by periods of diarrhea, often alternating with constipation.

Irritable bowel syndrome is estimated to affect 14 to 20% of the North American population. It accounts for 50 to 70% of all people with digestive compaints and represents 30 to 50% of all referrals to gastroenterologists, specialists in treating digestive disorders. It commonly occurs in individuals between the ages of 20 to 35 years, but can also occur in young children and the elderly. It is one of the most frequent causes of chronic diarrhea in young children. And although IBS occurs in the elderly, it is an uncommon cause of diarrhea in this age group.

Symptoms of irritable bowel syndrome include diarrhea, constipation; often alternating between periods of diarrhea and constipation, abdominal pain, cramping bloating, flatulence, beltching, nausea, vomiting, heartburn, variable appetite, poor digestion and difficult swallowing. Fever, gastro-intestinal bleeding and weight loss are not part of this syndrome and suggest a more serious underlying disorder.

The exact cause of irritable bowel syndrome is unknown. It is generally agreed that IBS is a disorder of movement of digestive material through the intestines. Factors that affect colon motility include psychological and emotional stressors, diet, especially lack of fiber and increased consumption of refined carbohydrates. There is also evidence to suggest that IBS is a learned behavior.

Diagnosis of irritable bowel syndrome is usually made after other serious gastro-intestinal disorders have been ruled out. Diagnosis is based upon history, presenting symptoms, and lab tests to rule out other disorders. Other diseases that can mimic IBS include excessive consumption of coffee, tea, colas and refined sugars, intestinal infection, ulcerative colitis, Crohn's disease, lactose intolerance, laxative abuse, drug induced intestinal inflammation, diverticulitis, malabsorption syndrome, diabetes, hypothyroidism and cancer.

Conventional medical treatment of irritable bowel syndrome focuses on drug therapy to provide relief of the symptoms associated with this disorder. Anti-cholinergic, anti-diarrhea, anti-ulcer and psychotropic drugs are routinely prescribed for this disorder. Prescribed medication includes the anti-cholinergic, Bentyl (dicyclomine), opiates such as Lomotil (diphenoxylate) and Imodium (loperamide), beta-blockers, prostaglandin inhibitors and a variety of psychotropic drugs and muscle relaxants.

Lifestyle

Stress is strongly associated with the development of irritable bowel syndrome. Stressors should be identified and reduced. Meditation, deep breathing exercises, yoga, biofeedback, counselling and behavioral modification are effective techniques that help the body relax. Exercise is a great way to reduce stress and should be a part of daily routine. The combination of behavioral modification and medical treatment is very effective in altering the course of IBS.

Diet

Avoid white sugar and refined carbohydrates. Refined carbohydrates can aggravate intestinal muscle spasm. Avoid coffee, tea, colas, chocolate and other caffeine containing beverages and foods. Caffeine increases muscle contraction in the intestines and will make diarrhea and cramping worse. Food sensitivities and allergies have been implicated as a possible triggering mechanism in IBS. Offending foods include wheat, milk, soy, beef, pork, food additives and colorings, corn, coffee and citrus fruits. Increase consumption of foods high in fiber, whole and unprocessed grains, fresh fruits and vegetables.

Vitamins and Minerals
(Daily unless otherwise stated)

Vitamin B-complex - 50-100 mg. Helps the body respond to stress and supplementation may be beneficial.
Folic acid - 10-20 mg. Supplementation may be beneficial in treating chronic diarrhea.

Calcium - 600-1200 mg. Helps to relax smooth muscle of the intestines relax and prevents intestinal cramping.
Magnesium - 400-800 mg. Helps to relax smooth muscle of the intestines and prevents intestinal cramping.

Food Supplements
(Daily unless otherwise stated)

Dietary fiber - 10-30 gm. Helps to increase stool bulk, increase transit time through the digestive system and prevent diarrhea.
Digestive enzymes and/or Hydrochloric acid - 1-2 tablets just after each meal. Supplementation has demonstrated to be effective in treating certain cases of chronic diarrhea.
Lactobacillus acidophilus - 2-4 capsules between meals. Supplementation may be beneficial in treating certain cases of chronic diarrhea.
Peppermint oil (enteric coated capsules) - 0.6-1.2 ml. Peppermint oil helps smooth muscle of the intestines to relax and prevents cramping of the colon. Enteric coated peppermint oil is successfully used in Europe to treat IBS.

Herbal Medicines

Specific plants and plant derivatives may be useful in treating irritable bowel syndrome. **Balm (Melissa officinalis), Chamomile (Matricaria chamomilla), Caraway (Carum carvi), Cramp bark (Viburnum opulus), Fennel (Foeniculum vulgare), Ginger (Zingiber officinalis), Peppermint (Mentha piperita), Rosemary (Rosemarinus officinalis) and Valerian (Valerian officinalis)** are useful plants in treating this disorder. One or more of these herbal medicines may be consumed as a tea, tincture, fluid extract, solid extract or supplement.

Highly Recommended

Decrease stress / avoid white sugar and refined carbohydrates/ avoid all caffeine sources / vitamin B-complex / calcium / magnesium / dietary fiber / Lactobacillus acidophilus / peppermint oil / Chamomile / Fennel / Ginger / Peppermint / Valerian.

CHAPTER 37

Kidney Stones

Kidney stones are solid accumulations that tend to form in the kidneys, but can occur throughout the urinary tract system. Pain, obstruction and secondary infection are the most common symptoms associated with kidney stones.

Kidney stones occur in approximately 6% of the population. They are responsible for one in a thousand of hospital admissions. They are twice as common in men as they are in women and tend to occur in adults over the age of 30 years.

Kidney stones may be present without producing any symptoms and may pass through the urinary tract without any complications. Back pain that occurs where the kidneys are located and flank pain that radiates across the abdomen, down the ureters and down the inner thigh and genital areas, are common symptoms. Nausea, vomiting, bloating and abdominal distention can occur. Excruciating intermittent pain usually indicates an acute obstruction of a stone within the kidney or along the ureters. Fever, chills, increased frequency of urination, blood in the urine and the presence of white blood cells in the urine usually indicate an infection. A stone obstruction can disrupt normal kidney function.

The exact cause of kidney stone formation is not entirely known. The identification of the type of kidney stone is important in determining the cause of stone formation and the appropriate treatment. Approximately 5% of calcium stones are associated with hyperparathyroidism, vitamin D excess, hyperthyroidism, sarcoidosis, kidney tubular acidosis, multiple myeloma, Cushing's disease and cancer. Diagnosis of kidney stones is based upon history and medical tests including a urinalysis, X-ray and intravenous pyelogram (IVP).

Conventional medical treatment of kidney stones includes the use of analgesics and muscle relaxants to alleviate the pain and surgery to remove the stones. No specific treatment is recommended for small, solitary kidney stones that do not cause obstruction or produce infection. Painkillers and muscle relaxants are prescribed to alleviate the pain associated with kidney stones. Surgery is recommended for multiple stones that can cause obstruction or produce infection. Shock wave lithotripsy uses ultrasound waves to disintegrate the stones.

Lifestyle

Chronic consumption of aspirin and lack of exercise can promote kidney stone formation. Daily exercise is a great way to stay in shape and improve kidney function. Long term use of antacids that are high in calcium can contribute to stone formation.

Lead, aluminum, mercury, uranium and cadmium toxicity can damage the kidneys and can promote stone formation. Sources of these heavy metals should be identified and eliminated.

Diet

Avoid sugar and refined carbohydrates. Avoid excess milk, cheese and other dairy products. Decrease consumption of salt, soft drinks and red meats. Decrease consumption of foods high in oxalic acids such as bean, cocoa, coffee, tea, chocolate, beet tops, rhubarb, spinach, kale, peanuts, pepper and beet tops. Increase consumption of whole, unprocessed foods and high fiber foods. A vegetarian diet may be beneficial. Avoid excess phosphates from red meat, soft drinks and refined foods. Excess phosphates upsets the calcium balance and promotes stone formation. Increase water consumption to 6 to 8 glasses per day. Increase consumption of cranberry and watermelon juices. Both are natural diuretics.

Vitamins and Minerals
(Daily unless otherwise stated)

Vitamin A - 10,000-20,000 IU. Deficiency can promote the development of kidney stones.
Vitamin B-complex - 50-100 mg. May be deficient. Intramuscular injections may be beneficial.
Vitamin B6 - 25-100 mg. May be deficient. Involved in the metabolism of oxalic acid and glutamic acid. Helps enzymes that breakdown oxalic acid.
Vitamin C - 500-2000 mg. Acidifies the urine and most stones will not form in acid urine. Avoid high doses, greater than 6 grams per day, for extended periods. High doses can promote formation of kidney stones.

Vitamin K - 200-400 mcg. May be deficient. Necessary for the production of proteins in the kidney that help to dissolve stones.

Magnesium - 400-800 mg. Improves the solubility of calcium stones. Works synergistically with vitamin B6.

Food Supplements
(Daily unless otherwise stated)

Glutamic acid - 250-500 mg. Decreases calcium oxylate precipitation.
Kidney glandular extract - 500-1000 mg. Supports the function of the kidneys.
Lysine - 500-1000 mg. A naturally occuring amino acid that may be deficient and deficiency increase urinary calcium levels.
Potassium citrate - 100-200 mg. Helps to decrease calcium oxylate precipitation.

Herbal Medicines

Specific plants and plant derivatives may be useful in treating kidney stones. Diuretic herbal medicines promote urination and the expulsion of stones. Diuretic herbal medicines include **Bearberry (Arctostaphylos uva-ursi), Buchu (Barosma betulina), Corn silk (Zea mays), Couchgrass (Agropyrens repens), Dandelion (Taraxacum officinalis), Horsetail (Equisetum arvense), Hydrangea (Hydrangea arborescens), Juniper (Juniper communis), Parsley (Petroselinum sativum), Parsley piert (Parietaria officinalis), and Stone root (Collinsonia canadensis).** Khella (Ammi visnaga) helps to relax the ureters and promote passage of the stone in the urine. One or more of these herbal medicines may be consumed as a tea, tincture, fluid extract, solid extract or supplement.

Highly Recommended

Avoid food high in oxylic acid / increase water consumption / vitamin B6 / vitamin C / magnesium / Bearberry / Buchu / Corn silk / Couchgrass / Hydrangea / Juniper / Stone root.

139

CHAPTER 38

Liver Disease

Liver disease is the term used to describe diseases that affect the liver. Diseases that affect the liver include acute and chronic hepatitis, fatty degeneration of the liver, cirrhosis and liver cancer.

An estimated 2 to 5% of the population are believed to suffer from liver disease. Men are affected slightly more than females. Liver disease is much more prevalent in individuals who consume large quantities of alcohol over long periods, have been exposed to toxic chemicals or have been exposed to certain viruses that are known to cause hepatitis.

The liver is a large, dark red gland located in the upper right portion of the abdomen, just beneath the diaphragm. The liver is the largest and most metabolically active organ in the entire body. It has over 500 different and important functions. These functions involve such broad categories as intermediate metabolism of carbohydrates, proteins and fats; production of many different proteins and enzymes including globulins and albumin that help to regulate fluid volume in the blood and initiate blood clotting; production of bile that aids in the digestion and absorption of fats; detoxification and removal of foreign material and toxins such as bacteria, drugs, alcohol and noxious chemicals; storage of protein, glycogen, vitamins and minerals; the liver can store up to 20% of its weight in glycogen and up to 40% of its weight in fats; maintains the balance of sex hormones in the body; breaks down worn out red blood cells and disposes of the them through the urine and feces and has many other important functions too numerous to list here.

The liver is one of the most frequently damaged organs in the body. It is fortunate that it has an incredible regeneration capacity. It has been experimentally shown that only 10% of the liver is required to maintain normal liver function.

Jaundice is the yellowish discoloration of the skin, white of the eye and other tissues due to excess circulating bilirubin in the blood. Jaundice is not a disease by it itself, but is usually a sign of underlying liver dysfunction. Bilirubin is a yellow or orange pigment producted by the breakdown of old red blood cells and hemoglobin by the liver. Cholestasis results when bile flow is impaired and always results in obstructive jaundice.

Hepatitis is an inflammatory process of the liver characterized by patchy degeneration of liver cells. The major causes of hepatitis are viruses types A, B, non-A, non-B, alcohol and drugs. Hepatitis A is spread primarily by fecal-oral contact and causes a "flu-like" illness. Hepatitis B is transmitted through blood and contaminated blood products. Hepatitis B is associated with a wide spectrum of liver disease from a sub-clinical carrier state to acute hepatitis, chronic hepatitis, cirrhosis and liver cancer. Hepatitis B may also cause a "flu-like" illness but can progress and ultimately cause fatal liver failure. Chronic hepatitis is an inflammation of the liver that lasts for 6 months or longer.

Ascites is the term used to describe excess fluid in the abdomen and always is due to a chronic diseases such as cirrhosis of the liver from alcoholism and liver cancer.

Fatty liver is the abnormal accumulation of fat in liver cells and is estimated to occur in 25% of all people. It is most common response of the liver to injury. It occurs when when there is chronic exposure to environmental toxins, excess consumption of alcohol and a diet high in fats and refined carbohydrates.

Fibrosis is due to excess accumulation of fibrous tissue in the liver. It may result from accumulation of old fibers and production of new fibrous tissue. It is a common response to liver damage.

Cirrhosis is used to describe disintegration of liver cells and widespread fibrosis throughout the liver. Cirrhosis is only exceeded by heart disease and cancer as the leading cause of death in the 45 to 65 year old age group in North America. Chronic and excess consumption of alcohol is the most common cause of cirrhosis.

Signs and symptoms of liver disease are numerous. Early signs of liver disease may include fatigue, poor appetite, nausea, vomiting and fever. Distaste for cigarettes is an early characteristic sign of hepatitis. Hives and joint pains may also occur. Jaundice, a yellowish disocoloration of the skin and cholestasis, bile flow obstruction may occur. Laboratory tests and X-rays are often required to make the diagnosis of liver disease.

Conventional medical treatment of liver disease focuses on drug therapy and surgery. In many instances no treatment is required for mild to moderate liver disease. In more serious instances anti-inflammatory drugs including steroids are prescribed. Surgery is indicated in those instances where drug therapy is not successful and part of the disease organ can be removed.

Lifestyle

Prevention is the most important factor in avoiding liver disease. Clean personal hygiene is very beneficial in preventing infectious liver disease. Avoiding excess exposure to environmental toxins and chemicals is imperative in preventing toxic liver disease. Avoid chronic and excess consumption of alcohol. Those individuals who have a problem controlling alcohol intake should seek appropriate therapy. Excellent counsellors, support groups and facilities are available to treat alcoholism.

Diet

Avoid all white sugar and refined carbohydrates. Excess consumption of sugar is associated with elevated liver enzymes, indicating liver inflammation and possible damage. Avoid excess coffee, tea, colas, chocolate and other caffeine containing beverages and foods. Large doses of caffeine can overwhelm an already overworked liver. Moderate consumption of coffee for short periods of time may be beneficial to the liver. Caffeine increases bile release from the liver into the small intestine. Avoid excess alcohol consumption. Chronic consumption of alcoholic beverages can lead to cirrhosis and permanent liver damage. Moderate consumption of alcohol may be beneficial. Increase consumption of whole and unprocessed foods, whole grains and cereals, fresh fruits and vegetables. Specifically increase consumption of carrots, beets and artichokes. They have a beneficial effect of stimulating bile flow and help to clean the liver.

Vitamins and Minerals
(Daily unless otherwise stated)

Vitamin B-complex - 50-100 mg. Helps the body respond to stress.
Vitamin B12 - 50-500 mcg. Required for DNA cell reproduction. Supplementation may help to increase appetite and decrease liver inflammation in individuals with viral hepatitis.

142

Folic acid - 400-800 mcg. Required for DNA cell reproduction. Supplementation together with vitamin B12 helps to improve symptoms and shorten the duration of illness in individuals with viral hepatitis.

Vitamin C - 2000-6000 mg. Has immune stimulating and antiviral effects. High dose vitamin C therapy may be very beneficial in improving the symptoms and shortening the duration of illness in individuals with viral hepatitis.

Food Supplements
(Daily unless otherwise stated)

Adrenal glandular extract - 500-1000 mg. Helps to support and stimulate adrenal gland function. The adrenal gland helps the body deal to stress.

Bioflavonoids - 1000-2000 mg. Specific bioflavonoids (catechin, quercitin) help to support liver function and decrease inflammation in the liver. Works synergistically with vitamin C.

Carnitine - 500-1500 mg. Helps to improve fat transport into liver cells and improve breakdown and elimination of fat soluble toxins.

Choline - 500-1500 mg. Choline is a lipotropic that aids in fat digestion and breakdown within liver cells and aids in the elimination of fat soluble toxins.

Liver glandular extract - 500-2000 mg. Helps to support and stimulate liver function. Is a rich source of fat soluble and B-complex vitamins and iron and other nutrients required by the liver.

Methionine - 500-1500 mg. Is a potent lipotropic that aids in fat digestion and breakdown within liver cells and aids in the elimination of fat soluble toxins.

Thymus glandular extract - 500-1000 mg. Helps to support and stimulate thymus gland function. The thymus gland is an important part of the immune system and supplementation may be beneficial in decreasing the effects of liver infection.

Herbal Medicines

Specific plants and plant derivatives may be useful in treating liver disease and improving liver function. **Artichoke (Cyanara scolymus), Black radish (Raphanus sativum), Dandelion (Taraxacum officinalis), Fringetree bark (Chionanthus virginicus), Goldenseal (Hydrastis canadensis), Greater celandine (Chelidoniun majus), Licorice (Glycyrrhiza glabra), Milk thistle (Silybum marianum) and Tumeric**

(**Curcuma longa**) help to protect the liver and prevent permanent damage from infection and inflammation. One or more of these herbal medicines may be consumed as a tea, tincture, fluid extract, solid extract, or supplement.

Highly Recommended

Avoid chronic and excess consumption of alcohol / decrease consumption of white sugar and refined carbohydrates / vitamin B-complex / vitamin C / adrenal glandular extract / bioflavonoids / choline / liver glandular extract / methionine / thymus glandular extract / Artichoke / Dandelion / Milk thistle.

CHAPTER 39

Macular Degeneration

The macula is the central area of the retina in the eye responsible for fine vision. Macular degeneration is caused by atrophy or degeneration of the macula and is one of the leading causes of decreased visual acuity.

Macular degeneration occurs in 2 to 5% of the population and typically affects elderly individuals. It affects both sexes equally and is much more common in white than in black people. Macular degeneration is the leading cause of decreased visual acuity in people aged 55 years and older in North America. It is second only to cataracts as the leading cause of decreased vision in people aged 65 years or older. Macular degeneration is responsible for blindness in 120,000 people in North America and accounts for 16,000 new cases of blindness each year.

A slow or sudden, painless loss of visual acuity may occur. Occasionally the first symptom is visual distortion from one eye. As the disease progresses there is progressive loss of visual acuity. Individuals with macular degeneration, though often legally blind, usually have good peripheral vision and useful color vision. Although blindness may occur in some cases, individuals with macular degeneration should be advised that they will not lose all sight.

The cause of macular degeneration is not entirely known. A decrease in visual acuity is a normal process of aging. Heredity is believed to play a strong role in the development of this disease. Risk factors that contribute to the development of this disease include atherosclerosis, hypertension, cigarette smoking and poor nutrition.

There is no effective conventional medical treatment for macular degeneration. Laser therapy may be beneficial in some instances. Optical devices used to enhance poor vision are available and low vision service counselling is advised.

Lifestyle

Avoid risk factors that may cause macular degeneration. Eliminate factors that contribute to the development of atherosclerosis and hypertension. Avoid cigarette smoking and immediately begin a program to quit smoking.

Diet

Avoid white sugar and refined carbohydrates. Limit the consumption of fats, especially saturated fats, which contributes to the development of atherosclerosis and hypertension. Avoid excess alcohol consumption. Increase consumption of whole and unprocessed foods, fresh fruits and vegetables. Especially increase consumption of vegetables high in vitamin A and beta-carotene including carrots, squash, beets and other green leafy vegetables.

Vitamins and Minerals
(Daily unless otherwise stated)

Vitamin A - 10,000-25,000 IU. A potent antioxidant, that helps to prevent damage to the retina, macula and blood vessels of the eye.
Beta-carotene - 50,000-100,000 IU. Precursor to vitamin A that doesn't have the side effects that vitamin A does in higher doses. Also acts as a potent antioxidant.
Vitamin C - 500-2000 mg. A potent antioxidant that helps to prevent damage to the retina, macula and blood vessels of the eye.
Vitamin E - 400-800 IU. A potent antioxidant that helps to prevent damage to the retina, macula and blood vessels of the eye.

Selenium - 200-400 mcg. A potent antioxidant that helps to prevent damage to the retina, macula and blood vessels of the eye.
Zinc - 50-100 mg. Required for proper function of the macula. Supplementation helps to prevent accelerated visual loss associated with macular degeneration.

146

Food Supplements
(Daily unless otherwise stated)

Bioflavonoids - 500-1500 mg. Helps to stabilize connective tissue around blood vessels of the eye.

Omega-3 oils (flaxseed, fish oil) - 1000-3000 mg. A rich source of essential oils. Supplementation helps to decrease atherosclerosis and hypertension.

Omega-6 oils (evening primrose, borage oil) - 1000-3000 mg. A rich source of essential oils. Supplementation helps to decrease atherosclerosis and hypertension.

Herbal Medicines

Specific plants and plant derivatives may be useful in treating macular degeneration and preventing further visual loss. **Bilberry (Vaccinium myrtillus), Gingko (Ginkgo biloba), Hawthorn (Crataegus oxyacantha)** may be beneficial in treating macular degeneration. A standardized extract containing 25% bilberry anthocyanosides is recommended at 75 to 150 mg per day. One or more of these herbal medicines may be consumed as a tea, tincture, fluid extract, solid extract or supplement.

Highly Recommended

Avoid cigarette smoking / avoid white sugar and refined carbohydrates / vitamin A / beta-carotene / vitamin C / vitamin E / selenium / zinc / bioflavonoids / Bilberry.

CHAPTER 40

Menopause

Menopause refers to the condition when the ovaries stop functioning and menstruation and childbearing cease. Menopause is often called "change of life" or climacteric and occurs to all women throughout the world. Menopause is a natural physiologic process that results from the normal aging of the ovaries.

15% of women experience no symptoms during menopause. 60 to 75% of women experience hot flushes to the face, neck, upper body and excessive perspiration, especially at night. Decreased menstrual flow, decreased bleeding during the period and periods spaced further apart are usually the first signs of menopause. Other symptoms include fatigue, insomnia, dizziness, tingling in extremities, rapid heart beat, heart palpitations, difficult and/or painful sexual intercourse, inability to hold urine, bladder infection, vaginitis, dry vagina, nausea, flatulence, constipation, joint and muscle pain. Decreased size of the ovaries, fallopian tubes, uterus and vagina occurs. Osteoporosis, or decreased bone mass can occur as a consequence of menopause. Menopause generally lasts from one to five years in duration, although hot flushes for more than ten years have been reported.

The ovaries are two small almond sized glands located in the lower abdomen on either side of the uterus. The ovaries have two functions: ovulation of eggs and production of hormones, chiefly progesterone and estrogen, which influence the female's physical characteristics and affect the reproductive process. During the female reproductive cycle, one ripe egg is released from one ovary and it begins its descent down the fallopian tubes into the uterus. In anticipation of fertilization various physiologic changes occurs in the uterus and vagina. If fertilization does not occur then the lining of the uterus is shed and menstruation occurs. Over 450 ripe eggs are released from the ovaries during the normal female reproductive life.

Natural menopause normally occurs between the ages of 40 and 58 years. The average age of onset of menopause is 49 to 50 years of age. If menopause occurs before the age of 40 years then it is refered to as premature menopause. If menopause occurs after the age of 58 years then it is refered to as delayed menopause. Menopause can occur earlier than normal if there is a history of hormone dysfunction, infection, surgery, radiation, cancer or use of certain drugs. Smoking can accelerate the onset of menopause by two years or more.

Conventional medical treatment of menopause includes the use of antidepressants, muscle relaxants and hormone replacement. Estrogen is typically prescribed at a dosage of 0.3 to 1.25 mg/day. A combination of estrogen and progesterone is used for patients that still have a uterus. Risk factors of estrogen use include endometrial cancer, breast cancer, hypertension, blood clots, liver disease, stroke, gall bladder disease and heart attacks. The risk factors and benefits of hormone therapy should be considered before estrogen is prescribed. Estrogen therapy should be reserved for those individuals at high risk for developing osteoporosis.

Lifestyle

Menopause can be a particularly stressful stage of life. Stressors should be identified and decreased. Concerns, fears and questions about menopause should be addressed. Misconceptions about menopause should be corrected. Menopause does not only happen to neurotic women. Menopause does not make a women less beautiful or less sexy. You can still enjoy a fulfilling sex life before and after menopause. After menopause many women feel that they have been freed from the responsibility of pregnancy.

Make exercise a part of daily routine. Walk, swim, ride a bicycle or do some form of aerobic exercise on a daily basis.

Use natural fiber clothes and support hosiery. Synthetic fibers can aggravate menopausal symptoms.

Diet

Avoid white sugar and refined carbohydrates. Avoid coffee, tea, chocolate, colas and other caffeine containing foods and beverages. Decrease consumption of fats, dairy, red meat, alcohol, spicy foods and processed foods. Increase consumption of whole, unprocessed foods, vegetables and fruits. Increase consumption of foods high in vitamin E content including liver, wheat germ, seeds and nuts. Increase consumption of fresh, unsweetened vegetable and fruit juices.

Vitamins and Minerals
(Daily unless otherwise stated)

Vitamin A - 10,000-25,000 IU. Helps to maintain the lining of the vagina and uterus. Also acts as a potent antioxidant and improves immune function.

Vitamin B-complex - 50-100 mg. Consists of the entire B-complex family including Vitamin B1 (Thiamine), B2 (Riboflavin), B3 (Niacin) and B12 (Cyanocobalamin). Known also as the "stress" vitamins that help to maintain a healthy nervous system. Intramuscular injections may be beneficial.

Vitamin B5 (Pantothenic Acid) - 250-500 mg. Helps to support the function of the adrenal glands and decrease symptoms of stress and fatigue.

Vitamin B6 (Pyridoxine) - 25-50 mg. Used by the liver to activate hormones such as estrogen and to eliminate toxins.

Vitamin C - 5000-3000 mg. Helps to decrease hot flushes and other symptoms of menopause.

Vitamin D - 400-800 IU. Required for intestinal absorption of calcium and helps to prevent osteoporosis.

Vitamin E - 400-1600 IU. Helps to decrease hot flushes and other symptoms of menopause.

Calcium - 800-1500 mg. Necessary for healthy bones and prevents osteoporosis. Helps symptoms of fatigue, stress, muscle spasms and abdominal cramps.

Magnesium - 600-1000 mg. Helps symptoms of fatigue, stress, muscle spasms, abdominal cramps and depression.

Food Supplements
(Daily unless otherwise stated)

Bee pollen - 500-1000 mg. Helps to decrease hot flushes and other symptoms of menopause. Bee pollen is a rich source of B-complex vitamins and vitamin E.

Digestive enzymes and/or Hydrochloric acid - 1-2 capsules with each meal. Many women over the age of 50 years have a lack of digestive enzymes and/or hydrochloric acid. Necessary for proper digestion and absorption of vitamins and minerals.

Herbal Medicines

Specific plants and plant derivatives may be useful in treating menopause and helping to relieve the symptoms associated with this condition. Many plants contain natural estrogen and estrogen precursors. Plant estrogens, though less active than synthetic estrogens, due exert biological activity. Plant estrogens can be a natural source of estrogen that can help to minimize the symptoms associated with menopause. Plant sources of estrogen include **Alfalfa (Medicago sativa), Black Cohosh (Cimicifuga racemosa), Blue Cohosh (Caulophyllum thalictroides), Chaste tree (Vitex agnus-castus), Dong quai (Angelica sinensis), False Unicorn root (Helonias opulus), Fennel (Foeniculum vulgare), Fo ti tieng (Polygonum multiforum), Ginseng (Panax ginseng) and Licorice (Glycyrrhiza glabra).** One or more of these herbal medicines may be consumed as a tea, tincture, fluid extract, solid extract or supplement.

Highly Recommended

Avoid white sugar and refined carbohydrates / avoid caffeine containing beverages / vitamin B-complex / vitamin E / calcium / magnesium / bee pollen / digestive enzymes / Alfalfa / Black cohosh / Blue cohosh / Dong quai / Fennel / Ginseng.

151

CHAPTER 41

Migraine Headache

A migraine headache is usually a severe headache often limited to one side of the head and may be accompanied by nausea and vomiting.

A conservative estimate indicates that 10% of the North American population or ten to 20 million people suffer from migraine attacks. Migraines occur slightly more commonly in females than in males.

Symptoms of migraine headaches include dull or sharp pain in the head. The pain may occur on one or more sides of the head and may extend to the neck. However, the pain is usually localized to one side of the head, typically in the frontal or temporal areas. Many migraine sufferers report that they sense the onset of a headache and describe an "aura" that may occur just preceding the headache. Visual disturbances, hearing disturbances, altered taste and smell and other sensory disturbances may occur. In addition, loss of mental acuity or consciousness and muscle function may occur. Immediate medical attention is required when a headache comes on suddenly from no apparent cause, there is associated neurological symptoms or from trauma to the head. High fever and stiffness of the neck accompanied by headache may indicate meningitis.

Although recurring headache may an early sign of serious disease in the body, relatively few headaches are caused by a serious, underlying organic disease. Most headaches result from dilation of blood vessels in the tissues surrounding the brain or from tension in the muscles of the neck and scalp.

A tension headache is associated with prolonged overwork, emotional strain and stress and typically occurs in the occipital region of the skull. Pain usually begins in the back of the head and extends down the neck. Pain may occur one or both sides and has been described as excruciating to a dull, peristent ache.

A cluster headache is a migraine-like disorder characterized by attacks of one-sided intense pain over the eye and forehead, with flushing and watering of the eyes and nose. Attacks usually last about one hour and occur in clusters of two or more headaches.

The exact cause of migraine headaches is not known. Up to 70% of individuals suffering from migraines have a family history for these headaches, suggesting a genetic link. Stress is the single most common precipitant of migraine headache. Other common precipitants include dietary factors, poor nutrition, hypoglycemia and hormonal changes. Certain foods have been described to provoke migraine attacks. Cheese, pickled herring, red wine and chocolate are believed to provoke attacks. Some individuals with migraines may have a disorder of carbohydrate metabolism and notice that missing a meal brings on an attack. Hypoglycemia or low blood sugar can trigger migraines and eating small frequent meals is strongly recommended.

Conventional medical treatment of migraines focuses on drug therapy to prevent the pain and inflammation associated with these headaches. Commonly prescribed medication include aspirin (ASA), Motrin (ibuprofen), Tylenol (acetaminophen), ergotamine and other ergot alkaloids, Inderal (propranolol), codeine, morphine and other narcotic analgesics. Drug therapy is beneficial in decreasing the pain and inflammation associated with migraines, but does not identify the cause and does not prevent future attacks.

Lifestyle

Stress can trigger migraine headaches. Stressors should be identified and reduced. Stress reduction techniques such as meditation, hypnotherapy, acupuncture and hydrotherapy may be helpful and provide relief. Exercise is an excellent way to reduce stress. Exercise should be a part of daily routine and include such as activities as walking, jogging, bicycling, swimming or other sports.

Diet

Caffeine consumption has been shown to increase incidence of migraine attacks. Coffee, tea, colas, chocolate and other caffeine containing foods and beverages should be eliminated. Food sensitivities and allergies are strongly associated with the development of headaches. At least 25 different foods have been described to evoke migraines. These foods or food and drug combinations include coloring and flavoring agents, food additives and preservatives, foods containing tyramine including red wine and cheese, pesticides, eggs, milk, cheese and dairy products, peanuts, curry, wheat and other grains. Intake of foods high in copper including chocolate and citrus fruits, can also trigger migraine headaches and should be avoided. Increase consumption of whole and unprocessed foods, fresh fruits and vegetables.

Vitamins and Minerals
(Daily unless otherwise stated)

Vitamin B-complex - 50-100 mg. Helps the body respond to stress and supplementation may be beneficial where stress is a factor in triggering migraines.
Vitamin E - 400-1200 IU. Has demonstrated anti-inflammatory and membrane stabilizing effects that may be beneficial in treating migraines.

Calcium - 800-1200 mg. Helps smooth muscle around blood vessels and skeletal muscle in the skull to relax.
Magnesium - 400-800 mg. Helps smooth muscle around blood vessels and skeletal muscle in the skull to relax.

Food Supplements
(Daily unless otherwise stated)

Adrenal glandular extract - 500-1000 mg. Helps to stimulate and support adrenal gland function. It promotes cortisol release from the adrenal glands which has potent anti-inflammatory activity.
Bromelain (1800-2200 m.c.u.) - 500-1000 mg. A sulfur containing proteolytic enzyme obtained from the pineapple plant. It activates anti-inflammatory prostaglandins in the body and promotes removal of fluid that causes inflammation and swelling. Take without food or between meals for best results.
Choline - 500-1000 mg. May be low in red blood cells and may be associated with migraines. Supplementation may be beneficial.
Omega-3 oils (flaxseed, fish oil) - 5-10 gm. A rich source of essential fatty acids that may be deficient in the body. Supplementation helps to inhibit platelet aggregation in blood vessels, produce anti-inflammatory prostaglandins and prevent migraine attacks.
Omega-6 oils (evening primrose, borage oil) - 5-10 gm. A rich source of essential fatty acids that may be deficient in the body. Supplementation helps to inhibit platelet aggregation in blood vessels, produce anti-inflammatory prostaglandins and prevent migraine attacks.

Herbal Medicines

Specific plants and plant derivatives may be useful in treating migraine headaches. **Devil's claw (Harpagophytum procumbens), Feverfew (Tanacetum parthenium), Licorice (Glycyrrhiza glabra), Tumeric (Curcuma longa), Valerian (Valerian officinalis), White willow (Salix alba) and Wintergreen (Gaultheria procumbens)** are useful plants. One or more of these herbal medicines may be consumed as a tea, tincture, fluid extract, solid extract or supplement.

Highly Recommended

Decrease stress / avoid food and environmental sensitivities and allergies / vitamin B-complex / calcium / magnesium / adrenal glandular extract / omega-3 oils / omega-6 oils / Feverfew.

CHAPTER 42

Multiple Sclerosis

Multiple sclerosis is a slowly progressive nerve disease characterized by demyelination of nerves in the brain and spinal cord. Myelin is a composed of fat and surrounds some nerves. Its main function is to protect the nerves from injury and increase nerve conduction. Myelin is broken down and nerves are more susceptible to injury and improper nerve conduction.

Multiple sclerosis occurs slightly more commonly in women than in men. The disease usually occurs in individuals between the ages of 20 and 40 years. The incidence of MS in tropical climates around the world is 1 in 10,000, whereas the incidence in northern temperate climates is 1 in 2000. Onset of the disease is insidious. Exacerbations and remissions lasting for months to years may occur. The disease is rarely fatal.

The most common symptom of MS is usually an abnormal sensation such as burning, tingling or prickling in the face, head, arm, hand, leg or foot. Muscle weakness, slight stiffness, unusual fatigability of an arm or leg, minor gait disturbances, difficult bladder control, vertigo (spinning sensation) and mild emotional disturbances can also occur. Excess heat can worsen symptoms. Nerve pain, optic neuritis, double vision, increased tendon reflexes, involuntary, rhythmic movement of the eyes, involuntary muscle tremors, increased or decreased frequency of urination, incontinence and sexual impotence in men are other physical symptoms. Depression, hysteria, apathy, lack of judgement, inattention, emotional lability, sudden weeping are other emotional symptoms. Symptoms can occur for months or years without a proper diagnosis.

The exact cause of multiple sclerosis is unknown. Genetics plays an important role. Family history of the disease increases the chances of children developing the disease. Immune dysfunction and auto-immune disorders possibly play a role in the development of Multiple sclerosis. Viral infection has been suggested to be an initiating factor, but the lack of identifying a virus does not support this theory. Environmental factors including airborne allergens, pesticides and other chemicals are associated with the development of the disease. Latitude seems to be associated with the disease. Additionally, areas where the consumption of milk and dairy products is highest tend to have the highest incidence of MS. The location of the first 15 years of life tends to affect the development of MS later in life.

Diagnosis of MS is quite difficult and is based on symptoms. All other possibilities should be considered and ruled out first. Stroke, herpes, Lou Gehrig's disease, anemia and arthritis are among the diseases that should be considered. A cerebrospinal fluid (CFS) sample from the areas around the brain and spinal cord is necessary. A computerized tomography (CT) scan or a magnetic resonance imaging (MRI) scan can confirm the diagnosis by the identification of plaques in the nervous system.

There is no specific conventional medical treatment for Multiple sclerosis. Cortisone and other steroid drugs are usually prescribed during acute exacerbations of MS, but their long term use is unjustified. Physical therapy is often recommended as a part of the treatment regime. It is important to emphasize that no single treatment is effective and a holistic approach is often the best.

Lifestyle

Stress can aggravate Multiple sclerosis. Stressors should be identified and reduced. Stress reduction techniques such as meditation, biofeedback and yoga are useful. Exercise is a great way to reduce stress and a daily exercise is strongly recommended.

Environmental sensitivities and allergies have been associated with the development of MS. Fungi, molds, pollens, pesticides, herbicides and other toxic chemicals have been implicated. Mercury amalgam toxicity and lead toxicity should also be considered in the evaluation of individuals with MS.

Massage, muscle and strength training and physical therapy are beneficial and should be included in a treatment program for MS.

Diet

Avoid all fats and oils, especially saturated fats. Saturated fats should be decreased to less than 10 grams per day, while unsaturated fats should be decreased to less than 50 grams per day. Avoid milk, butter, cheese, eggs and other dairy products. Decrease consumption of white sugar and refined carbodydrates, coffee, tea, chocolate, alcohol, and refined and processed foods. Increase consumption of whole, unprocessed foods, complex carbohydrates, fresh fruits and vegetables.

Vitamins and Minerals
(Daily unless otherwise stated)

Vitamin B-complex - 100 mg. Necessary for proper nerve function and helps the body respond to stress. Intramuscular injections may be beneficial.
Vitamin B1 (Thiamine) - 5-10 mg. May be deficient and supplementation may be beneficial.
Vitamin B3 (Niacin) - 20-25 mg. May be deficient and supplementation may be beneficial.
Vitamin B6 (Pyridoxine) - 50-200 mg. May be deficient and is necessary for proper nerve function.
Vitamin C - 500-1000 mg. A potent antioxidant that helps to prevent damage to nerve cells.
Vitamin D - 400-800 IU. Helps to regulate fat metabolism and is involved in the production of myelin around nerve cells.
Vitamin E - 400-800 IU. A potent antioxidant that helps to prevent damage to nerve cells.

Calcium - 800-1200 mg. Helps to regulate fat metabolism and is involved in the production of myelin around nerve cells.
Magnesium - 400-800 mg. Necessary for proper nerve and muscle function and helps the body deal with stress.
Potassium - 1000-3000 mg. Necessary for chemical reactions and regulates electric impulses within nerve cells.
Selenium - 200-400 mcg. A potent antioxidant that helps to prevent damage to nerve cells.

Food Supplements
(Daily unless otherwise stated)

Adrenal gland - 500-1000 mg. Enhances function of the adrenal gland and improves overall energy.
Calcium EAP (Ethanolamine phosphate) - 800-1200 mg. A vital constituent of myelin and nerve cell membranes. Also available as Magnesium EAP and Potassium EAP. Helps to prevent demyelination.

D-phenylalanine - 2-4 gm. A naturally occuring amino acid that is used to make chemical transmitters between nerve cells and supplementation may be beneficial.

Omega-3 oils (flaxseed, fish oil) - 1000-3000 mg. A rich source of esssential oils that support the function of the nervous system, aid in fat metabolism and decrease inflammation in nerve cells.

Omega-6 oils (evening primrose, borage oil) - 1000-3000 mg. A rich source of essential oils that support the function of the nervous system, aid in fat metabolism and decrease inflammation in nerve cells.

Proteolytic enzymes - 3-6 capsules. Decreases inflammation in nerve cells and decreases the autoimmune process.

Thymus glandular extract - 500-1000 mg. Supplementation enhances immune function.

Unsaturated fats (olive, sunflower, cod liver oil) - 5-10 gm. Supplementation may be beneficial.

Herbal Medicines

Specific plants and plant derivatives may be useful in treating multiple sclerosis. **Ginkgo biloba** (24% heterosides) at 120 mg per day increase blood flow to the nervous system and could have potential benefit in the treatment of individuals with MS.

Highly Recommended

Decrease stress / Avoid environmental sensitivities and allergies / physical therapy / avoid fats and oils, especially saturated fats / vitamin B-complex / vitamin B12 / vitamin E / calcium / magnesium / potassium / calcium EAP / omega-3 oils / omega-6 oils / unsaturated oils.

159

CHAPTER 43

Obesity

Obesity is defined as excess total body fat and is one of the most prevalent chronic disorders in the western hemisphere.

15 to 20% of the North American population are overweight and 5 to 8% of the population are classified as obese. Men and women are affected equally and all age groups are at risk. Increased age and increased caloric intake are strongly associated with the development of obesity.

Major consequences of obesity include high blood pressure, breathing problems, diabetes mellitus, gallstones, muscle and joint instability and pain, back pain and cancer. Obesity can be also be associated with personality problems and unhappiness. Food and eating may be used as a substitute for other activities and may be a replacement for boredom, loneliness and stress.

By nature females have a higher body fat composition than males. Females who have body fat in excess of 30% of total weight are considered overweight. A more desirable composition for females would be 15 to 25% body fat. Males who have body in excess of 20% are considered overweight. A more desirable composition for males would be 10 to 20% body fat.

The exact cause of obesity is not known. Both genetic and environmental factors contribute to overeating and weight gain. It has been recognized a long time ago that obesity and weight control problems occur in families. Energy imbalances occur when energy intake from food sources exceeds daily energy expenditure. Endocrine and metabolic disturbances have been used as an excuse for obesity for many individuals. Although these imbalances do occur they are rarely the primary cause of obesity and are usually secondary as a result of being overweight.

Changes in eating pattern and weight gain can be a symptom of depression. In many obese individuals the major caloric intake occurs during the evening meal or bedtime snack. Treatment of the underlying disorder is strongly recommended. Early life patterns and emotional responses to food are considered major factors in the development of obesity later in life. Food is often viewed as a reward. Especially significant are the responses learned in early childhood when a child is rewarded for good behavior with food and often high calorie foods.

Poor diet and eating habits are common causes of weight gain and the development of obesity. In North America, the typical diet is composed of 40 to 45% carbohydrates, 15 to 20% protein and 35 to 40% fat. Fat contains twice as many calories as either carbohydrates or proteins. The standard American diet is much too high in fat. In addition, calorie dense foods, high in calories but low in volume, are also consumed too much. A high fat and simple carbohydrate diet associated with physical inactivity and a sendentary lifestyle contributes to the development of obesity.

Conventional medicat treatment of obesity focuses on drug therapy and occasionally surgery. Commonly prescribed and over-the-counter medication for appetite suppression contain known stimulants such as caffeine, ephedrine and pseudo-ephedrine. These substances are nervous system stimulants. They increase metabolic rate and are effective for short term use. The long term use of appetite suppressants is strongly discouraged and may have serious side effects. Adverse side effects of appetite suppressants include nervousness, irritability, emotional lability, insomnia, heart palpitations, increased blood pressure, heart arrhythmias, increased frequency of urination and sweating. Occasionally hypothyroidism is the cause of obesity and weight gain and thryoid hormone replacement is indicated. Thyroxine or other thyroid hormones should not be used in the absence of clinical hypothyroidism in the treatment of obesity. Surgical intervention is restricted to those individuals who are grossly overweight and who are at risk for life threatening consequences of their condition. The purpose of surgery is to decrease the size of the stomach or intestines and decrease the absorption of food. Patients who are treated by surgical intervention need lifetime followup to monitor the treatment.

Lifestyle

Psychological and emotional factors are strongly associated with eating habits and the development of obesity. Behavioral patterns associated with overeating should be identified and modified. Psychological and dietary counselling may be necessary to identify causes and develop an appropriate treatment.

Lack of exercise and a sedentary lifestyle are strongly associated with the development of obesity and weight gain. Daily exercise is strongly recommended. Moderate aerobic exercise such as walking, jogging, cycling, swimming, hiking or other forms of exercise is encouraged.

Poor eating habits can be an outlet for stress. Stressors should be identified and reduced. Stress reducing techniques such as deep breathing exercises, meditation, hypnotherapy and yoga are recommended.

Diet

Caloric expenditure should exceed dietary caloric intake. A low calorie diet together with increased physical activity and exercise should be the foundation of any weight loss program. Avoid white sugar and refined carbohydrates. These are calorie dense foods, low in weight but very high in calories. Decrease fats, especially saturated fats. Fats have twice the caloric value of carbohydrates and proteins. Increase consumption of dietary fiber. A high fiber diet increases non-caloric bulk and causes a feeling of fullness and decreases appetite. Indigestible fiber has no caloric value. Increase consumption of whole and unprocessed foods, whole grains and cereals, fresh fruits and vegetables.

Vitamins and Minerals
(Daily unless otherwise stated)

Vitamin B-complex - 50-100 mg. Helps the body respond to stress and supplementation may be beneficial.
Vitamin C - 500-2000 mg. Supplementation may help to contribute to weight loss.

Iodine - 100-200 mcg. May be deficient. Used by the thyroid gland in the production hormones to regulate body metabolism. Deficiency may cause hypothyroidism and contribute to weight gain.

Food Supplements
(Daily unless otherwise stated)

Carnitine - 500-1500 mg. Involved in fat metabolism and energy production. Supplementation may help to increase fat utilization.

Co-enzyme Q10 - 30-60 mg. May be deficient in some individuals with chronic obesity.

Fiber - 5-30 gm. The indigestible portion of plants and vegetables. Helps to increase bulk of stool, increases feeling of fullness, decreases hunger and helps to decrease digestion and absorption of sugar and simple carbohydrates. Supplementation is very beneficial in promoting weight loss.

Glucomannan - 5-10 gm. An unabsorbable complex carbohydrate from Konjak root. Supplementation results in weight loss despite no change in eating and exercise habits.

Glutamine - 500-1000 mg. A naturally occuring amino acid that may decrease carbohydrate cravings and food bingings.

Guar gum - 5-10 gm. An unabsorbable complex carbohydrate. Supplementation results in reduced hunger in obese individuals and influences carbohydrate and fat metabolism in a beneficial manner aiding in weight loss.

Omega-3 oils (flaxseed, fish oil) - 1000-3000 mg. A rich source of essential oils that helps to improve fat metabolism. Supplementation may benefit those individuals who fail to lose weight on calorie restricted diets.

Omega-6 oils (evening primrose, borage oil) - 1000-3000 mg. A rich source of essential oils that helps to improve fat metabolism. Supplementation may benefit those individuals who fail to lose weight on calorie restricted diets.

Thyroid glandular extract - 250-500 mg. Helps to support and nourish the thyroid gland which is responsible for regulating body metabolism.

Herbal Medicines

Specific plants and plant derivatives may be useful in treating obesity and promoting weight loss. **Green tea (Camellia sinensis), Kola (Cola nitida), Ma Huang (Ephedra sinensis)** may be beneficial. Ephedra is the natural source of the alkaloid, ephedrine, that is widely used in many over-the-counter weight loss drugs. Ephedra stimulates body metabolism and increases fat metabolism and breakdown. Plants high in fiber such as **Psyllium (Plantago ovata)** help to increase feeling of fullness, decrease appetite and promote weight loss. One or more of these herbal medicines may be consumed as a tea, tincture, fluid extract, solid extract or supplement.

Highly Recommended

Identify and modify behavior pattern associated with poor eating habits / moderate daily aerobic exercise / avoid white sugar and refined carbohydrates / decrease consumption of fats / increase high fiber foods / vitamin B-complex / iodine / dietary fiber / glucommanan / glutamine / guar gum / omega-3 oils / thyroid glandular extract / Ephedra.

CHAPTER 44

Osteoarthritis

Osteoarthritis is a non-inflammatory degenerative joint disease marked by breakdown of cartilage around bone and buildup of bone at bone margins. Osteoarthritis is also called degenerative joint disease.

Osteoarthritis is the most common form of arthritis and it affects 20% of the population. Osteoarthritis is uncommon before the age of 35 years and more frequent above the age of 65 years. The incidence of osteoarthritis increases with age and affects 85% of individuals over the age of 75 years. Osteoarthritis affects females more commonly than males.

Symptoms of osteoarthritis vary from mild to severe, depending on the amount of degeneration that has take place. Pain that is worse in the morning and is usually worse with motion is the most common symptom. Osteoarthritis produces no inflammation and no joint swelling occurs. Joint stiffness, deformity, decreased range of motion and bony calcification and bone spurs are common. The weight bearing joints are more commonly affected including the wrist, elbow, shoulder, low back, hip, knee and ankles. The diagnosis of osteoarthritis is based upon history, blood tests and X-rays. Other diseases that must be ruled out include rheumatoid arthritis, gout, ankylosing spondylitis, infection and an endocrine, metabolic or neurologic dysfunction.

The exact cause of osteoarthritis is not entirely known. Osteoarthritis is a part of the degeneration that occurs as part of the normal aging process. Genetics plays a role in the development of the disease. Other factors include increased age, obesity, sedentary lifestyle, congenital abnormalities, trauma, fractures, surgery, excessive joint wear and tear.

Osteoarthritis is caused by disintegration of the cartilage that covers the ends of the bones. Cartilage has a poor blood supply and takes a long time to heal once damaged. As the cartilage wears away, the roughened surface of the bone is exposed and pain and stiffness result. Exposed bone proliferates. In severe cases the center of the bone wears away and a bony ridge is left around the edges. This ridge may restrict movement of the joint.

Conventional medical treatment of osteoarthritis focuses on drug therapy to reduce the pain associated with this disease. Commonly prescribed medication include aspirin (ASA), Motrin (ibuprofen), Indocid (indomethacin), Fenopron (fenoprofen), Naprosyn (naproxen), Tolectin (tolmetin) and Clinoril (sulindac). Side effects of these commonly used non-steroidal anti-inflammatories (NSAID's) include nausea, vomiting, headaches, dizziness, tinnitus and digestive upset. In addition, the use of these NSAID's should be reserved for short periods of treatment since their prolonged use decreases cartilage repair. Steroids are occasionally prescribed but their use is limited. Surgery to the affected joint, such as hip and knee replacements, is reserved for those individuals with advanced osteoarthritis and where more conservative treatments are ineffective.

Lifestyle

Increase daily exercise as tolerated. Regular exercise helps to build healthy bones, reduces stress and decreases the pain associated with osteoarthritis. Epsom salt baths may beneficial. Physical therapy may also be effective in relieving pain. Hot and cold applications, massage, diathermy, ultrasound, TENS (transcutaneous electrical neural stimulation) and other physical modalities may be effective.

Diet

Decrease consumption of sugar and refined carbohydrates, fats and refined and processed foods. Food senstivities and allergies can aggravate osteoarthritis and make this condition worse. A food sensitivity or allergy test may be necessary to identify offending foods. Avoid vegetables from the Nightshade (Solanaceae) family including tomatoes, potatoes, egg plant, green peppers and tobacco. Avoid citrus fruits if they aggravate symptoms. Increase consumption of complex carbohydrates, fiber and whole and unprocessed foods.

Vitamins and Minerals
(Daily unless otherwise stated)

Vitamin B3 (Niacinamide) - 1000-3000 mg. Start at 500 mg per day then increase slowly up to 3000 mg per day as tolerated. Increases blood supply to joints, increases joint mobility and decreases pain.

166

Vitamin B-complex - 100 mg. May be deficient. Supplement with Niacinamide.

Vitamin B5 (Pantothenic acid) - 250-500 mg. May be deficient.

Vitamin C - 1000-3000 mg. Important in connective tissue growth and maintenance. Supplementation may be beneficial.

Vitamin E - 400-1200 IU. Decreases pain associated with osteoarthritis.

Calcium - 800-1200 mg. Helps to build and maintain strong bones, connective tissue and muscle.

Copper - 2-3 mg. May be deficient and supplementation helps to relieve joint pain and inflammation.

Magnesium - 400-800 mg. Helps to relieve muscle spasms around joints that may be affected by osetoarthritis. Works synergistically with calcium.

Zinc - 10-25 mg. May be deficient.

Sulfur - 500-1000 mg. May be deficient. Sulfur baths may be effective.

Food Supplements
(Daily unless otherwise stated)

Adrenal glandular extract- 500-1000 mg. Stimulates adrenal gland function and supplementation may be beneficial.

Chondroitin sulphate - 500-2000 mg. Necessary for proper growth and repair of connective tissue.

Glycosaminoglycans - 2-6 gm. Necessary for proper growth and repair of connective tissue. Supplement for one month.

Green lipped mussel (Perma canaliculus) - 3-6 capsules. Rich in glycosaminoglycans, especially chondroitin sulphate, that is necessary for connective tissue growth and repair.

Methionine - 1-2 gm. A sulfur containing amino acid that is required for proper growth of cartilage.

Omega-3 oils (flaxseed, fish oil) - 1000-3000 mg. A rich source of essential oils that are used by the body to support joint structure and decrease inflammation.

Omega-6 oils (evening primrose, borage oil) - 3-6 capsules. A rich source of essential oils that are used by the body to support joint structure and decrease inflammation.

Superoxide dismutase (SOD) - 250-500 mg. A potent naturally occuring antioxidant that helps to decrease damage to joint structure and connective tissue. Intramuscular injections may be effective.

Herbal Medicines

Specific plants and plant derivatives may be useful in treating osteoarthritis and improving symptoms associated with this condition. **Autumn crocus (Colchicum autumnale), Blue cohosh (Cimicifuga racemosa), Burdock (Arctium lappa), Chapparal (Larrea tridentata), Dandelion (Taraxadum officinale), Devil's claw (Harpagophytum procumbens), Fenugreek (Trigonella foenum-graecum), Licorice (Glycyrrhiza glabra), Pipsissewa (Chimaphila umbellata), Tansy (Tanacetum vulgare), White willow (Salix alba), Wintergreen (Gaultheria procumbens) and Yucca** may be effective in relieving the symptoms associated with osteoarthritis. Topical application of a 10-20% solution of Wintergreen oil acts as an anti-rheumatic and counter-irritant and may be effective. Chapparal, Devil's claw and Yucca alone or in combination may be effective in reducing the pain and inflammation associated with osteoarthritis. One or more of these herbal medicines may be consumed as a tea, tincture, fluid extract, solid extract or supplement.

Highly Recommended

Moderate daily exercise / physical therapy / avoid food sensitivities and allergies / vitamin B3 / vitamin E / calcium / copper / magnesium / chondroitin sulfate / glycosaminoglycans / omega-3 oils / omega-6 oils / Chapparal / Devil's claw / Wintergreen oil / Yucca.

CHAPTER 45

Osteoporosis

Osteoporosis literally means "porous bone" and refers to an abnormal decrease in bone mass. Bones become abnormally brittle and break much easier than normal.

Osteoporosis affects 20 to 25 million individuals in North America and accounts for more than 1.2 million fractures per year in people over age 45 years. One-third of all American women and one-sixth of all American men will develop osteoporosis serious enough to cause a fracture. Fractures typically involving the vertebra, hip and wrist are a common consequence of advanced osteoporosis. Fractures involving the hip are the most serious. 20% die within one year because of complications such as pneumonia or pulmonary emboli and half of these individuals require long term nursing care. The estimated medical costs of osteoporosis-related fractures are between 7 and 10 billion dollars annually.

There are 206 separate bones in the human body. Bones are responsible for providing a rigid structure for the support of the human body. Bones offer a site for attachment for muscles, ligaments and tendons. Some bones have a chiefly protective function, such as the skull, which encloses the brain, the spinal cord, the eye and the inner ear. Other bones are involved primarily in movement, such as the jaw and is responsible for chewing food. The marrow contained within bones manufactures blood cells and plays an important role in the development of a healthy immune system. The bones themselves act as a storehouse of calcium, which must be maintained at a certain level in the blood for the body's normal chemical functioning. The basic chemical in bone responsible for giving bone its hardness and strength is calcium phosphate. Loss of the mineral content of bone is the major problem in osteoporosis and results in bone that is more susceptible to fracture.

Contrary to popular opinion bones are not solid, static structures. Bones are constantly in a dynamic state where they are constantly being reformed and remodelled. Normally there is balance between the rate at which bone is formed and the rate at which bone is broken done. Generally, bones are formed faster than they are broken down, until adulthood. In adulthood bone begins to be broken down at a faster rate than at which it is formed. Osteoporosis is a condition where bone is being broken down at a much faster rate than bone is being formed. Bones lose their strength and hardness and become brittle and break easily. Fractures of the hip, wrist and vertebra are common in many individuals with advanced osteoporosis.

Although fractures due to osteoporosis are more common in elderly people, it is important to realize that accelerated bone loss begins in early adulthood. Inappropriate diet and lifestyle throughout life are responsible for causing osteoporosis. Risk factors for osteoporosis include advanced age, fair skin, female sex, early menopause, women who have not produced any children, smoking, alcohol abuse, slender build, physical inactivity, family history of osteoporosis, low calcium intake, low vitamin D intake and other vitamin and minerals. Hyperparathyroidism, hyperthyroidism, anorexia nervosa, cortisone therapy, liver disease and bone cancer can also cause osteoporosis.

Osteoporosis is often asymptomatic and is only diagnosed when a fracture has occured. In the absence of fractures, X-rays can often detect the extent of reduced bone mass. Decreased height, a humpback and chronic pain are commonly observed in individuals with advanced osteoporosis.

Conventional medical treatment of osteoporosis includes the use of pain killers, muscle relaxants, hormone replacement and calcium supplements. Estrogen is typically prescribed at a dosage of 0.3 to 1.25 mg/day. Although estrogen therapy retards bone loss, it does not completely prevent it. Fractures still do occur, though less frequently. Risk factors of estrogen use include endometrial cancer, breast cancer, hypertension, blood clots, liver disease, stroke, gall bladder disease and heart attacks. The risk factors and benefits of estrogen therapy should be carefully weighed before estrogen is prescribed. Estrogen therapy should be reserved for those individuals at high risk for developing osteoporosis. Calcium supplements are usually prescribed in dosages of 800 to 1500 mg per day. Calcium deficiency can cause osteoporosis and supplementation plays an important role in the prevention of bone loss. However, it is becoming increasingly clear that calcium supplementation alone is not enough to prevent osteoporosis. Thiazide diuretics, thyroid hormone drugs or anticoagulants can lead to increased rate of calcium removal from the body. Individuals on these medications require extra calcium supplementation.

Lifestyle

A moderately active lifestyle is beneficial. Exercise is strongly recommended. The equivalent of a brisk 30 minute walk four to seven days a week is the recommended minimum and should be supplemented with light weight training where possible. Weight bearing forms of exercise are important for building strong bones. Smoking is strongly discouraged and should be discontinued as quickly as possible. In addition to causing hypertension, stroke, heart disease and lung cancer, smoking is associated with accelerated bone loss.

Diet

Avoid white sugar, refined carbohydrates, chocolate, fats, meat, coffee, tea, alcohol and processed foods. Avoid foods and fluids high in phosphates, such as red meat, alcohol and soft drinks. Phosphates lead to increased calcium removal from the body. Avoid foods high in oxalic acid, such as almonds, peanuts, cashews, rhubarb, beet greens and spinach. Oxalic acid inhibits calcium absorption. Increase consumption of whole, unprocessed foods, vegetables and fruits. Increase consumption of foods high in calcium including most vegetables, broccoli, kale, turnip greens, peas, brussel sprouts, cabbage, whole wheat products, wheat germ, oats, buckwheat, molasses, milk, buttermilk, cheese, yogurt, kefir, nuts and seeds especially sunflower and sesame seeds. Increase consumption of fresh, unsweetened fruit and vegetable juices.

Vitamins and Minerals
(Daily unless otherwise stated)

Vitamin A - 10,000-25,000 IU. Necessary for proper growth and repair of connective tissue and bone.
Vitamin B6 (Pyridoxine) - 25-50 mg. Involved in the crosslinking of connective tissue and elimination of toxins in the liver that can accelerate bone loss.
Folic Acid - 400-800 mcg. Involved in the detoxification of toxins in the liver that can accelerate bone loss.
Vitamin C - 500-1000 mg. Involved in the crosslinking of connective tissue which results in strong bone.
Vitamin D - 400-800 mcg. Required for intestinal absorption of calcium.
Vitamin K - 2-3 mcg. Required for the production of the protein matrix upon which calcium is deposited to form bone.

Boron - 1-3 mg. Involved in the activation of steroid hormones, including estrogen and vitamin D.

Calcium - 800-1500 mg. Main chemical responsible for the hardness and strength of bone. Often deficient in individuals with osteoporosis.

Copper - 1-3 mg. Deficiency associated with osteoporosis. Involved in the crosslinking of connective tissue.

Magnesium - 800-1000 mg. Involved in numerous biochemical reactions that takes place in bone. Involved in the conversion of inactive vitamin D to active vitamin D.

Manganese - 10-20 mg. Required for bone mineralization and for production of connective tissue.

Silicon - 1-3 mg. Necessary for crosslinking of connective tissue and bone.

Strontium - 1-2 mg. Occurs in relatively large concentrations in bones and teeth, where it is thought to replace a small fraction of calcium.

Zinc - 10-25 mg. Deficiency associated with osteoporosis. Essential for normal bone formation and activation of vitamin D.

Food Supplements
(Daily unless otherwise stated)

Digestive enzymes and/or Hydrochloric acid - 1-2 capsules with each meal. Helps to improve digestion and absorption of calcium and other vitamins and minerals necessary for bone. Lack of digestive enzymes and/or Hydrochloric acid is common in older adults and often results in poor digestion and absorption of vitamins and minerals.

Herbal Medicines

Specific plants and plant derivatives may be useful in treating osteoporosis and preventing bone loss. Some plants contain natural estrogen and estrogen precursors. Plant estrogens, though less potent than synthetic estrogens, due exert biological activity. Plant estrogens can be a natural source of estrogen that can help to minimize bone loss in postmenopausal women. Plant sources of estrogen include **Alfalfa (Medicago sativa), Black Cohosh (Cimicifuga racemosa), Blue Cohosh (Caulophyllum thalictroides), Chaste tree (Vitex agnus-castus), Dong quai (Angelica sinensis), False Unicorn root (Helonias opulus), Fennel (Foeniculum vulgare), Fo ti tieng (Polygonum multiforum) and Licorice (Glycyrrhiza glabra). Horsetail (Equisetum arvense)** contains a relatively high source of silica and may be used as a supplement.

One or more of these herbal medicines may be consumed as a tea, tincture, fluid extract, solid extract or supplement.

Highly Recommended

Moderate daily exercise / quit cigarette smoking / avoid white sugar and refined carbohydrates / increase whole and unprocessed foods / multiple vitamin and mineral complex / vitamin A / vitamin C / vitamin D / vitamin K / boron / calcium / magnesium / silicon / zinc / digestive enzymes and/ or hydrochloric acid / plant estrogens.

CHAPTER 46

Parasites and Worms

Parasites and worms are common infections of the digestive system and are characterized by indigestion, abdominal bloating, gas and diarrhea. In severe infection there may be fever, joint pain and vomiting.

Giardia is the most common parasitic infection in North America and is estimated to occur in 5 to 10% of the population. Giardiasis is caused by the parasite, Giardia lamblia and is most common in the Rocky mountain area. It is usually caused by drinking water contaminated with the parasite.

Entamoebiasis is caused by the parasite, Entamoeba histolytica and is estimated to occur in 3 to 10% of the world population. Chance of infection increases with foreign travel. Symptoms associated with Entamoeba infection include diarrhea and lower abdominal discomfort.

Lyme disease is caused by the parasite Borrelia burgdorferi and is transmitted through the deer tick. Infection usually results in inflammed skin, joint pain and heart and nerve abnormalities.

Worms account for approximately one billion infections worldwide per year. Round worms, flukes and tapeworms are common worm infections. Over 50 million infection occur in North America alone. Pinworm infection caused by the worm Enterobius vermicularis is common among children. Peri-anal itching is the most common symptom associated with pinworm infection.

Conventional medical treatment of parasites and worms focuses on drug therapy. Frequently prescribed medication include Chloroquine, Flagyl (metronidazole), Quinacrine, Mobendazole, Praziquantel and Niclosamide. These drugs are relatively toxic and side effects include nausea, vomiting, digestive upset, liver damage, kidney dysfunction and nervous system dysfunction.

Lifestyle

Poor personal hygiene can contribute to parasite and worm infection. Consumption of contaminated drinking water is the most common cause of infection. Drinking water should be carefully analyzed before it is orally consumed.

Avoid uncooked or poorly cooked meats. They may be infected with parasites and worms.

Diet

Avoid white sugar and refined carbohydrates. Excess consumption of refined sugar can impair host immune response and increase susceptibility to infection. Food sensitivities and allergies can cause indigestion and can promote parasite and worm infection. Food sensitivities and allergies should be identified and avoided. Increase consumption of whole and unprocessed foods, fresh fruits and vegetables. Specifically increase consumption of garlic, pumpkin seeds and papaya.

Vitamins and Minerals
(Daily unless otherwise stated)

Vitamin A - 10,000-25,000 IU. Supplementation helps to stimulate the immune system and fight infection.
Beta-carotene - 50,000-100,000 IU. A precursor to vitamin A without the toxic side effects at high doses. Supplementation helps to stimulate the immune system and fight infection.
Vitamin C - 500-3000 mg. Supplementation helps to stimulate the immune system and fight infection.
Vitamin E - 400-800 IU. Supplementation helps to stimulate the immune system and fight infection.

Zinc - 25-50 mg. Supplementation helps to stimulate the immune system and fight infection.

Food Supplements
(Daily unless otherwise stated)

Digestive Enzymes and/or Hydrochloric acid - 1-2 tablets with meals. May be deficient and supplementation helps to increase digestive juices and improve digestion.

Fiber - 5-20 gm. Fiber increases stool transit time, promotes healthy bacteria in the digestive system and aids in the elimination of waste.

Thymus glandular extract - 500-1000 mg. Supplementation helps to stimulate thymus gland function and stimulate immune function.

Herbal Medicines

Specific plants and plant derivatives may be useful in treating parasitic infections. **Black walnut (Juglia nigra), Garlic (Allium sativum), Goldenseal (Hydrastis canadensis), Papaya leaf (Carica papaya), Pumpkin seed (Curcubita pepo) and Wormwood (Artemesia absinthium)** may be beneficial. One or more of these herbal medicines may be consumed as a tea, tincture, fluid extract, solid extract or supplement.

Highly Recommended

Clean personal hygiene / consume uncontaminated drinking water / avoid white sugar and refined carbohydrates / vitamin A / beta-carotene / vitamin C / zinc / digestive enzymes and/or hydrochloric acid / Black Walnut / Garlic / Goldenseal / Papaya / Pumpkin seeds / Wormwood.

176

CHAPTER 47

Parkinson's Disease

Parkinson's disease is a a slowly progressive nervous system disorder that is characterized by muscle rigidity, slowness of movement, postural instability and resting muscle tremors.

Parkinson's disease affects approximately 1% of the population greater than 50 years old. The incidence of this disease increases with advance age. 75 to 80% of individuals with Parkinson's disease are between the ages of 70 and 80 years. The average age of onset of this disease is 60 years. Parkinsons's disease affects males slightly more than females.

Parkinson's disease usually appears gradually and progresses slowly. Slowness of movement and slight tremors of the hands and neck are common. Many individuals with this disease have muscle rigidity as the only symptom. Hands, arms and legs may be affected by muscle tremors. The jaw, tongue, eyelids and forehead are occasionally affected. 50-80% of individuals with this disease have a pill rolling tremor of one or both hands at rest. Tremors are better with movement and absent with sleep. As the disease progresses symptoms also get worse. Progressive muscle rigidity, slowness of movement, muscle aches and fatigue, difficulty walking, lack of balance, dull, monotone speech, mask-like, lack of eyelid blinking and expressionless facial features are common symptoms. Lead-pipe and cogwheel rigidity of the arms and legs can occur. Increased tendon reflexes occurs. Dementia and depression may also occur in 50% of individuals with this disease.

The exact cause of Parkinson's disease is not known. There is a loss of nerve cells in the mid-brain. This results in a decrease in the neurotransmitter, dopamine, responsible for conduction of nerve impulses. An imbalance between two opposing neurotransmitters, acetylcholine and dopamine, results. When dopamine is depleted, the functional overactivity of acetylcholine produces the symptoms of Parkinson's disease.

No underlying cause responsible for the destruction of nerve cells in the mid-brain is found in 90% of individuals with Parkinson's disease.

Secondary causes that interfere with the function of dopamine include a degenerative disease affecting the brain, viral infection, drugs or toxins including anti-psychotic medication and lithium, carbon dioxide poisoning, manganese toxicity, chronic exposure to herbicides and pesticides, nutritional deficiencies, stroke and brain tumors.

Conventional medical treatment of Parkinson's disease is symptomatic and supportive. Most individuals require life long therapy consisting of drug therapy, counselling, physical therapy and rarely, surgical therapy. Commonly used medication include dopamine precursors such as l-dopa and carbidopa, amantidine, bromocryptine (parlodel), antihistamines such as Benadryl (diphenhydramine), tricyclic antidepressants (amitryptiline), propranolol and deprenyl. L-dopa and carbidopa are chemical precursors to dopamine that help to increase dopamine levels in the brain. Side effects of l-dopa include nausea, vomiting, heart palpitations, arrhythmias, hypotension, abnormal muscle movements and incoordination, delerium and hallucinations. A popular combination of l-dopa and carbidopa (Sinemet) is commonly used and counteracts the unpleasant side effects of levodopa alone. The major disadvantage of this drug is that its effectiveness is limited and tolerance can develop.

Lifestyle

The individual's mental outlook and motivation can affect the extent to which they can successfully cope with this disease. Counselling should be available to explain the extent and nature of the disease and give realistic hopes for forstalling or preventing more serious effects.

Physical therapy including muscle stretching and massage may be highly beneficial in preventing muscle cramps and increasing range of motion.

Diet

A low protein diet is recommended. L-dopamine is an amino acid and like other amino acids must compete for absorption in the digestive system. Restricting protein and amino acids, improves the absorption and availability of l-dopamine. Alcohol should also be restricted, because large amounts can antagonize the effects of dopamine in the brain. Increase consumption of whole, unprocessed and unrefined foods.

Vitamins and Minerals
(Daily unless otherwise stated)

Vitamin B-complex - 50-100 mg. Helps the body respond to stress. Intramuscular injections may be beneficial.

Vitamin B1 (Thiamine) - 5-10 mg. Supplementation may be beneficial.

Niacin - 10-25 mg. Increases l-dopamine levels in individuals taking l-dopa.

Vitamin B6 (Pyridoxine) - 50-100 mg. Helps to increase production of dopamine. Intramuscular or intravenous injections may be beneficial. However, do not take vitamin B6 when taking l-dopa alone. Vitamin B6 and l-dopa both increase brain dopamine levels and this may counteract the effectiveness of l-dopa alone.

Vitamin C - 500-2000 mg. Helps to counteract the negative effects of L-dopa.

Vitamin E - 400-1200 IU. A potent antioxidant that may help to prevent destruction of nerve cells in the brain.

Selenium - 200-400 mcg. A potent antioxidant.

Zinc - 10-25 mg. May be deficient. Helps to increase levels of L-dopa by reducing the effects of vitamin B6.

Food Supplements
(Daily unless otherwise stated)

Glutathione - 1-2 capsules or as directed on the label. A powerful antioxidant.

Lecithin (Phosphatidyl choline) - 5-10 gm. Supplies the raw material needed to produce acetylcholine, an excitatory brain neurotransmitter.

Leucine - 5-10 gm. May be deficient. Supplementation helps to prevent atrophy of parts of the mid-brain. Effective in a minority of individuals with Parkinson's disease.

Octacosanol - 10-20 mg. Available as wheat germ oil. High in vitamin E. Supplementation may be beneficial.

Omega-6 oils (evening primrose, borage oil) - 1000-3000 mg. Helps to improve fat metabolism and decrease inflammation. Supplementation may be beneficial.

Phenylalanine - 2-5 gm. A naturally occuring amino acid that supplies the raw material needed to produce dopamine in the brain.

Superoxide dismutase (SOD) - 1-2 capsules or as directed on the label. A powerful antioxidant.

L-Tyrosine - 2-4 gm. Supplies the raw material needed to produce dopamine in the brain. Increases production and turnover of dopamine. Supplementation may be beneficial.

Herbal Medicines

Specific plants and plant derivatives may be useful in treating Parkinson's disease. The **Windsor bean** found in Switzerland is the original source used to produce l-dopa. The **Cowhage bean (Macuna pruriens)** found in India has been used in traditional Ayurvedic medicine to effectively reduce the symptoms associated with this disease. **Ginkgo (Ginkgo biloba)** contains bioflavonoids that increase blood supply to the brain. This is important in preventing destruction of nervous tissue and aiding in regeneration. One or more of these herbal medicines may be consumed as a tea, tincture, fluid extract, solid extract or supplement.

Highly Recommended

Physical therapy / increase whole and unprocessed foods / vitamin B-complex / vitamin B3 / vitamin B6 / vitamin E / zinc / lecithin / leucine / octacosanol / omega-6 oils / phenylalanine / tyrosine / Ginkgo biloba.

CHAPTER 48

Peptic Ulcers

Peptic ulcers are ulcerations or excavations that occur in the lining of the stomach and duodenum.

Peptic ulcers occur in 5 to 10% of the North American population and involve twice as many men as women. The disease is considered to be an illness of young and middle aged adults, but can occur at any age.

The most common symptom of peptic ulcers is upper abdominal pain that may be described as burning, gnawing, cramping or aching. The pain may last for several minutes to two hours and may come in waves. The daily pattern of pain is related to the production of hydrochloric acid in the stomach. Pain is usually better in the morning and following a meal, with food in the stomach to buffer the effects of acid. Pain is worse before meals and before bedtime. The pain will often last for three or four days and then subside and then reappear weeks or months later. Other symptoms of uncomplicated peptic ulcers include nausea, loss of appetite and weight loss. Vomiting may occur with duodenal ulcers. Three major complications of peptic ulcers include hemorrhage, perforations and obstruction. Bleeding may vary from a small amount of hidden blood that occurs over a period of time, to massive hemorrhage requiring immediate treatment.

The cause of ulcer formations is rarely due to excessive secretion of acid alone. Most cases represent an imbalance between acid, enzymes and other potentially damaging agents that protect the delicate lining of the digestive system. The protective lining of the digestive system, called a mucous membrane, consists of a group of sugars known as polysaccharides and proteins and enzymes. These substances line the stomach and duodenum and prevent hydrochloric acid from digesting through the stomach wall. Ulcers are caused when there is a weakening of the mucous membrane and stomach acid is allowed to irritate the mucous lining.

Conventional medical therapy focuses on drug therapy to reduce stomach acid secretions. Tagamet (cimetidine) and Zantac (ranitidine) are two of the most common drugs routinely prescribed in ulcer therapy.

These drugs are histamine-2 receptor antagonists and they markedly inhibit hydrochloric acid production. Histamine is usually released from nerve endings that supply parietal cells of the stomach which stimulates hydrochloric acid production in these cells. Histamine-2 receptor antagonists, such as Tagamet and Zantac, bind to sites on parietal cells and prevent stimulation from histamine. The net result is that the production of hydrochloric acid in the stomach is markedly decreased. However, decreasing stomach acid is only part of the problem. Common side effects caused by these drugs include drowsiness, lethargy, dizziness, diarrhea, skin rash and liver damage.

Lifestyle

Stress can cause and aggravate peptic ulcers. Stressors should be identified and reduced. Exercise is an excellent way to reduce stress. Exercise such as walking, hiking, cycling, swimming or other sports should be a part of daily routine. Meditation, deep breathing exercises, biofeedback and yoga are other effective stress reducing techniques that should be considered.

Diet

Avoid all white sugar and refined carbohydrates. Avoid coffee, tea and other caffeine containing beverages which stimulate acid secretion. Avoid milk. It is a common misconception that milk decreases stomach acidity and should be consumed in large quantities in an individual who has a peptic ulcer. Milk has only a transient effect in neutralizing stomach acidity, followed by a rebound effect where the stomach produces more acid. Avoid spicy and irritating foods that may aggravate peptic ulcers. Food sensitivities and allergies may be associated with the development of ulcers. Increase consumption of fiber and high fiber foods. Consume 1 to 2 liters of fresh cabbage juice for several weeks. Cabbage juice contains glutamine that helps to heal the damaged lining of the mucous membrane. Increase consumption of bananas. They also contain natural factors that help to heal the damaged mucous membrane of the stomach. Increase consumption of whole and unprocessed foods, fresh fruits and vegetables.

Vitamins and Minerals
(Daily unless otherwise stated)

Vitamin A - 10,000-25,000 IU. Necessary for proper development and maintenance of epithelial tissue. Supplementation helps to reduce the number and size of stress ulcers.
Vitamin B-complex - 50-100 mg. Helps the body respond to stress.
Vitamin B5 (Pantothenic Acid) - 500-1000 mg. Helps the body respond to stress that might be a important factor in the development of peptic ulcers.
Vitamin B6 (Pyridoxine) - 25-50 mg. May be deficient. Supplementation may help to heal stress ulcers.
Vitamin C - 500-2000 mg. May be lower in individuals with peptic ulcers. Important for strengthening connective tissue in the digestive system. Supplementation helps to improve the healing time of ulcers. Excess vitamin C consumed on an empty stomach can also aggravate stomach pain.
Vitamin E - 400-800 IU. May provide protection against stress related ulcers.

Zinc - 25-50 mg. Helps to inhibit the release of histamine and other substances from stomach cells that contribute to ulcer formation.

Food Supplements
(Daily unless otherwise stated)

Adrenal glandular extract - 500-1000 mg. Helps to support and stimulate adrenal gland function which is the main gland responsible for helping the body deal with stress.
Bioflavonoids - 500-1000 mg. Helps to inhibit histamine release from nerve endings that supply the stomach and prevents excess acid secretion. Works synergistically with vitamin C.
Bromelain - 600-1200 mg (1800-2400 m.c.u.) Has anti-inflammatory and protein digesting ability.
Glutamine - 1000-2000 mg. Is involved in the production of mucous lining the stomach and duodenum and protects these structures from hydrochloric acid. Supplementation helps to improve the quality and quantity of mucous.

Herbal Medicines

Specific plants and plant derivatives may be useful in treating peptic ulcers. **Aloe vera** juice is soothing and healing to the damaged lining of the stomach. **Licorice (Glycyrrhiza glabra)** protects the lining of the stomach and improves the quality and quantity of mucous produced. **Blessed thistle (Cnictus benedictus), Chamomile (Matricaria chamomilla), Ginger (Zingiber officinalis), Lemon Balm (Melissa officinalis), Peppermint (Mentha piperita), Rosemary (Rosemarinus officinalis) and Valerian (Valerian officinalis)** contain aromatic oils that help to relax and soothe the inflammed and irritated lining of the stomach. Robert's formula is a popular combination of herbal medicines that have been used to treat peptic ulcers. Constituents of this formula include **Marshmallow (Althea officinalis), Geranium (Geranium maculatum), Goldenseal (Hydrastis canadensis), Purple coneflower (Echinacea angustifolia), Slippery Elm (Ulmus fulva), Bromelain (1800-2400 m.c.u.) and Cabbage powder.** One or more of these herbal medicines may be consumed as a tea, tincture, fluid extract, solid extract or supplement.

Highly Recommended

Decrease stress / avoid white sugar and refined carbohydrates / avoid caffeine containing foods and beverages / avoid food senstivities and allergies / fresh vegetable juices / vitamin A / vitamin B-complex / vitamin C / zinc / bromelain / glutamine / Aloe / Chamomile / Licorice / Marshmallow / Peppermint / Slippery elm.

CHAPTER 49

Periodontal Disease

Periodontal disease is a disease which destroys the gums and bony structures that support the teeth. Periodontal disease includes, gingivitis; inflammation of the gums and periodontitis; inflammation and loss of the bony structures of the teeth. Periodontal disease is also called pyorrhea.

Periodontal disease is one of the most common diseases to affect humans. It affects 60% of young adults, 80% of middle aged adults and over 90% of people over the age of 65 years.

Periodontal disease is caused by many different factors. Poor oral hygiene is the most common cause of periodontal disease. Food allergies, diabetes, anemia, bacterial infection, heavy metal toxicity including lead, mercury and bismuth, vitamin deficiencies including vitamins B3, B12, folic acid and C, long term use of certain drugs such as phenytoin, cancer and other debilitating diseases can also cause periodontal disease. Other factors that contribute to this condition include chronic food impaction, unreplaced or missing teeth, malocclusion, tongue thrusting, teeth grinding, toothbrush trauma, breastfeeding, poor structure and integrity of connective tissue, amalgam fillings, cigarette smoking and chewing tobacco.

Early signs of periodontal disease include swelling, redness, change in the normal contours of the gum margin, watery discharge and bleeding from gums. Gums become friable and bleed easily after only slight trauma such as brushing and flossing of teeth. Pain is usually absent.

Conventional medical treatment of periodontal disease focuses on prevention and the use of antibiotics to prevent bacterial infection. If conservative treatment is ineffective in preventing the disease process then surgery might be recommended.

Lifestyle

Poor oral hygiene can cause this disease. Prevention consists of routine plaque control. Regular brushing and flossing is mandatory to prevent this disease. Routine teeth cleaning by a dentist every four to six months is effective in removing plaque and retarding the disease process.

Diet

Avoid sugar and refined carbohydrates and refined and processed foods. Increase consumption of fiber, whole and unprocessed foods. Food sensitivities and allergies may contribute to the development of this disease. A food sensitivity or allergy test may be necessary to identify offending foods.

Vitamins and Minerals
(Daily unless otherwise stated)

Vitamin A - 10,000-25,000 IU. May be deficient. Important for developing strong connective tissue to support the gums and teeth. Also improves wound healing and stimulates immune function.
Vitamin B-complex - 50-100 mg. May be deficient.
Vitamin B3 (Niacin) - 10-25 mg. May be deficient and can cause pellagra.
Vitamin B12 - 50-100 mcg. May be deficient.
Folic acid - 1-5 mg. May be deficient. Important in the development and maintenance of epithelial tissue. Supplementation helps to decrease gingival inflammation, bleeding, gum tenderness, discharge and plaque formation. A 0.1% oral solution can be used as mouthwash twice daily. May be combined with zinc for best results.
Vitamin C - 1000-3000 mg. May be deficient. Important for developing strong connective tissue to support the gums and teeth. Also improves would healing and enhances immune function.
Vitamin E - 400-800 IU. A potent antioxidant that helps to prevent free radical damage.

Selenium - 200-400 mcg. A potent antioxidant that helps to prevent free radical damage.
Zinc - 15-30 mg. May be deficient. Stabilizes connective tissue, helps to increase collagen production, stimulates immune function and decreases allergic histamine release. A 5.0% oral solution may be used as a mouthwash twice daily. May be combined with folic acid for best results.

186

Food Supplements
(Daily unless otherwise stated)

Bioflavonoids - 1000-2000 mg. Increases the strength of connective tissue, decrease inflammation, allergic histamine release and membrane permeability. Works synergistically with vitamin C.
Lactobacillus acidophilus - 1-2 capsules between meals. Part of the normal flora of the mouth and intestines. Supplementation helps to repopulate Lactobacillus and prevent infection from other bacteria.

Herbal Medicines

Specific plants and plant derivatives may be effective in treating periodontal disease. **Barberry (Berberis vulgaris), Calendula (Calendula officinalis), Eucalyptus (Eucalyptus globulus), Garlic (Allium sativum), Goldenseal (Hydrastis canadensis), Myrrh (Commiphora molmol) and Purple coneflower (Echinacea angustifolia)** are antiseptics that can be used. Topical application of Myrrh may be particularly effective. **Bilberry (Vaccinium myrtillus)** and other dark berries are rich in bioflavonoids that are important for the development and maintenance of the connective tissue of the gums. One or more of these herbal medicines may be consumed as a tea, mouthwash or supplement or applied topically.

Highly Recommended

Floss and brush regularly / avoid white sugar and refined carbohydrates / avoid food sensitivities and allergies / vitamin A / folic acid / vitamin C / zinc / bioflavonoids / Lactobacillus acidophilus / Calendula / Garlic / Myrrh.

CHAPTER 50

Premenstrual Syndrome

Premenstrual syndrome (PMS) is the term used to describe the group of symptoms that occur prior to the onset of menstruation in the normal female menstrual cycle.

PMS has been reported to affect 70 to 90% of the female population. Between 20 and 40% of females report some degree of temporary mental and physical dysfunction and 2 to 5% of women may become incapacitated. It has been estimated that 20 to 40% of all women seek professional help with PMS symptoms. PMS is cross-cultural and affects women of all races, socio-economic status and professions. Increased age seems to play a role in the development of symptoms with approximately 50% of women between the ages of 30 and 40 years showing three or more symptoms of PMS. The risk of PMS increases with certain events such as puberty, pregnancy, childbirth, tubal ligation, menopause, use of oral contraceptives, hysterectomy and major life stressors.

Common symptoms of PMS include anxiety, irritability, mood swings, increased appetite, headache, fatigue, dizziness, palpitations, depression, crying, forgetfulness, insomnia, fluid retention, weight gain, swollen extremities, breast tenderness and abdominal bloating.

The exact of PMS is unknown, although a dysfunction involving the brain and ovary axes is believed to occur. Current theories suggest that PMS is secondary to estrogen excess, progesterone deficiency, low progesterone to estrogen ratio, or a precipitous drop in progesterone levels. Vitamin B6 and magnesium deficiencies have been implicated in the cause of PMS. In addition, hypoglycemia (low blood sugar), psychomotor and stress related factors and elevated prolactin levels have also been suggested to play a role in the development of PMS.

Conventional medical treatment of PMS focuses on drug therapy to help alleviate the symptoms associated with this disorder. Commonly prescribed medication includes analgesics, aspirin (ASA), ibuprofen, diuretics, oral contraceptives pills, progesterone, bromocryptine and anti-prostaglandin drugs. Drug therapy is only marginally effective in relieving the symptoms associated with PMS.

Lifestyle

Psychological and social stressors are closely associated with the development and severity of PMS. Women should be encouraged to evaluate stressors in their life and reduce the demands they make on themselves and others. PMS may be a time for introspection and a time for a woman to become more aware and sensitive to her body, especially her menstrual cycle. Stess reduction techniques such as relaxation, deep breathing, meditation, visualization and hypnosis should be explored. Supportive therapy and counselling may be beneficial.

Regular exercise, at least three to four times per week, throughout the month, especially during premenstrual time, is an important means of stress reduction. A brisk walk, swimming, cycling or other forms of aerobic exercise are very beneficial.

Diet

Avoid coffee, tea and other caffeine containing beverages and foods. Avoid white sugar and refined carbohydrates. Avoid excess salt and salty foods. Limit milk, cheese and other dairy products. Food sensitivities and allergies can aggravate PMS. A food sensitivity or allergy test may be necessary to identify offending foods. Increase consumption of whole and unprocessed foods, fresh fruits and vegetables.

Vitamins and Minerals
(Daily unless otherwise stated)

Vitamin A - 10,000-25,000 IU. Supplementation during the second half of the female cycle may be beneficial in reducing the symptoms associated with PMS.
Vitamin B-complex - 50-100 mg. Supplementation may be beneficial and may help the body respond to stress.
Vitamin B6 (Pyridoxine) - 25-100 mg. May be deficient. Vitamin B6 is required for proper fat metabolism and to maintain proper magnesium levels. Supplementation may reduce symptoms associated with PMS.
Vitamin E - 400-800 IU. Supplementation may be beneficial and may reduce symptoms associated with PMS.

Calcium - 800-1200 mg. Supplementation may help to relieve menstrual cramping pains.

189

Magnesium - 400-800 mg. May be deficient. Deficiency can cause adrenal gland growth, fluid retention and emotional lability that occurs with PMS. Supplementation with magnesium relieves PMS symptoms.

Food Supplements
(Daily unless otherwise stated)

Omega-3 oils (flaxseed, fish oil) - 1000-3000 mg. A rich source of essential oils that helps to decrease symptoms of PMS.
Omega-6 oils (evening primrose, borage oil) - 1000-3000 mg. A rich source of essential oils that helps to decrease symptoms of PMS.

Herbal Medicines

Specific plants and plant derivatives may be useful in treating PMS. Phyto-estrogens are plant sources of estrogens and estrogen precursors. Phyto-estrogens are 1:400 as active as estrogens found in animal sources, but plant estrogens due exert biological activity. Plants containing phyto-estrogens have been traditionally used to treat female disorders, including menstrual disorders, menopause and PMS. **Alfalfa (Medicago sativa), Black cohosh (Cimicifuga racemosa), Blue cohosh (Caulophyllum thalictroides), Chaste tree (Vitex agnus castus), Dong quai (Angelica sinensis), Fennel (Foeniculum vulgare) and Unicorn root (Aletris farinosa)** are estrogen containing plants. One or more of these herbal medicines may be consumed as a tea, tincture, fluid extract, solid extract or supplement.

Highly Recommended

Decrease stress / regular exercise / avoid white sugar and refined carbo-hydrates / avoid caffeine containing beverages and foods / vitamin B-complex / vitamin B6 / vitamin E / calcium / magnesium / omega-3 oils / omega-6 oils / Black cohosh / Blue cohosh / Dong quai.

CHAPTER 51

Prostate Enlargement

Prostate enlargement is an abnormal enlargement of the prostate gland, causing variable degrees of bladder outlet obstruction.

Benign prostatic hyperplasia (BPH) is estimated to affect 50% of the men over the age of 50 years. 80% of the men of 80 years old or older are affected by BPH.

The prostate is a walnut shaped gland located around the urethra at the outlet of bladder. The prostate gland contributes to seminal fluid a secretion containing acid phosphatase, citric acid and proteolytic enzymes, which accounts for the liquefaction of semen. The rate of production of prostate fluid increases during sexual stimulation.

Symptoms of BPH include increased frequency of urination, urination at night, incomplete bladder emptying, inability to void, overflow incontinence and terminal dribbling. Hesitancy and intermittency with decreased size and force of urinary stream occur.

The exact cause of prostate enlargement is not entirely known, but hormone imbalances are known to play an important role in its development. BPH is caused by an abnormal enlargement of the prostate gland which irritates the bladder and urethra. Because of its position around the urethra, enlargement of the prostate quickly interferes with the normal passage of urine from the bladder. Urination becomes increasingly difficult and the bladder never feels completely emptied. If left untreated, continued enlargement of the prostate eventually obstructs the bladder completely and emergency measures may become necessary to empty the bladder. If the prostate is markedly enlarged, chronic obstruction may result.

Diagnosis of benign prostatic hyperplasia by a physician should be based on symptoms, physical exam and blood work. A regular checkup and prostate exam is reommended once per year after the age of 50 years. Prostate cancer may initially present with similar symptoms. Prostate cancer is the second leading cause of cancer in all males.

Conventional medical treatment of prostate enlargement focuses on surgery to rectify abnormal prostate enlargement. A surgical procedure called transurethral resection of the prostate (TURP) is the medical treatment of choice. Occasionally certain drugs are prescribed that help to decrease the symptoms associated with prostate enlargement.

Diet

Avoid coffee, tea, colas, chocolate and other caffeine containing foods and beverages. Caffeine is a natural diuretic that increases urinary discharge. Food sensitivities and allergies can aggravate symptoms associated with prostate enlargement. A food sensitivity or allergy test may be necessary to identify offending foods. Avoid white sugar and refined carbohydrates. Increase consumption of whole and unprocessed foods, especially foods high in zinc.

Vitamins and Minerals
(Daily unless otherwise stated)

Vitamin A - 10,000-25,000 IU. A potent antioxidant helps to decrease free radical damage to the prostate gland. It is also required for normal production of prostate fluid.
Vitamin E - 400-800 IU. A potent antioxidant that helps to decrease inflammation in the prostate gland.

Selenium - 200-400 mcg. Selenium protects against cadmium induced prostate enlargement.
Zinc - 50-100 mg. Zinc is involved in the production of prostate hormones. Supplementation reduces the size of prostate gland and significantly improves symptoms associated with prostate enlargement.

Food Supplements
(Daily unless otherwise stated)

Amino acids (glutamic acid, alanine, glycine) - 2-8 gm. Supplementation may be beneficial and can decrease symptoms associated with prostate enlargement. These amino acids inhibit nervous irritation on the bladder and urethra caused by prostate enlargement.

Omega-3 oils (flaxseed, fish oil) - 1000-3000 mg. Supplementation may be beneficial and can decrease symptoms associated with benign prostate enlargement. These oils inhibit prostate enlargement by inhibiting the action of testosterone.

Omega-6 oils (evening primrose, borage oil) - 1000-3000 mg. Supplementation may be beneficial and can decrease symptoms associated with prostate enlargement. These oils inhibit prostate enlargement by inhibiting the action of testosterone.

Herbal Medicines

Specific plants and plant derivatives may be useful in treating BPH and improving the symptoms associated with prostate enlargement. **African pyegium (Pyegium africanum) and Saw palmetto berries (Serenoa repens)** may be beneficial. One or more of these herbal medicines may be consumed as a tea, tincture, fluid extract, solid extract or supplement. A dosage of 200-400 mg of a 80 to 95% liposterolic extract of Saw palmetto berries is recommended.

Highly Recommended

Avoid caffeine containing beverages and foods / avoid food sensitivities and allergies / vitamin A / vitamin E / selenium / zinc / alanine / glutamic acid / glycine / omega-3 oils / omega-6 oils / Saw palmetto berries.

CHAPTER 52

Psoriasis

Psoriasis is usually a chronic, recurrent skin disease marked by discrete bright red patches covered with silvery scales. Psoriasis most often appears on the scalp, knees and elbows and occasionally on the chest, back and buttocks. Sometimes the fingernails are affected, causing pitting, cracking, and ridging of the nails.

Psoriasis is usually a lifelong disease that affects 2 to 4% of the population and equally affects males and females. Psoriasis may first appear in childhood, but most often begins during the third decade of life. In most instances it remains throughout adulthood, often improving during summer and during pregnancies in females. Most individuals suffering from psoriasis only experience mild itching, but the scaly patches are unsightly and may interfere with work, social relationships and self image.

The underlying cause of the disease remains unknown, but it is probably genetic in origin. One third of all individuals with psoriasis usually have another family member with the disease. Psoriasis can be aggravated by stress, sunburn, allergies, illness, surgery, infection and by certain drugs.

Skin cells reproduce at a rate one thousand times the normal rate in individuals with psoriasis. The rate at which skin cells reproduce is controlled by the delicate balance between the chemicals cAMP and cGMP. Individuals with psoriasis have decreased levels of cAMP and increased levels of cGMP.

Conventional medical treatment of psoriasis focuses on the use of cortisone, retinoids, anthralin, methotrexate and other drugs that have potentially serious side effects.

Lifestyle

Stress can aggravate psoriasis. Stressors should be identified and decreased. Exercise should be a part of daily routine and is great way to reduce stress. Exposure to sunshine and artificial light can be beneficial. Long wave ultraviolet light (UVA) may also be beneficial. Topical application of coal tar reduces the inflammation of the psoriatic skin patches. The oldest form of natural therapy is the Goekerman routine which combines coal tar with ultraviolet light.

Diet

Food sensitivities and allergies can aggravate psoriasis. A food sensitivity or allergy test may be necessary to identify offending foods. Avoid white sugar, refined carbohydrates, fats, red meat, coffee, tea, chocolate, alcohol, citrus fruits, nuts, corn, tomato and wheat. Increase consumption of whole, unprocessed foods, vegetables and fruits. Therapeutic fasting for short periods may be very beneficial in reducing skin inflammation associated with psoriasis.

Vitamins and Minerals
(Daily unless otherwise stated)

Vitamin A - 50,000-100,000 IU. Required for the development and maintenance of healthy skin. Inhibits the production of toxins that aggravate psoriasis. High doses of vitamin A may have serious adverse effects and should be administered only under proper medical care.
Vitamin B12 - 10-1000 mcg. Supplementation may reduce the size of psoriatic skin patches.
Folic acid - 200-400 mcg. May be deficient and is involved in skin cell reproduction.
Vitamin C - 500-3000 mg. Involved in normal growth and repair of skin and connective tissue.
Vitamin D - 400-800 IU. Necessary for proper calcium absorption and skin nutrition. Topical application of vitamin D may be beneficial.

Selenium - 400-800 mcg. A potent antioxidant that activates enzymes that reduce skin inflammation.
Zinc - 10-25 mg. May be deficient.
Nickel - 1-3 mg. May be deficient.

Food Supplements
(Daily unless otherwise stated)

Digestive enzymes and/or Hydrochloric acid - 1-2 capsules with each meal. May be deficient and supplementation may help to improve digestion and absorption of food and vitamins and minerals.
Lecithin (Phosphatidyl choline) - 5-20 gm. Supplementation helps to improve fat metabolism.
Omega-3 oils (flaxseed, fish oil) - 1000-3000 mg. Involved in fat metabolism and decreases inflammation of psoriatic skin patches.
Omega-6 oils (evening primrose, borage oil) - 1000-3000 mg. Involved in fat metabolism and decreases inflammation of psoriatic skin patches.

Herbal Medicines

Specific plants and plant derivatives may be useful in treating psoriasis. Plants that have been traditionally used to treat psoriasis include **Burdock (Arctium lappa), Chaparral (Larrea tridentata), Dandelion (Taraxacum officinale), Sarsaparilla (Smilax officinalis and Yellow dock (Rumex crispus).** Although the constituents of these plants differ, they are collectively known as alteratives or blood cleansers. One or more of these herbal medicines may consumed as a tea, tincture, solid extract, fluid extract or capsule. Topical application of **Comfrey root (Symphytum officinale) and Licorice (Glycyrrhiza glabra)** may be beneficial. Comfrey root is soothing and healing to the skin. Licorice root decreases the inflammation of psoriatic skin patches.

Highly Recommended

Decrease stress / topical coal tar applications / UV light / avoid food sensitivities and allergies / vitamin A / vitamin C / vitamin D / digestive enzymes and/or hydrochloric acid / omega-3 oils / omega-6 oils / Burdock / Comfrey / Licorice / Yellow dock.

196

Rheumatoid Arthritis

Rheumatoid arthritis (RA) is a chronic disease characterized by symmetrical inflammation of the joints of the arms and legs.

Approximately 1% of all populations are affected with RA. Women are affected two to three times more commonly than men. An estimated 2 to 3 million people are afflicted with RA. Onset may occur at any age, but it most often occurs between the ages of 25 and 50 years.

Characteristic symptoms of classic rheumatoid arthritis include morning stiffness, joint tenderness, pain on motion, swelling and occasionally subcutaneous nodules. Onset of RA may be abrupt with simultaneous inflammation of multiple joints and with insidious, progressive joint involvement.

The exact cause of RA is still unkown. In chronically affected joints the delicate synovial membrane abnormally thickens and develops numerous folds leading to inflammation, fibrosis and necrosis. The synovial cells lining the joint become inflammed and contribute the pain and swelling.

Conventional medical treatment of RA consists of drug therapy to decrease the pain and inflammation. Analgesics, corticosteroids, immuno-suppressive drugs and surgery are commonly used therapies. Commonly prescribed anti-inflammatory medication includes aspirin (ASA), Tylenol (acetaminophen), Indocid (indomethacin), Fenopron (Fenoprofen), Naprosyn (naproxen), Tolectin (tolmetin) and Clinoril (Sulindac). There are many unpleasant side effects if using non-steroidal anti-inflammatory medication. The prolonged use of these NSAID's should be limited for short durations since their prolonged use could actually inhibit tissue repair and wound healing.

Lifestyle

Moderate daily exercise is recommended. Exercising joints through full range of motion helps to increase flexibility. Topical application of ice is very beneficial in reducing acute inflammation. Physical therapy including ultrasound, diathermy and interferential treatment may be beneficial in reducing inflammation, decreasing muscle spasms and increasing joint function.

Diet

Avoid white sugar and refined carbohydrates. A low fat diet may be beneficial in reducing symptoms associated with RA. Food sensitivities and allergies are strongly associated with the development of rheumatoid arthritis. A food sensitivity or allergy test may be necessary to identify offending foods. Fasting and elimination diets may be very beneficial in reducing symptoms associated with RA and subsequent food challenges may produce acute exacerbations. Dairy, wheat, animal protein, food additives and preservatives have been implicated as potential agents for allergies. Increase consumption of whole and unprocessed foods, fresh fruits and vegetables.

Vitamins and Minerals
(Daily unless otherwise stated)

Vitamin B-complex - 50-100 mg. Helps the body respond to stress.
Vitamin B3 (Niacin) - 50-300 mg. Helps to increase blood flow to affected joints and decreases inflammation.
Vitamin B5 (Calcium pantothenate) - 500-1000 mg. May be deficient with the degree of deficiency related to the severity of symptoms.
Vitamin C - 500-3000 mg. May be decreased and supplementation may be beneficial.
Vitamin K - 15-30 mg. Stabilizes the delicate synovial cells lining joints and decreases inflammation in joints.

Copper - 2-3 mg. May be decreased with the degree of deficiency related to the severity of symptoms. Copper supplementation decreases pain and inflammation within joints. Copper may be in the form of elemental copper, copper salicylate or topical copper bracelets.
Manganese - 10-20 mg. May be decreased and supplementation may be beneficial.
Selenium - 200-400 mcg. May be deficient and supplementation may be beneficial.
Sulfur - 500-1000 mg. May be deficient and supplementation may improve symptoms of RA.

Zinc - 50-100 mg. Supplementation improves symptoms associated with RA including joint swelling, morning stiffness and walking time.

Food Supplements
(Daily unless otherwise stated)

Bromelain (1800-2200 m.c.u.) - 500-1000 mg. A sulfur containing proteolytic enzyme obtained from the pineapple plant. It activates anti-inflammatory prostaglandins in the body. Supplementation decreases inflammation and promotes removal of fluid in swollen areas.
Digestive enzymes and/or Hydrochloric acid - 1-2 capsules before each meal. May be deficient in some individuals with RA. Supplementation may help to improve digestion and symptoms associated with RA.
Histidine - 500-1000 mg. May be decreased in individuals with RA and supplementation may be beneficial.
Omega-3 oils (flaxseed, fish oil) - 1000-3000 mg. Supplementation decreases pain and inflammation of affected joints. Supplementation significantly reduces pain, swelling and morning stiffness.
Omega-6 oils (evening primrose, borage oil) - 1000-3000 mg. Supplementation decreases pain and inflammation of affected joints. Supplementation significantly reduces pain, swelling and morning stiffness.

Herbal Medicines

Specific plants and plant derivatives may be useful in reducing the pain and inflammation associated with rheumatoid arthritis. **Blue cohosh (Caulophyllum thalictroides), Black cohosh (Cimicifuga racemosa), Devil's claw (Harpagophytum procumbens), Licorice (Glycyrrhiza glabra), Tumeric (Curcuma longa), Valerian (Valerian officinalis), White willow bark (Salix alba), Wintergreen (Gaultheria procumbens)** may be beneficial. One or more of these herbal medicines may be consumed as a tea, tincture, fluid extract, solid extract or supplement.

Highly Recommended

Physical therapy / avoid food sensitivities and allergies / vitamin B-complex / vitamin B3 / vitamin C / vitamin K / copper / zinc / bromelain / digestive enzymes and/or hydrochloric acid / omega-3 oils / omega-6 oils / Devil's claw / Licorice / Tumeric / Valerian / White willow / Wintergreen.

CHAPTER 53

Seborrhea

Seborrhea is an inflammatory condition of the skin of the scalp with yellowish, greasy scaling of the skin, more commonly known as dandruff. It may spread to other areas of the face, neck, central part of the trunk and the armpit area.

Seborrhea has been estimated to affect 2 to 5% of the population and affects men and women equally. It commonly occurs between the ages of 20 and 50 years.

Sebaceous glands, oil producing glands, located at the base of the skin become overactive and the hair and the scalp become excessively oily. The scales are greasy, yellowing and crusty. Burning, itching and redness of the involved area may occur. There is also a dry form of the condition, in which the scales are hard, dry and whitish grey in color and the hair is dry and brittle.

The underlying cause of the disease is unknown. There is no specific cure for seborrhea, although various measures are used to control and relieve it. The most imperative action is cleanliness of the hair scalp, combs and brushes.

Conventional medical treatment of seborrhea includes the use of antibiotics, cortisone and sulfur containing creams and Resorcinol. These medications provide symptomatic relief and are only moderately effective in treating psoriasis.

Diet

Food sensitivities and allergies can aggravate seborrhea. A food sensitivity or allergy test may be necessary to identify offending foods. Avoid white sugar, refined carbohydrates, chocolate, fats, oils, coffee, tea, alcohol, citrus fruits, nuts, corn and wheat. Increase consumption of whole, unprocessed foods, vegetables and fruits.

Vitamins and Minerals
(Daily unless otherwise stated)

Vitamin A - 10,000-50,000 IU. Necessary for healthy skin and hair. Deficiency can cause seborrhea.

Biotin - 200-400 mcg. May be deficient and supplementation improves symptoms of seborrhea.

Folic Acid - 400-800 mcg. May be deficient and supplementation improves symptoms of seborrhea.

Vitamin B6 (Pyridoxine) - 25-50 mg. Topical application of vitamin B6 in an ointment base significantly improves symptoms of seborrhea.

Vitamin B12 - 100-1000 mcg. Intramuscular injections of vitamin B12 improves symptoms of seborrhea.

Vitamin E - 400-800 IU. Improves healing of the skin and is a potent antioxidant.

Selenium - 200-400 mcg. A potent antioxidant that works synergistically with vitamin E.

Sulfur - 500-1000 mg. Helps to eliminate toxins and has antibacterial action. Topical application is effective.

Food Supplements
(Daily unless otherwise stated)

Digestive enzymes and/or Hydrochloric acid - 1-2 capsules with each meal. Deficiency has been observed with some patients with seborrhea and supplementation can improve symptoms of seborrhea.

Herbal Medicines

Specific plants and plant derivatives may be useful in treating seborrhea. Plants that have been traditionally used to treat seborrhea include **Burdock (Arctium lappa), Chaparral (Larrea tridentata), Dandelion (Taraxacum officinale), Sarsaparalla (Smilax officinalis), and Yellow dock (Rumex crispus).** Although the constituents of these plants differ, they are collectively known as alteratives or blood cleansers. One or more of these herbal medicines may be consumed as a tea, tincture, fluid extract, solid extract or supplement.

Highly Recommended

Avoid food sensitivities and allergies / vitamin A / biotin / folic acid / vitamin B6 / selenium / sulfur / digestive enzymes and/or hydrochloric acid / Burdock / Chaparral / Dandelion / Yellow dock.

CHAPTER 55

Stroke

A stroke or cerebro-vascular accident is a disease involving one or more of the blood vessels of the brain. It involves a rupture or blockage of a blood vessel in the brain, depriving parts of the brain of blood supply, resulting in loss of consciousness, paralysis or other symptoms depending on the site and extent of injury.

Strokes are a major cause of death and disability and the third leading cause of death in western society. It is estimated that 3 to 5% of the population are affected by cerebro-vascular accidents. Men and women are equally affected.

Strokes are more common than is generally realized. It is estimated that by the age of 30 years, one out of four persons has sufficient change in the cerebral arteries to provide a setting for a stroke at any time. Autopsy studies show that nearly half of those who die from other causes have had minor strokes without ever having been aware of them. The impact on society is far reaching. 75% of all stroke victims are 65 years or older. Increased age, especially greater than 65 years, is a noted risk factor to the development of stroke. Those individuals who have had one stroke are at high risk for the development of another stroke. Other high risk factors include cigarette smoking, lack of physical activity, high blood pressure and high fat diet.

There are three main causes of strokes that are usually a severe complication of atherosclerosis or hardening of the arteries involving blood vessels of the brain. They are brain embolism, thrombus and hemorrhage. Other causes include compression of brain blood vessels are a result of tumors or swelling and arterial spasms.

An embolism is a small mass of material circulating in blood vessels. It can consist of air, fat or other material introduced into the circulatory system. It travels in the arterial system until it is too large to pass any further. It blocks blood flow and deprives the brain of oxygen.

A thrombus is the most common cause of stroke. A thrombus is a small clot or collection of fat, cholesterol and blood cells that slowly develops and blocks arteries in the brain. The thrombus eventually blocks blood flow through the artery and deprives the brain of vital oxygen and nutrients.

A hemorrhage is a rupture of a blood vessel, usually an artery within the brain. Hemorrhage is most frequently associated with pre-existing high blood pressure. With athersclerosis there is a hardening of the blood vessel wall. It loses its elasticity and becomes more prone to rupture. In another condition the blood vessel wall may become weak-ened by an aneurysm and is susceptible to rupture and hemorrhage into brain tissue.

Symptoms of strokes vary according to the type and area of the brain affected. As a consequence of the blockage of these arteries, the brain is deprived of necessary blood supply and oxygen. If the left side of the brain is affected, the opposing right side of the body is affected. Early symptoms of stroke include dizziness, headache, mental confusion and poor coordination. Speech disturbances also are related to the area of the brain affected. The speech center is located in the left side of the brain. If the left side of the brain is affected then speech disturbance may occur. Emotional disturbance may also accompany a stroke. A stroke victim may have difficulty controlling their emotions and may laugh or cry with little or no provocation. Sometimes urinary and fecal incontinence may accompany a stroke. There may be loss of consciousness, paralysis of one or more limbs, and convulsion. Sudden death rarely occurs as a result of a stroke. Depending upon the extent and duration of injury, brain damage may be transient or permanent.

Strokes that last from a few minutes to less than 24 hours are called transient ishemic attacks (TIA). This term arises from the nature of attack, which is only temporary and leaves no noticeable permanent damage. These attacks are considered warnings that a more severe attack will probably occur unless steps are taken to improve blood flow through the arteries.

Conventional medical treatment of arteries focuses on drug therapy and surgery. Anticoagulant drugs such as warfarin and coumadin are prescribed only when risk of hemorrhage is low and clot formation has been found to be either the potential or actual cause of decreased blood flow. Anti-hypertensive medication is frequently prescribed to lower blood pressure and reduce the risk of rupture. Occasionally brain surgery may be necessary to prevent further and permanent damage and death. Arterial endarectomy is a surgical procedure employed to remove the material that blocks an artery. The procedure is delicate and complications may arise.

Lifestyle

Stress can raise blood pressure and precipitate a cerebro-vascular accident. Stressors should be identified and reduced. Meditation, biofeedback and exercise are excellent stress reduction techniques. Exercise should be a part of daily routine. Walking, cycling, swimming or other aerobic exercises are excellent ways to increase circulation to the brain and can reduce atherosclerosis and hypertension. The amount of activity allowed following a stroke depends on the cause and extent of the stroke.

Diet

Avoid white sugar and refined carbohydrates. Avoid a high fat diet, especially saturated fats. Avoid coffee, tea, colas, chocolate and other caffeine containing beverages and foods. Avoid excessive consumption of alcohol. Increase consumption of whole and unprocessed foods, fresh fruits and vegetables.

Vitamins and Minerals
(Daily unless otherwise stated)

Vitamin A - 10,000-25,000 IU. Involved in the production and maintenance of connective tissue in blood vessel walls.
Vitamin B-complex - 50-100 mg. Helps the body respond to stress and supplementation may be beneficial.
Vitamin B3 (Niacin) - 100-500 mg. Helps to dilate arteries and increase blood flow to the brain.
Vitamin C - 500-2000 mg. Involved in cross-linking of connective tissue around blood vessels and helps to maintain strong and healthy artery walls.
Vitamin E - 400-1200 IU. Helps to decrease platelet stickiness and decrease atherosclerosis in the brain.

Calcium - 500-1000 mg. Helps to relax smooth muscle around blood vessels and increases blood flow and decreases blood pressure.

Magnesium - 400-800 mg. Helps to relax smooth muscle around blood vessels and increase blood flow and decrease blood pressure.

Food Supplements
(Daily unless otherwise stated)

Bioflavonoids - 500-1500 mg. Helps to strengthen connective tissue around blood vessels of the brain. Works synergistically with vitamin C.
Omega-3 oils (flaxseed, fish oil) - 1000-3000 mg. A rich source of essential oils that helps to decrease atherosclerosis and high blood pressure.
Omega-6 oils (evening primrose, borage oil) - 1000-3000 mg. A rich source of essential oils that helps to decrease atherosclerosis and high blood pressure.

Herbal Medicines

Specific plants and plant extracts may be useful in treating strokes and preventing further strokes. **Capsicum (Capsicum frutescens), Garlic (Allium sativum), Ginger (Zingiber officinalis), Ginkgo (Ginkgo biloba), Gotu kola (Centella asiatica) and Tumeric (Curcuma longa)** may be beneficial in helping stroke victims. Ginkgo contains natural flavonoids that help to dilate blood vessels and increase both blood supply and oxygen to the brain. One or more or these herbal medicines may be consumed as a tea, tincture, fluid extract, solid extract or supplement.

Highly Recommended

Decrease stress / quit smoking / moderate daily aerobic exercise / avoid fats, especially saturated fats / avoid caffeine containing beverages and foods / avoid excess alcohol / vitamin B-complex / vitamin E / magnesium / omega-3 oils / Capsicum / Garlic / Ginkgo / Gotu kola / Tumeric.

CHAPTER 56

Urinary Tract Infections

Urinary tract infections (UTI's) are a common infection of the urinary tract and typically involves the ureters, bladder and urethra and in more serious cases, the kidneys.

Urinary tract infections are experienced by 10 to 20% of the population with a much higher incidence in females than in males. The rate if UTI's is ten times higher in females than in males. 10% of infants and adolescents, 2-3% of adults aged 20 to 60 years and 10-20% of adults greater than the age of 60 years suffer from UTI's. There is a high rate of recurrence with urinary tract infections.

Urine produced in the kidneys is usually sterile. Bacteria including E. coli, Klebsiella, Proteus, Enterobacter and Pseudomonas are common causes of UTI's. E. coli, a normally occuring non-disease producing bacteria, causes up to 85% of all UTI's. These bacteria enter through the urethra and may travel up the urinary tract and cause infection.

Lower urinary tract infections commonly involve the bladder causing cystitis and are characterized by difficult and painful urination and increased urgency and frequency of urination. Other symptoms include fever, chills and flank pain, low back pain and abdominal discomfort. In more serious cases, symptoms include blood in the urine, diarrhea, vomiting and kidney dysfunction. The association of urinary tract infections with sexual intercourse in women is known as "honeymoon cystitis." Infection occurs within 24 hours following sexual intercourse. Infection will recur in up to 50% of individuals within one year.

Conventional medical treatment of UTI's focuses on antibiotic therapy to eliminate bacterial infection. Commonly prescribed medication includes Amoxicillin, Ampicillin, Cefaclor, Doxycycline, Nitrofurantoin, Sulfonamides and Trimethoprim.

Lifestyle

Poor personal hygiene habits may contribute to the development of urinary tract infections. Cleaning the urethral opening after urination with tissue may help to prevent spread of bacteria.

Diet

Avoid white sugar and refined carbohydrates because they may feed the bacteria causing infection and can depress immune function. Food sensitivities and allergies have been associated with the development of urinary tract infections. Food sensitivities and allergies should be identified and eliminated. Drink large amounts of water, up to 4 liters per day. Water will aid in elimination throught the urinary tract and help to flush out bacteria. Drink large amounts of unsweetened cranberry juice, up to 3 liters per day. Cranberry juice contains natural antibiotics that help to prevent bacteria from adhering to the cells lining the urinary tract.

Vitamins and Minerals
(Daily unless otherwise stated)

Vitamin A - 10,000-25,000 IU. Helps to activate the immune system and helps to fight bacterial infection of the urinary tract.
Vitamin B6 (Pyridoxine) - 25-50 mg. May be deficient and may impair the ability of cells lining the urinary tract to resist bacterial attachment.
Vitamin C - 1000-5000 mg. Helps to activate the immune system and helps to fight bacterial infection in the urinary tract.

Magnesium - 400-800 mg. May be deficient and helps to relax smooth muscle of the urinary tract.
Zinc - 25-50 mg. Helps to activate the immune system and helps to fight bacterial infection in the urinary tract.

Food Supplements
(Daily unless otherwise stated)

Thymus glandular extract - 500-1000 mg. Helps to activate the immune system and to resist infection of the urinary tract.
Kidney glandular extract - 500-1000 mg. Helps to support and nourish the kidneys and urinary tract. Supplementation may be beneficial.

Herbal Medicines

Specific plants and plant derivatives may be useful in treating common urinary tract infections. **Bearberry (Arctostaphylos uva-ursi), Buchu (Barosma betulina), Corn silk (Zea mays), Couchgrass (Agropyron repens), Dandelion (Taraxacum officinalis), Horsetail (Equisetum arvense), Hydrangea (Hydrangea arborescens), Juniper (Juniper communis), Parsley (Petroselinum sativum), Parsely piert (Parietaria officinalis) and Stone root (Collinsonia canadensis)** are useful plants in treating UTI's. One or more of these herbal medicines may be consumed as a tea, tincture, fluid extract, solid extract or supplement.

Highly Recommended

Personal hygiene habits / avoid food sensitivities and allergies / avoid white sugar and refined carbohydrates / increase water consumption / unsweetened cranberry juice / vitamin A / vitamin C / magnesium / zinc / thymus glandular extract / Bearberry / Buchu / Corn silk / Couch grass / Dandelion / Juniper / Stoneroot.

CHAPTER 57

Varicose Veins

Varicose veins are dilated, elongated, tortuous superficial veins that typically occur in the legs.

Varicose veins occur in 50% of middle aged adults. They are four times more common in females than in males. Varicose veins occur more frequently in individuals who must stand or sit motionless for prolonged periods.

Obvious signs of varicose veins include dilated, twisted and enlarged superficial veins in the legs although they can occur throughout the body. Other symptoms that can occur include muscle fatigue, muscle aches, localized itching, heaviness in the legs, bruising or bluish discoloration of veins involved and leg swelling and edema. Complications of varicose veins include ulceration, blood stasis and phlebitis.

Varicose veins are caused by congenitally absent or incompetent valves within the veins. Heredity plays an important role in their development and they are more common when another another family member has them. Prolonged standing or sitting impairs venous blood flow and leads to blood flow congestion. Risk factors for increased chances of developing varicose veins include obesity, pregnancy and any disease that impairs muscle movement in the legs. Other potential causes of poor circulation and muscle aches include osteoarthritis, nerve inflammation, diabetic or alcoholic nerve dysfunction, arterial insufficiency and intermittent claudication.

Conventional medical treatment of varicose veins is limited as the disease is regarded as incurable. A popular technique called injection sclerotherapy involves injecting a chemical substance into the vein. This causes hardening of the vein and prevents further dilation as the disease progresses. Surgical stripping and ligation of the varicose veins is generally reserved for advanced stages of the disease.

Lifestyle

Treatment of mild cases of varicose veins includes rest periods at intervals during the day. The individual should lie flat with their feet raised slightly above the level of the heart. Bathing the legs in warm water and epsom salts helps to stimulate blood flow.

Avoid standing for prolonged periods. Use support good hosiery or stocking. Tight stockings, garters or tight clothing should not be worn because they could further restrict blood flow.

Exercise is strongly encouraged. Regular leg exercises or walking, jogging, cycling or swimming are great ways to stimulate blood flow through the legs. Those who have a predispositon to varicose veins should make such activities a part of their regular routine. If possible, they should avoid occupations that require them to stand or sit motionless for long periods of time or should make it a point to walk about and exercise their leg muscles at frequent intervals during working hours.

Diet

Decrease sugar and refined carbohydrates. Avoid refined and processed foods. Increase whole and unprocessed foods. Increase consumption of fiber. Increase consumption of vegetables and fruits, legumes and whole grains. Increase consumption of garlic, onions, ginger and cayenne because they help to prevent decreased blood flow and clot formation within veins.

Vitamins and Minerals
(Daily unless otherwise stated)

Vitamin A - 10,000-25,000 IU. Important in the development and maintenance of the lining of the veins, arteries and capillaries.
Vitamin B-complex - 50-100 mg. May be deficient. Helps the body respond to stress.
Vitamin C - 500-3000 mg. Important in the development of strong connective tissue that surrounds veins and enhances immune function.
Vitamin D - 200-400 IU. Helps to prevent leg cramps when combined with calcium and magnesium.
Vitamin E - 400-800 IU. Helps to decrease inflammation, important in wound healing and improves blood viscosity.

Calcium - 800-1200 mg. Helps to prevent leg cramps when combined with vitamin D and magnesium.
Magnesium - 400-800 IU. Helps to prevent leg cramps when combined with calcium and vitamin D.
Zinc - 15-30 mg. Necessary in wound healing and helps to increase the strength of the blood vessel wall. The topical application of zinc oxide ointment may be effective.

Food Supplements
(Daily unless otherwise stated)

Bioflavonoids - 500-1000 mg. Important in the development of strong connective tissue that surrounds veins. Works synergistically with vitamin C.
Bromelain (2000 m.c.u.) - 1000-2000 mg. Take between meals. A proteolytic enzyme that has anti-inflammatory activity and helps to dissolve fibrin clots within blood vessels.
Fiber (psyllium, oat bran, guar gum) - 5-10 gm. Deficiency has been associated with the development of varicose veins and hemorrhoids. Supplementation may be beneficial.

Herbal Medicines

Specific plants and plant derivatives may be useful in treating varicose veins. **Bilberry (Vaccinium myrtillus), Butcher's broom (Ruscus aculeatus), Gotu kola (Centella asiatica), Hawthorn (Crataegus oxyacantha), Horse chestnut (Aesculus hippocastanum), Marshmallow (Althea officinalis) and Prickly Ash (Zanthoxylum americanum)** contain substances that help to strengthen and support vein walls. One or more of these herbal may be applied topically or consumed as a tea, tincture, fluid extract, solid extract or supplement.

Highly Recommended

Moderate exercise / support hosiery / epsom salt baths / dietary fiber / vitamin A / vitamin C / vitamin E / calcium / magnesium / zinc / bioflavonoids / Butcher's broom / Gotu kola / Horse chestnut.

212

CHAPTER 58

Vitiligo

Vitiligo is a skin disorder characterized by white, hypopigmented patches that typically occur in the arms, upper trunk and back and head regions. Skin pigment cells called melanocytes produce the pigment, melanin, that is responsible for providing skin tone and color. With vitiligo skin pigment cells are destroyed and there is a lack of melanin. Snow white patches with a darkened borders are classic manifestations of this disorder.

Approximately 1% of the population have vitiligo to varying degrees. Slightly more females are affected than males. Age on onset is between the ages of 10 and 30 years, although it may occur later in life.

The exact cause of vitiligo is unknown. Genetics is known to play an important role and vitiligo tends to occur in families. Vitiligo also occurs more often in individuals with diabetes, hypothyroidism, anemia, hypoadrenalism and immune dysfunction. Skin areas affected tend to be more susceptible to sunburn and individuals with vitiligo should be forewarned about the sun's possible adverse affect.

Conventional medical treatment of vitiligo includes the use of psoralens or phototoxic drugs, cosmetic creams used to cover up skin patches, sunscreens, ultraviolet A light and Dy-o-derm.

Lifestyle

Overexposure to sunlight can aggravate vitiligo and lead to sunburn of affected areas. Individuals with vitiligo are advised to use sunscreens to protect themselves from the adverse effects of sunshine. However, long wave ultraviolet light (UVA) may be beneficial.

Diet

Increase consumption of foods high in para-amino-benzoic acid (PABA) including kidney, liver, molasses and whole grains. Increase consumption of foods high in the amino acids phenylalanine and tyrosine including meats, legumes, nuts and whole grains.

Vitamins and Minerals
(Daily unless otherwise stated)

Vitamin A - 10,000-25,000 IU. Required in the normal production of skin pigment cells.
Vitamin B-complex - 50-100 mg. May be deficient and supplementation may be beneficial.
PABA (Para-amino-benzoic acid) - 250-500 mg. May be deficient and supplementation may improve the skin condition. PABA is a potent antioxidant that absorbs ultraviolet light, helps to breakdown and utalize proteins, and improves the activity of folic acid and pantothenic acid. PABA injections along with B-complex may be beneficial.

Copper - 2-3 mg. May be deficient and supplementation may help. Copper is required to produce melanin.

Food Supplements
(Daily unless otherwise stated)

Digestive enzymes and/or Hydrochloric acid - 1-2 capsules capsules with each meal. Deficieny may occur in some individuals with vitiligo leading to poor absorption of protein and vitamins and minerals.
Phenylalanine - 2-4 gm. A naturally occuring amino acid required for the production of melanin.
Tyrosine - 2-4 gm. A naturally occuring amino acid required for the production of melanin.

Highly Recommended

Avoid over-exposure to sunlight / use sunscreens / vitamin A / PABA / copper / digestive enzymes and/or hydrochloric acid / phenylalanine / tyrosine.

214

CHAPTER 59

Warts

Warts or verrucae are benign, semi-contagious growths of the outer layer of the skin. Warts are caused by viruses and tend to occur in the hands, arms, face, upper trunk, legs, feet, anal and genital areas. The most common types of warts include the common wart, plantar warts and genital warts.

Warts are generally more common among children and young adults than among older persons. Appearance, size and location of warts can vary. Most warts are less than one half centimeter in diameter. They may be flat or raised, dry or moist. Usually they have a rough, pitted surface, either flesh-colored or darker than the surrounding skin.

Warts tend to develop on the exposed areas of the skin including the hands, elbows, face, knees, feet and other areas. Warts may be single or multiple and tend to occur in areas of repetitive friction. When they occur on especially vulnerable areas such as the knee or elbow, they can become irritated and tender. Plantar warts are flat warts that occur commonly on the soles of the feet. They can become irritated and tender due to the repetitive motion of walking. A butcher's wart occurs on the hands and arms of meat cutters. Warts can occur in the nostril and can obstruct breathing by blocking a nostril. Laryngeal warts in the larynx or voice box may occur and irritate the throat. Genital warts occur in or on the genitalia of males and females. They are often sexually transmitted and can cause a tremendous amount of stress due to their location and their effect on human sexuality. Condyloma and the human papilloma virus (HPV) can cause genital and peri-anal warts, especially in females. HPV virus has been associated with the development of cervical dysplasia and cervical cancer. Women with veneral warts should consult a physician and get a PAP test to identify abnormal cells in the cervix. Anal warts occur on the anus and can cause a lot of itching.

A wart develops between one and eight months after exposure to virus and the virus becomes lodged in the outer layer of the skin. Afterwhich time, a benign, unsightly growth may develop. Warts are highly resistant to therapy and have a high rate of recurrence. Warts are spread by scratching, rubbing and razor cuts. In a half of all cases, warts disappear spontaneously without any treatment. However, warts may recur and remain for years.

The exact cause of warts is not entirely known. Warts like any other virus or bacteria tend to occur when the immune system is depressed. Nutritional deficiences can lead to the development of warts.

Conventional medical treatment of warts includes the use of removal by acids (salicylic, bichloroacetic acid, nitric acids), burning, freezing (liquid nitrogen) and electrodessication. The use of antiviral agents such bleomycin and alpha interferon have been used. These methods may be effective, although warts are highly recurrent and resistant to therapy. Scarring of the skin may occur as a result of treatment.

Lifestyle

Psychological state can affect the growth and outcome of warts. Positive, focused mental concentration on the elimination and disappearance of the wart can be effective in reducing their size and recurrence.

Diet

Decrease consumption of white sugar, refined carbohydrates, fats and oils and refined, processed foods. Increase consumption of complex carbohydrates and whole, unprocessed foods. Topical application of papaya, banana peel or potato may be effective.

Vitamins and Minerals
(Daily unless otherwise stated)

Vitamin A - 10,000-25,000 IU. May be deficient and supplementation can improve immune function.
Vitamin C - 1000-3000 mg. May be deficient and supplementation can improve immune function and fight viral infections.
Vitamin E - 400-1200 IU. May be deficient. Topical application of vitamin E oil to the wart may be effective.

Zinc - 10-25 mg. May be deficient and supplementation can improve immune function.

216

Food Supplements
(Daily unless otherwise stated)

Thymus glandular extract - 500-1000 mg. Helps to support and stimulate thymus gland function. The thymus gland plays an important role in immune function.

Herbal Medicines

Specific plants and plant derivatives may be useful in treating common warts. **Cypress spurge (Euphorbia cypaissiae), Dandelion (Taraxacum officinale), Garlic (Allium sativum), Greater celandine (Chelidonium majus), American Mandrake (Podophyllum pellatum), Milk Thistle (Silybum marianum), White Willow (Salix alba), Tea Tree oil (Maleleuca officinalis) and Yellow Cedar (Thuja occidentalis)** have been used successfully to treat warts. The topical application of the milky juice from these plants applied to the surface of the wart, then covered with a bandaid is effective. A 10-20% solution of **salilcylic acid,** derived from white willow, can be used. A 10-25% **podophyllum tincture** with 75 to 90% benzoin may be applied to the wart. **Thuja tincture and tea tree oil** are also effective. Care should be taken when applying these substances to the skin. They are highly irritating and can damage the surrounding tissue.

Highly Recommended

Visualization / avoid white sugar and refined carbohydrates / vitamin A / vitamin C / vitamin E / zinc / Garlic / Greater celandine / American mandrake / Tea tree oil / Yellow cedar / salicylic acid / podophyllum tincture.

CHAPTER 60

Yeast Infection

Chronic yeast infection is the term used to describe persistent infections of the skin, mouth, digestive system, vagina and in more rare forms involve the lungs, heart or blood.

The exact prevalence of yeast infection is not known. Yeast can be cultured from the skin, mouth, digestive system and vagina in virtually every individual, making the diagnosis of yeast infection difficult. 5 to 10% of the population have active yeast infection.

Yeast are a group of single celled organisms that belong to the fungus (mushrooms, molds) family. Unlike plants, yeast do not possess chlorophyll and reproduce by highly resistant spores. Candida albicans is a common yeast that is normally part of the human flora. Candida overgrowth can lead to chronic yeast infection.

Symptoms of chronic yeast infection are specific to the area of the body involved. General symptoms include fatigue, lethargy, feeling of being drained, drowsiness, inability to concentrate, feeling of "spaciness" or unreality", depression, mood swings, headaches, dizziness or loss of balance, pressure above the ears, feeling of head swelling and tingling, recurrent infections, ear pain or deafness, blurred vision, burning or tearing eyes, itchy eyes, nasal congestion or discharge, post-nasal drip, itchy nose, dry mouth, rash or blisters in the mouth, sore throat, cough, bad breath, pain or tightness in the chest, wheezing or shortness of breath, heartburn, indigestion, excessive beltching, abdominal pain, bloating, constipation, diarrhea, excessive flatulence, hemorrhoids, rectal itching, painful or burning urination, frequent urination, frequent bladder infections, persistent vaginal itch, persistent vaginal burning, impotence, loss of sexual desire, menstrual cramps and/or other menstrual irregularities, premenstrual tension, muscle aches, muscle weakness and/or paralysis, pain and/or swelling of joints, skin rashes and increased sensitivities to foods and environmental allergens.

Risk factors for chronic yeast infection include the use of anti-ulcer drugs, broad spectrum antibiotics, steroids, oral contraceptives, excessive consumption of sugar, immune deficiency, diabetes mellitus, intravascular

218

catheters, intravenous drug use, lack of digestive enzymes, nutrient deficiency and prolonged white blood cell deficiency. Antibiotic use is the single most common cause of chronic yeast infection.

Conventional medical treatment of yeast infection focuses on drug therapy, both oral and topical, to eradicate the organisms. Commonly prescribed medication include Flagyl (metronidazole), Monistat (miconazole), Lotrimin (clotrimazole), Ketoconazole, Griseofulvin, Amphotercin B and Nystatin. Side effects of these medication include nausea, vomiting, digestive disturbance, anorexia, muscle cramps, joint pains, hives, skin rash, peripheral neuropathy, convulsions, seizures, decreased white blood cell count and liver damage.

Lifestyle

Avoid risk factors that contribute to chronic yeast infection. Indiscriminate use of antibiotics can cause chronic yeast infection. Antibiotics may be necessary in certain medical conditions, but long term and unnecessary use of antibiotics may be detrimental. Additionally, use of other immune suppressing drugs may contribute to chronic yeast infection.

Diet

Decrease consumption of yeast and yeast containing foods including breads, pastries, alcoholic beverages, malt products, condiments, sauces and vinegar containing foods, processed and smoked meats, dried and candied fruits, edible fungi, cheeses, packaged and processed foods. Avoid white sugar and refined carbohydrates because it feeds yeast and depresses immune function. Increase consumption of whole and unprocessed foods, fresh fruits and vegetables.

Vitamins and Minerals
(Daily unless otherwise stated)

Vitamin A - 10,000-25,000 IU. Supplementation helps to stimulate the immune system and fight infection.
Beta-carotene - 50,000-100,000 IU. Precursor to vitamin A without the side effects at high doses. Supplementation helps to stimulate the immune system and fight infection.

219

Vitamin B-complex - 25-50 mg. May be deficient. Helps the body respond to stress.
Vitamin B2 (Riboflavin) - 10-25 mg. May be deficient.
Vitamin B6 (Pyridoxine) - 25-50 mg. May be deficient.
Folic Acid - 200-400 mcg. May be deficient.
Vitamin C - 1000-3000 mg. Supplementation helps to stimulate the immune system and fight infection.

Iron - 10-25 mg. May be deficient
Magnesium - 400-800 mg. May be deficient.
Selenium - 200-400 mcg. May be deficient.
Zinc - 25-50 mg. May be deficient. Supplementation helps to stimulate the immune system and fight infection.

Food Supplements
(Daily unless otherwise stated)

Caprylic acid - 1-2 gm. A naturally occuring medium chain fatty acid that disintegrates yeast cell walls. Time release preparations are recommended, so that the fatty acid is not digested in the stomach. May be used at the same time with acidophilus supplements and antibiotics.
Fiber - 20-40 gm. Important in promoting colon health. Dietary fiber increases stool transit time, increases pancreatic digestive juices, increases bile production, increases production of short chain fatty acids and maintains a healthy bacterial population in the digestive system.
Lactobacillus acidophilus - 2-4 capsules (4 billion bacteria per capsule). One of a group of naturally occuring bacteria that normally inhabit the intestines in healthy individuals. Acidophilus bacteria produce many substances that are harmful to unwanted yeast and other potentially infectious organisms. Supplementation helps to repopulate the digestive system and/or vagina with good, healthy bacteria.
Omega-3 oils (flaxseed, fish oil) - 1500-3000 mg. May be deficient. A rich source of essential fatty acids that is required by the body for proper immune function.
Omega-6 oils (evening primrose, borage oil) - 1500-3000 mg. May be deficient. A rich source of essential fatty acids that is required by the body for proper immune function.
Undecylenic acid - 1-2 gm. A naturally occuring medium chain fatty acid that disintegrates yeast cell walls.

Herbal Medicines

Specific plants and plant derivatives may be useful in treating chronic yeast infection. **Chamomile (Matricaria chamomilla), Garlic (Allium sativum), Goldenseal (Hydrastis canadensis), Lemon Balm (Melissa officinalis) and Pau D'arco (Tabebuia avellanedae)** may be beneficial. **Australian tea tree oil (Meleleuca alternifolia)** contains an aromatic oil that has significant antifungal activity. Topical application of tea tree oil preparations is very beneficial in treating a wide variety of fungal infection. Many other botanical medicines contain aromatic oils that demonstrate significant antifungal activity. **Balm (Melissa officinalis), Chamomile (Matricaria chamomilla), Cinnamon (Cinnomomum verum), Ginger (Zingiber officinalis), Peppermint (Mentha piperita) and Rosemary (Rosmarinus officinalis)** are rich in oils that have significant antifungal activity. One or more of these herbal medicines may be consumed as a tea, tincture, fluid extract, solid extract or supplement.

Highly Recommended

Avoid indiscriminate use of drugs that decrease immune function / avoid yeast and yeast containing beverages and foods / avoid white sugar and refined carbohydrates / vitamin A / beta-carotene / vitamin C / zinc / caprylic acid / fiber / Lactobacillus acidophilus / omega-6 oils / Garlic / Ginger / Goldenseal / Pau D' arco / Australian tea tree oil.

CHAPTER 61

Other Common Diseases

Allergies (general): Decrease stress / avoid smoking / vitamin B6 / vitamin B12 / vitamin C / vitamin E / molybdenum / bioflavonoids / catechin / quercitin / pantethine / omega-3 oils (flaxseed, fish oils) / omega-6 oils (evening primrose, borage oils) / Lactobacillus acidophilus and bifidus / adrenal glandular extract / thymus glandular extract / rule out food and environmental sensitivities including wheat, dairy, corn, citrus fruits, peanuts, strawberries, dust, molds, pollens, aspirin (ASA), sodium salicylate, sodium bisulfite, monosodium glutamate (MSG), BHT, BHA, tartrazine and other sensitivities.

Angina pectoris: Avoid coffee, tea and other caffeine containing beverages / decrease alcohol / avoid smoking / decrease stress / avoid all stimulants / increase daily exercise as tolerated / vitamin E / magnesium / L-carnitine / co-enzyme Q-10 / Hawthorn (Crataegus oxycantha).

Anemia: Vitamin A / beta-carotene / vitamin B-complex / vitamin B1 / vitamin B2 / vitamin B5 / vitamin B6 / vitamin B12 / folic acid / vitamin C (increases iron absorption) / vitamin E / copper / iron (may be deficient) / zinc / rule out food sensitivities / rule out digestive enzymes and hydrochloric acid deficiency.

Ankylosing spondylitis (Marie-Strumpell Disease): Decrease stress / avoid smoking / avoid all food sensitivities and allergies / decrease consumption of processed and refined foods and increase consumption of whole, unprocessed foods / vitamin B6 / vitamin B-12 / vitamin C / vitamin E / calcium / magnesium / bioflavonoids / omega-3 oils (flaxseed, fish oils) / omega-6 oils (evening primrose, borage oils) / digestive enzymes and/or hydrochloric acid / bromelain / Devil's claw (Harpagophytum procumbens) / White willow (Salix alba) / Tumeric (Curcuma longa).

Anorexia nervosa: Increase consumption of whole and unprocessed foods, fresh fruits and vegetables / zinc (may be deficient and helps to improve taste, smell and appetite) / essential fatty acids (may be deficient).

Athlete's foot: Wash frequently and keep feet dry / vitamin A / vitamin C / vitamin E (topical) / zinc / topical tea tree oil (Maleleuca alternifolia) / topical thuja oil / copper sulphate soaks / UV light / Garlic and Berberis soaks.

Anxiety: Avoid coffee, tea and other caffeine containing beverages / avoid white sugar and refined carbohydrates / rule out hypoglycemia / avoid alcohol / vitamin B-complex (may be deficient) / vitamin B1 / vitamin B3 / vitamin B6 / calcium / magnesium.

Appetite (poor): Decrease stress / avoid refined and processed foods / increase whole, unprocessed foods, fresh fruits and vegetables / foods to increase digestion such as lemon juice, beets, ginger, papaya / protein supplement may be necessary to maintain weight / vitamin A / vitamin B-complex / magnesium / zinc / digestive enzymes and/or hydrochloric acid / thyroid glandular extract / Capsicum (Capsicum frutescens) / Catnip (Nepeta cataria) / Dandelion (Taraxacum officinalis) / Fennel (Foeniculum vulgare) / Fenugreek (Trigonella foenum-graecum) / Gentian (Gentian lutea) / Ginger (Zingiber officinalis) / Ginseng (Panax ginseng) / Peppermint (Mentha piperita) / Wormwood (Artemisia absinthium).

Autism: Vitamin B6 (high doses administered only under medical supervision) / magnesium (decreases irritability) / rule out food and environmental sensitivities and/or allergies.

Autoimmune Disorders (General): Vitamin E / omega-3 oils (flaxseed, fish oil) / omega-6 oils (evening primrose, borage oil).

Bad Breath (Halitosis): Detoxification Diet / avoid refined and processed foods / increase consumption of whole and unprocessed foods / chlorophyll / digestive enzymes and hydrochloric acid / Lactobacillus acidophilus.

Backache: Important to identify the exact origin of back pain / exercise and stretching is important in preventing back injury / ice packs applied topically help to reduce pain and inflammation / vitamin B-complex (helps to the body respond to stress) / vitamin B-6 / vitamin B-12 / vitamin C / calcium / magnesium / bromelain / cysteine / White willow (Salix alba) / Tumeric (Curcuma longa).

Baldness (Alopecia): Vitamin A / vitamin B-complex / vitamin B6 / biotin / inositol / choline / vitamin C / vitamin E / essential fatty acids / kelp / thyroid glandular extract.

223

Bedwetting (Enuresis): Rule out urinary tract infections, kidney disease and diabetes / avoid sugar and refined carbohydrates / eliminate dairy, wheat, citrus fruits, eggs, corn, peanuts, tomatoes and any other food sensitivities or allergens / limit fluid intake before bedtime / increase consumption of cranberry and celery juices / alternating hot and cold packs to bladder region / vitamin A / beta-carotene / B-complex / vitamin E / calcium / magnesium / Celery (Apium graveolens) / Cinnamon (Cinnamomum zyelanicum) / Cleavers (Galium aparine) / Cramp bark (Viburnum opulus) / Goldenseal (Hydrastis canadensis) / Green oats (Avena sativum) / Saint John's wort (Hypericum perforatum).

Bipolar Disorder: Vitamin B-complex / vitamin B12 (may be deficient) / folic acid (may be deficient) / omega-6 oils (evening primrose, borage oils) / L-phenylalanine (an amino acid used as a neurotransmitter) / L-tryptophan (an amino acid used as a neurotransmitter) / lecithin / avoid excess L-glutamine (an excitatory amino acid).

Body Odor: Magnesium / zinc / essential fatty acids / chlorophyll / dietary fiber / lecithin / Lactobacillus acidophilus / Burdock (Arctium lappa) / Oregon grape root (Berberis vulgaris) / Purple coneflower (Echinacea angustifolia) / Yellow dock (Rumex crispus).

Boils: Hot pack applications / hot epsom salt baths / vitamin A / beta-carotene / vitamin C / vitamin E / zinc / Calendula (Calendula officinalis) / Garlic (Allium sativum) / Goldenseal (Hydrastis canadensis).

Bruises: Vitamin C / vitamin E / vitamin K / zinc (deficiency associated with purpura) / bioflavonoids (helps to stabilize connective tissue) / Arnica montana (homeopathic remedy).

Bruxism (Tooth Grinding): Avoid stress / avoid sugar and refined carbohydrates / vitamin B-complex / vitamin B5 / calcium / magnesium / vitamin C / zinc / adrenal glandular extract.

Burns: Cold water and ice / vitamin A / vitamin C / vitamin E (topically) / PABA (topically) / zinc / essential fatty acids / chlorophyll / Aloe vera gel (topically) / Calendula succus (topical) / comfrey (topical) / wheat grass / wheat germ oil / sodium bicarbonate / adrenal glandular extract / topical antibacterial ointment (Neosporin, Polysporin) may be beneficial.

Bursitis: Ice applications topically may be beneficial in reducing the pain and inflammation / Vitamin A / vitamin B-complex / vitamin B12 (intramuscular injections may be beneficial) / vitamin C / vitamin E / zinc

/ bioflavonoids / bromelain / adrenal glandular extract / physical therapy including acupuncture, ultrasound and transcutaneous electrical neural stimulation (TENS) may be beneficial.

Bronchitis: Important to identify organism causing disease and can be caused by viruses, bacteria and fungi / avoid white sugar and refined carbohydrates / avoid mucous forming foods such as milk, cheese and other dairy and wheat / increase fluid consumption / a hot water bottle and local heat application may be beneficial / rest and sleep as necessary / antibiotics may be required in some cases / postural drainage to help break up the mucous / vitamin A / beta-carotene / vitamin C / zinc / thymus glandular extract / expectorants such as Bloodroot (Sanguinaria canadensis) / Coltsfoot (Tussilago farfara) / Gum plant (Grindelia officinalis) / Licorice (Glycyrrhiza glabra) / White horehound (Marrubium vulgare) / Wild cherry bark (Prunus serotina) / Garlic (Allium sativum) / Goldenseal (Hydrastis canadensis) / Purple coneflower (Echinacea angustifolia) / topical mustard poultice (1 part mustard seeds to 4 parts flour).

Calcium Deposits: Avoid large quantities of calcium in the diet (dairy, nuts) / avoid large quantities of oxalic acids (chocolate, rhubarb, spinach) / vitamin B6 / vitamin C / vitamin D (increases calcium absorption) / magnesium / silica / digestive enzymes and hydrochloric acid / bioflavonoids.

Cardiac Arrhythmias: Avoid coffee, tea and other caffeine containing beverages / avoid smoking / avoid all stimulants / vitamin E / magnesium (helps to stabilize heart rate) / copper (may be deficient) / potassium (may be deficient) / L-carnitine / co-enzyme Q-10 / taurine (stabilizes heart rate and rhythm) / rule out food and environmental sensitivities / Cactus (Cactus grandiflora) / Hawthorn (Crataegus oxyacantha).

Cardiomyopathy: Avoid alcohol / vitamin E / selenium / L-carnitine / co-enzyme Q-10.

Cellulite: Decrease consumption of sugar, refined carbohydrates and all fats / increase consumption of whole and unprocessed foods / make exercise a part of daily routine / vitamin B-complex / vitamin C / Butcher's broom (Ruscus aculeatus) / Gotu kola (Centella asiatica) / Horse chestnut (Aescus hippocastanum).

Childhoods Diseases (Chicken pox, Measles, Mumps): Rest and sleep as needed / may be contagious / limit exposure to other children and immune suppressed individuals / avoid sugar and refined carbohydrates / increase fluid intake / tepid, warm water baths with baking soda, apple cider vinegar and oatmeal / vitamin A / beta-carotene / vitamin B-complex / vitamin C / zinc / thymus glandular extract / calamine lotion / Burdock (Arctium lappa) / Chamomile (Matricaria chamomilla) / Garlic (Allium sativum) / Goldenseal (Hydrastis canadensis) / Indian tobacco (Lobelia inflata) / Licorice (Glycyrrhiza glabra) / Mullein (Verbascum thapsus) / Nettle (Urtica urens) / Pokeroot (Phytolacca decandra) / Purple coneflower (Echinacea angustifolia) / Yarrow (Achillea millefolium).

Colic (Intestinal): Identify and eliminate any food sensitivities or allergies / baking soda (Sodium bicarbonate) and water (helps to relieve intestinal gas) / gripe water / Chamomile (Matricaria chamomilla) / Fennel (Foeniculum vulgare) / Green oats (Avena sativa) / Peppermint (Mentha piperita).

Congestive Heart Failure: Vitamin E / calcium / magnesium / potassium / L-carnitine / co-enzyme Q-10 / taurine / Hawthorn (Crataegus oxyacantha).

Conjunctivitis: Vitamin A / vitamin C / vitamin E / zinc / cold compresses to the eye (helps to reduce swelling and inflammation) / Viavi eye drops / Eyebright (Euphrasia officinalis) / Goldenseal (Hydrastis canadensis).

Costochondritis: Vitamin B-complex / vitamin B-6 / vitamin B-12 / calcium / magnesium / massage / physcial therapy including acupuncture and manipulation.

Cradle Cap: Vitamin B6 (topical) / zinc / oils applied topically to scalp.

Cystic fibrosis: Avoid foods that increase mucous production / decrease consumption of milk, cheese and dairy, sugar and refined carbohydrates and white flour / increase consumption of fresh fruits and vegetables / drink plenty of water and other unsweetened fluids / protein supplement may be necessary to maintain weight / multi-vitamin and mineral supplement / vitamin A / vitamin B-complex / vitamin B-12 / vitamin C / vitamin E / vitamin K / selenium / zinc / digestive enzymes and/or hydrochloric acid / essential fatty acids (flaxseed, fish oil, evening primrose oils) / pancreas glandular extract / thymus glandular extract / Garlic (Allium sativum) / Goldenseal (Hydrastis canadensis) / Purple coneflower (Echinacea angustifolia) / Yarrow (Achillea millefolium).

Dandruff: Identify and eliminate stressors / avoid white sugar and refined carbohydrates / limit coffee, tea and other caffeine containing beverages / identify and eliminate food allergens and sensitivities including wheat, dairy and citrus fruits / increase consumption of whole and unprocessed foods / vitamin A / beta-carotene / vitamin B-complex / vitamin B6 / biotin / inositol / vitamin E / zinc / selenium / cod liver oil / omega-6 oils (evening primrose, borage oils) / lecithin / thymus glandular extract / digestive enzymes and/or hydrochloric acid.

Dermatitis Herpetiformis: PABA (Para-amino-benzoic acid), selenium / rule out food and environmental sensitivities including allergies to wheat, oats, rye and other gluten containing grains.

Diaper Rash: Avoid sugar and refined carbohydrates / keep diaper region clean and dry / avoid using soaps to wash diaper region / change diapers frequently and use cotton diapers / vitamin A / beta-carotene / vitamin D / vitamin E / zinc / essential fatty acids / omega-6 oils (evening primrose, borage oils) / oatmeal (topical) / lanolin (topical) / olive oil (topical) / Calendula (Calendula officinalis) / Comfrey (Symphytum officinalis) / Goldenseal (Symphytum officinale) / Slippery Elm (Ulmus fulva) / talc powder / zinc stearate / ointments including Aloe (Aloe vera) / Cabasil (mineral oxides) / Tea tree oil (Maleleuca alterniflora).

Diverticulitis: Avoid white sugar and refined carbohydrates / increase consumption of whole and unprocessed foods, fresh fruits and vegetables / increase consumption of fiber / hot epsom salt baths / vitamin A / beta-carotene / vitamin B-complex / vitamin C / vitamin E / vitamin K / digestive enzymes and/or hydrochloric acid / pancreatic enzymes / chorophyll / Lactobacillus acidophilus and bifidus (friendly bacteria) / Aloe (Aloe vera) / Anise (Pimpinella anisum) / Chamomile (Matricaria chamomilla) / Comfrey (Symphytum officinalis) / Garlic (Allium sativum) / Goldenseal (Hydrastis canadensis) / Marshmallow (Althea officinalis) / Peppermint (Mentha piperita) / Purple coneflower (Echinacea officinalis) / Slippery elm (Ulmus fulva).

Dry Eyes: Avoid food sensitivities and allergies / this may be associated with rheumatoid arthritis / vitamin A / vitamin B-complex / essential fatty acids (flaxseed, fish, evening primrose oils) / Viavi eye drops / Eyebright (Euphrasia officinalis).

Dumping Syndrome: High fiber diet / fiber supplement / folic acid / Lactobacillus acidophilus.

Dupuytren's Contracture: Vitamin B-complex / vitamin E (high doses) / silica / massage / manipulation / acupuncture / range of motion exercises / ultrasound.

Dysmenorrhea: Vitamin B3 / vitamin B6 / vitamin E / vitamin K / iron (may be deficient) / essential fatty acids / Dong quai (Angelica sinensis).

Edema: Avoid salt and salty foods / increase fresh fruit and vegetable juices / increase exercise as tolerated / vitamin A / beta-carotene / vitamin B-complex / vitamin B3 / vitamin B6 / vitamin C / vitamin E / vitamin K / zinc / bioflavonoids / essential fatty acids / amino acids / protein supplement / adrenal glandular extract / thymus glandular extract / chlorophyll / Bearberry (Arctostaphylos uva-ursi) / Buchu (Barosma betulina) / Burdock (Arctium lappa) / Cactus (Cactus grandiflora) / Cleavers (Galium aparine) / Couch grass (Agropyrens repens) / Hawthorn (Crataegus oxyacantha) / Hydrangea (Hydrangea arborescens) / Lily of the valley (Convallaria majus) / Juniper (Juniperus communis) / Parsley (Petroselinum sativum) / Pipsissewa (Chimaphila umbellata) / Watermelon seed (Citrullus vulgaris).

Emphysema: Avoid white sugar and refined carbohydrates / limit consumption of mucous forming foods including milk, cheese and other dairy products / aerobic exercises including walking, bicycling and swimming as tolerated / vitamin A (high doses administered only under proper medical supervision / vitamin B-complex / vitamin C / vitamin E / adrenal glandular extract / thymus glandular extract / amino acids / protein supplement / Boneset (Eupatorium perfoliatum) / Comfrey (Symphytum officinale).

Flatulence: Avoid refined and processed foods / avoid flatus forming foods including milk and dairy, beans, cabbage, onions and high fiber foods / food sensitivities and allergies may aggravate flatulence and should be eliminated / flaxseed oil / Lactobacillus acidophilus and bifidus (friendly bacteria) / digestive enzymes and/or hydrochloric acid / chlorophyll / Anise (Pimpinella anisum) / Caraway (Carum carvi) / Fennel (Foeniculum vulgare) / Garlic (Allium sativum) / Goldenseal (Hydrastis canadensis) / Peppermint (Mentha piperita) / Slippery elm (Ulmus fulva).

Fever: Increase consumption of water and other unsweetened fluids / cold baths / epsom salt baths / aspirin or acetaminophen suppositories / vitamin A / beta-carotene / vitamin C / vitamin E / thymus glandular extract / propolis (bee resin extract) / Boneset (Eupatorium perfoliatum) / Catnip (Nepeta cataria) / Elderberry (Sambucus nigra) / Garlic (Allium sativum) / Lemon balm (Melissa officinalis) / Peppermint (Mentha piperita) / Pleurisy root (Asclepius tuberosa) / Purple coneflower (Echinacea angustifolia) / White willow bark (Salix alba) / Yarrow (Achillea millefolium).

Fibrocystic Breast Disease: Avoid methylxanthines found in coffee, tea, soda beverages, chocolate and other foods / vitamin A / vitamin B6 / folic acid / vitamin C / vitamin E / magnesium / iodine (may be deficient) / omega-6 oils (evening primrose, borage oils) / Lactobacillus acidophillus / choline (helps support liver function) / methionine (helps support liver function) / avoid ginseng use.

Fractures: Increase consumption of whole, unprocessed foods, fresh fruits and vegetables / vitamin A / vitamin C / vitamin D / calcium / magnesium / silica / zinc / bioflavonoids / liver glandular extract.

Frigidity: Counselling may be required to identify and eliminate possible psychological causes / vitamin B-complex / vitamin C / vitamin E / zinc / bioflavonoids / essential fatty acids (flaxseed, evening primrose, borage oils) / bee pollen / Damiana (Turnera diffusa) / Ginseng (Panax ginseng).

Glaucoma: Acute glaucoma is a medical emergency / avoid white sugar and refined carbohydrates / vitamin B-complex / vitamin B1 / vitamin B2 / vitamin B6 / vitamin C / vitamin E / calcium / magnesium / chromium / potassium / bioflavonoids / Bilberry (Vaccinium myrtillus) / rule out food sensitivities.

Heart Attack: Avoid high fat foods / decrease sugar and refined carbohydrates / avoid dietary excess / avoid coffee, tea and other caffeine containing foods and beverages / increase consumption of high fiber foods / increase consumption of whole, unprocessed foods, fresh fruits and vegetables / exercise as tolerated (only after recovered from acute attack / make daily exercise a part of your routine / vitamin B-complex (helps the body respond to stress / vitamin E / calcium / magnesium / carnitine / co-enzyme Q-10 / bioflavonoids / omega-3 oils (flaxseed, fish oils) / Garlic (Allium sativum) / Ginkgo (Ginkgo biloba) / Hawthorn (Crataegus oxyacantha).

Heartburn: Avoid white sugar and refined carbohydrates / avoid coffee, tea, soda pop, alcohol, chocolate and other candy, citrus fruits, peanuts and spicy foods / limit consumption of heavy protein meals / limit consumption of milk and other dairy products / yogurt, kefir and sour milk are allowed / increase consumption of whole and unprocessed foods, fresh fruits and vegetables / increase consumption of enzyme fruits including papaya, kiwi and pineapple / fresh fruit and vegetable juices / vitamin A / beta-carotene / vitamin B-complex / vitamin B12 / folic acid / vitamin C (non-acid type) / vitamin E / zinc / charcoal tablets (absorb toxins) / Lactobacillus acidophilus (friendly bacteria) / fiber supplement / digestive enzymes and/or hydrochloric acid / pepsin (protein digesting enzyme) / pancreatic enzymes / Aloe juice (Aloe vera) / Angelica (Angelica sinesis) / Anise (Pimpinella anisum) / Chamomile (Matricaria chamomilla) / Comfrey (Symphytum officinalis) / Dandelion (Taraxacum officinale) / Fennel (Foeniculum vulgare) / Ginger (Zingiber officinalis) / Goldenseal (Hydrastis canadensis) / Licorice (Glycyrrhiza glabra) / Peppermint (Mentha piperita) / Slipper Elm (Ulmus fulva).

Heavy Metal Toxicity: Excess exposure and/or ingestion of aluminum, cadmium, lead, mercury / important to identify and eliminate origin of toxic metals / found in industrial chemicals, paint, water, foods, cosmetics, amalgam fillings / detoxification diet / avoid processed and refined foods / increase consumption of whole, unrefined foods, fresh fruits and vegetables / drink distilled water / eat high fiber foods / multi-vitamin and mineral complex / vitamin A / vitamin B-complex / vitamin B6 / vitamin C (high doses) / vitamin E / calcium / magnesium / potassium / zinc / dietary fiber supplement (helps to bind heavy metals) / pectin / bioflavonoids / chlorophyll / cysteine / methionine / Aloe (Aloe vera) / Garlic (Allium sativum) / intravenous chelation therapy may be beneficial.

Heavy Periods: May be caused by local irritation including fibroids of the uterus, polyps, increased uterine growth and endometriosis / rule out thyroid dysfunction / vitamin A / vitamin C / vitamin E / vitamin K / bioflavonoids / essential fatty acids / chlorophyll (vitaming K source) / Spotted cranesbill (Geranium maculatum) / Birthroot (Trillium pendulum) / Blue cohosh (Caulophyllum thalictroides) / Witch hazel (Hamamelis virginicus) / Shepherd's purse (Capsella bursa-pastoris).

Herpes Zoster: Vitamin B-complex / vitamin B12 (intramuscular injections may be beneficial) / vitamin C / vitamin E / zinc / thymus glandular extract / Licorice (Glycyrrhiza glabra) / Purple coneflower (Echinacea angustifolia).

Hiatal Hernia: Avoid white sugar and refined carbohydrates / avoid irritating foods such as coffee, chocolate, fatty foods, fried foods, alcohol and spicy foods / eat small, frequent meals / avoid food sensitivities and allergies / increase consumption of whole, unprocessed foods, fresh fruits and vegetables / multiple vitamin and mineral supplement / vitamin A / vitamin B-complex / vitamin C / zinc / digestive and pancreatic enzymes / pepsin (proteolytic enzyme) / Aloe (Aloe vera) / Goldenseal (Hydrastis canadenis) / Licorice (Glycyrrhiza glabra).

Hives (Urticaria): Vitamin A / beta-carotene / vitamin B-complex / vitamin B12 (intramuscular injections may be beneficial) / vitamin C / rule out food and environmental sensitivities / bioflavonoids.

Hyperestrogenism: Avoid white sugar and refined carbohydrates / decrease fats, oils and cholesterol / avoid coffee, tea and other caffeine containing beverages / increase consumption of complex carbohydrates and protein / increase consumption of fiber / vitamin B-complex / vitamin B6 / vitamin E / selenium / bioflavonoids / Lactobacillus acidophilus.

Hyperthyroidism: Avoid stimulants such as cigarette smoking, coffee, tea, chocolate and other caffeine containing foods / increase consumption of broccoli, cauliflower, cabbage, brussel sprouts (contains substances that inhibit thyroid function) / avoid food sensitivities and allergies / vitamin A / vitamin B-complex / vitamin C / iodine (potassium iodide) / Blue flag (Iris versicolor) / Irish moss (Chondrus crispus).

Impetigo: Usually caused by a Staphylococcus bacteria / Avoid white sugar and refined carbohydrates / vitamin A / vitamin C / vitamin E / zinc / thymus glandular extract / Comfrey (Symphytum officinalis) / Eucalyptus (Eucalyptus globulus) / Garlic (Allium sativum) / Goldenseal (Hydrastis canadensis) / Oil of bitter orange (Citrus aurantium) / Tea tree oil (Maleleuca alternifolia).

Impotence: Foods high in zinc including oysters, liver, nuts and beans / vitamin A / vitamin B-complex / vitamin B6 / vitamin E / zinc / essential fatty acids / wheat germ oil / Damiana (Turnera diffusa) / Ginkgo (Ginkgo biloba) / Ginseng (Panax ginseng) / Potency wood (Ptychopetalum olacoides) / Saw palmetto berries (Serenoa repens) / Yohimbe (Coryanthe or Pausinystalia yohimbe) / Deer antler.

Infertility: Vitamin B-complex / vitamin B6 / vitamin C / zinc / L-arginine / Ginseng (Panax ginseng) / bee pollen / royal jelly.

Kidney Disease: Avoid high protein diet / decrease consumption of white sugar and refined carbohydrates / vitamin A / vitamin B-complex / vitamin B-3 / vitamin B-6 / vitamin C / vitamin E / choline / magnesium / lecithin / thymus glandular extract / Bearberry (Arctostaphylos uva-ursi)

/ Buchu (Barosma betulina) / Chamomile (Matricaria chamomilla) / Couch grass (Agropyrons repens) / Horsetail (Equisetum arvense) / Juniper (Juniperus communis) / Mullein (Verbascum thapsus) / Parsley (Petroselinum sativum) / Stinging nettle (Urtica urens) / Watermelon seeds (Citrulla vulgaris).

Learning Disabilities: Avoid sugar and refined carbohydrates / rule out food and environmental sensitivities / rule out sensitivities to food additives and preservatives / iron (may be deficient) / manganese (may be deficient) / zinc (may be deficient) / avoid excess selenium / rule out heavy metal toxicity including lead, mercury and cadmium.

Lou Gehrig's Disease (Amyotrophic lateral sclerosis): Vitamin B-complex (helps the body respond to stress) / vitamin B-6 / vitamin B-12 / branch chain amino acids (valine, leucine and isoleucine) / threonine / essential fatty acids (flaxseed, evening primrose, borage oils).

Lupus (SLE): Avoid white sugar and refined carbohydrates / have a low calorie, low fat diet / avoid beef, pork and dairy products / rule out food and environmental sensitivities / vitamin A / beta-carotene / vitamin B-complex / vitamin B12 (may be deficient) / vitamin E / selenium / omega-3 oils (flaxseed, fish oil) / omega-6 oils (evening primrose, borage oil) / rule out digestive enzyme and/or hydrochloric acid deficiency / decrease consumption of alfalfa.

Mastitis: Avoid white sugar and refined carbohydrates / vitamin A / vitamin C / vitamin E / zinc / thymus glandular extract / Calendula (Calendula officinalis) / Garlic (Allium sativum) / Goldenseal (Hydrastis canadensis) / Purple coneflower (Echinacea angustifolia) / topical application of Calendula, castor oil or ice packs / Bellis perennis / continue nursing.

Meniere's Disease: Avoid aspirin and all drugs containing salicylic acid / vitamin A / beta-carotene / vitamin B-complex / vitamin B2 / vitamin B6 / vitamin C / vitamin E / bioflavonoids / thymus glandular extract / lithium.

Mitral Valve Prolapse: Vitamin B-complex / magnesium (may be deficient) / Hawthorn (Crataegus oxyacantha).

Motion Sickness: Eat small, frequent meals and avoid overeating / drink moderate amounts of water and fluids and keep well hydrated / vitamin B-complex / vitamin B6 / magnesium / charcoal tablets / Ginger (Zingiber officinalis) / Peppermint (Mentha piperita) / over-the-counter medication such as Dramamine (dimenhydrinate) may be effective. However these medications may cause sleepiness as a side effect.

Morning Sickness (Pregnancy): Small frequent meals / avoid white sugar and refined carbohydrates and coffee, tea and other stimulants / vitamin B6 / vitamin C / vitamin K / choline / methionine / Chamomile (Matricaria chamomilla) / Ginger (Zingiber officinalis) / Peppermint (Mentha piperita).

Muscle Cramps: Eat foods high in potassium including bananas / ensure proper fluid hydration / increase consumption of water and unsweetened fluids / vitamin B-complex / vitamin E / calcium / magnesium / potassium.

Muscular Dystrophy: Increase whole and unprocessed foods, fresh fruits and vegetables / vitamin E / inositol / selenium / lecithin.

Narcolepsy: Avoid food allergies and sensitivities / vitamin B-complex / vitamin B-6 / vitamin B-12 (intramuscular injections may be beneficial) / iodine / thyroid glandular extract / tyrosine (amino acid used to make brain neurotransmitter dopamine).

Neuralgia and Neuropathy: Vitamin B-complex / vitamin B3 / vitamin B6 / vitamin B12 (may be deficient) / essential fatty acids.

Neuromuscular Degeneration: Vitamin B-complex / vitamin B6 / vitamin B12 / folic acid / vitamin E / L-carnitine / calcium / magnesium.

Organic Brain Disorder: Vitamin B-complex / vitamin B6 / vitamin B12 / folic acid / calcium / magnesium / phosphorus / potassium / sodium / zinc / avoid excess copper / rule out food and environmental sensitivities / rule out heavy metal toxicity including lead, arsenic, mercury, cadmium and aluminum.

Poison Ivy: Avoid food allergies and sensitivities / vitamin A / vitamin C / vitamin E / zinc / bioflavonoids / quercitin / adrenal glandular extract / oral antihistamines such as Benadryl may be necessary / topical anti-itch cream such as calamine lotion / Watch for secondary infection if severe / antibiotics may be necessary in some cases.

Pneumonia: Important to identify organism causing disease / consider virus, bacteria and fungus / avoid white sugar and refined carbohydrates avoid mucous forming foods such as milk, cheese and other dairy and wheat / increase fluid consumption / a hot water bottle and local heat application may be beneficial / rest and sleep as necessary / antibiotics may be necessary / postural drainage may help to break up mucous / vitamin A / beta-carotene / vitamin C / zinc / thymus glandular extract / herbal expectorants / Bloodroot (Sanguinaria canadensis) / Coltsfoot (Tussilago farafara) / Gum plant (Grindelia officinalis) / Licorice (Glycyrrhiza glabra) / White horehound (Marrubium vulgare) / Wild cherry bark (Prunus serotina) / herbal antibiotics / Garlic (Allium sativum) / Goldenseal (Hydrastis canadensis) / Purple coneflower (Echinacea angustifolia) / mustard poultice (1 part mustard seeds to 4 parts flour).

Pregnancy: Eat a well balanced diet including 60-100 grams of protein / avoid alcohol and cigarette smoking / a general multiple vitamin and mineral supplement / vitamin B6 / folic acid (helps prevent neural tube defects) / vitamin E / vitamin K (may be deficient) / calcium (1.0-1.5 grams while pregnant and up to 2.0 grams while lactating) / magnesium / copper (may be deficient) / iron (may be deficient) / zinc (may be deficient) / citrus bioflavonoids (helps to prevent spontaneous abortions) / omega-6 oils (helps to prevent high blood pressure) / avoid excess vitamin A (may cause birth defects at high doses).

Prostatitis: Vitamin A / vitamin C / vitamin E / magnesium / selenium / zinc / prostate glandular extract / thymus glandular extract / essential fatty acids (flaxseed, evening primrose, borage oils) / pumpkin seeds / Bearberry (Arctostaphylos uva-ursi) / Buchu (Barosma betulina) / Couchgrass (Agropyren repens) / Gravel root (Eupatorium purpureum) / Goldenseal (Hydrastis canadensis) / Juniper (Juniper communis) / Marshmallow (Althea officinalis) / Parsley (Petroselinum sativum) / Saw palmetto (Serenoa repens).

Radiation Exposure: Increase dietary fiber / increase consumption of whole, unprocessed foods, fresh fruits and vegetables / vitamin A / beta-carotene / vitamin B-complex / vitamin B5 / vitamin B6 / vitamin C / vitamin E / selenium / zinc / bioflavonoids / lecithin / inositol / cysteine / methionine / essential fatty acids (flaxseed, evening primrose, borage oils) / liver glandular extract / Garlic (Allium sativum).

Raynaud's Syndrome: Vitamin E / omega-6 oils (evening primrose, borage oils) / rule out food and environmental sensitivities / alternating hot and cold water soaks of affect extremities (helps to regulate neurological control).

Restless Leg Syndrome: Avoid coffee, tea, soda beverages and other caffeine containing beverages / avoid stimulants / vitamin B12 / folic acid (may be deficient) / vitamin E (may be deficient) / calcium / magnesium (helps to prevent muscle cramps) / potassium.

Rheumatism: Moderate exercise / muscle stretching / vitamin B-complex / vitamin B6 / copper (topical application may be effective) / rule our food and environmental sensitivities / omega-3 oils (flaxseed fish oil) / omega-6 oils (evening primrose, borage oil) / bromelain / Devil's claw (Harpagophytum officinalis).

Sarcoidosis: Increase consumption of whole, unprocessed foods, fresh fruits and vegetables / identify and eliminate food sensitivities and allergies / vitamin A / vitamin B-complex / vitamin C / vitamin E / bioflavonoids / digestive enzymes and/or hydrochloric acid / liver glandular extract / thymus glandular extract.

Schizophrenia: Avoid coffee and other caffeine containing foods and beverages / rule out hypoglycemia / rule out food and environmental sensitivities / short term fasting may be beneficial / vitamin B-complex / vitamin B3 (high doses administered only under medical supervision) / vitamin B6 (high doses administered only under medical supervision) / vitamin B12 (may be deficient) / folic acid (may be deficient) / vitamin C (may be deficient) / manganese (may be deficient) / zinc / omega-6 oils (evening primrose, borage oil) / avoid excess dietary copper / avoid excess dietary serine (amino acid).

Scleroderma: PABA (Para amino benzoic acid) / vitamin E / omega-6 oils (evening primrose, borage oil).

Sinus Infection: Avoid white sugar and refined carbohydrates / avoid mucous forming foods such as milk, cheese, dairy, wheat and other starchy vegetables / rule out food allergies including milk, wheat, eggs, citrus fruits, and peanut butter / increase consumption of fluids / rest as needed / vitamin A / beta carotene / zinc / thymus glandular extract / Garlic (Allium sativum) / Goldenseal (Hydrastis canadensis) / menthol or eucalyptus packs over sinuses / hot packs over sinuses may be beneficial / diathermy (deep heat) / intra-nasal douche with salt and/or goldenseal extract / swab nasal passages with bitter orange oil.

Sore throat: Avoid sugar and refined carbohydrates / gargle with salt water, goldenseal and/or dilute bitter orange oil / Vitamin A / beta-carotene / vitamin C / zinc / thymus glandular extract / Garlic (Allium sativum) / Goldenseal (Hydrastis canadensis) / Purple coneflower (Echinacea angustifolia).

Tardive Dyskinesia: Vitamin B3 (high doses administered only under medical supervision) / vitamin B6 / manganese (may be deficient) / vitamin C / vitamin E / omega-6 oils (evening primrose, borage oils) / L-tryptophan / lecithin.

Tinnitus (ringing in ears): Avoid white sugar and refined carbohydrates / decrease fats, oils and cholesterol especially saturated fats / avoid coffee, tea and other caffeine containing beverages / rule out hypoglycemia / rule out food and environmental sensitivities / vitamin A (may be deficient) / vitamin D (may be deficient) / calcium / sodium fluoride / magnesium / potassium / omega-3 oils (flaxseed, fish oils) / rule out lead and aluminum toxicity / Ginkgo (Ginkgo biloba).

Tiredness: Avoid white sugar and refined carbohydrates / avoid coffee, tea and other caffeine containing beverages / vitamin B-complex / vitamin B5 (for adrenal glands) / vitamin B6 / vitamin B12 / folic acid / vitamin C / iron (only if deficient) / zinc / aspartic acid / L-carnitine / co-enzyme Q-10 / N,N dimethyl glycine / L-glutamine (excitatory neurotransmitter) / octacosanol / PAK (Pyridoxine alpha ketoglutarate) / Rule out food and environmental sensitivities / adrenal glandular extract / liver glandular extract / Chinese ginseng (Panax ginseng) / Licorice (Glycyrrhiza glabra) / Siberian ginseng (Eleutherococcus senticosus).

Tonsillitis: Avoid all white sugar and refined carbohydrates / gargle with salt / vitamin A / vitamin C / vitamin E / zinc / thymus glandular extract / Calendula (Calendula officinalis) / Cleavers (Galium aparine) / Garlic (Allium sativum) / Goldenseal (Hydrastis canadensis) / Myrrh (Commiphora molmol) / Pokeroot (Phytolacca decandra) / Purple coneflower (Echinacea angustifolia).

Toothache: Bitter orange oil (Citrus aurantium) / Clove oil (Euginia carophyllus) / Eucalyptus oil (Eucalyptus globulus) / Garlic (Allium sativum) / Goldenseal (Hydrastis canadensis) / Myrrh (Commiphora molmol) / Purple coneflower (Echinacea angustifolia) / Peppermint oil (Mentha piperita) / Wintergreen (Gaultheria procumbens).

Trigeminal Neuralgia: Dental work may be required / Vitamin B-complex / vitamin B-6 / vitamin B-12 / vitamin C / calcium / magnesium / essential fatty acids (flaxseed, evening primrose, borage oil) / acupuncture may be effective.

Vasculitis: Vitamin E (topical may be beneficial) / selenium / rule out food sensitivities.

Wrinkles: Avoid continual exposure to the sun / egg shell membrane facial / equal parts brewer's yeast and yogurt / cocoa butter (topically) / vitamin A / vitamin E / essential fatty acids (flaxseed, evening primrose, borage oils).

Vaginitis: Important to identify cause of inflammation / avoid sugar and refined carbohydrates / decrease consumption of refined and processed foods / sitz baths / 3% boric acid solution douche (1-2 tbsp to 1 quart water 2X per day) / yogurt douche (1 tbsp to 1 quart water 2X per day) / apple cider vinegar douche (2 tbsp to 1 quart water 2X per day) / vitamin A / beta-carotene / vitamin C / vitamin E / zinc / Lactobacillus acidophilus (may be applied as a vaginal suppository) / thymus glandular extract / Calendula (Calendula officinalis) / Garlic (Allium sativum) / Eucalyptus (Eucalyptus globulus) / Goldenseal (Hydrastis canadensis) / Purple coneflower (Echinacea angustifolia) / Tea tree oil (Maleleuca alternifolia) / Thuja (Thuja occidentalis).

Vertigo (Spinning sensation): Avoid heavy meals / eat frequent, small meals / rule out hypoglycemia / vitamin B-complex / Chamomile (Matricaria chamomilla) / Ginkgo (Ginkgo biloba) / Ginger (Zingiber officinalis) / Peppermint (Mentha piperita).

CHAPTER 62

Vitamins and Minerals

For most people who walk into a health food store it is often a bewildering experience. There are a wide variety of vitamin, mineral and herbal supplements that are often unknown to the average consumer. Confusing scientific words are often used to describe various vitamins and minerals. Different forms of the same vitamin and mineral exist. Units of measurements are equally confusing. Controversy about vitamin and mineral supplementation and dosages still exists and recommendations often vary considerably. As a naturopathic physician I am often asked about vitamin and mineral supplementation. I intend to offer some practical information on this topic in order that you make wise descisions when shopping for your specific vitamin and mineral supplement.

A vitamin is simply an organic substance that contains carbon and is necessary for life. Vitamins are generally needed in small quantities in the diet and are essential for specific chemical reactions in our body. With the exception of vitamin D and vitamin K, our body cannot make vitamins and we must get them from our diet. Different vitamins have very different functions. Vitamins regulate metabolism, help convert fat and carbohydrate into energy, assist in forming bones and other tissues and aid in enzyme function.

A mineral is simply an inorganic substance that does not contain carbon and is also necessary for life. Minerals are generally needed in small to medium quantities in the diet. Minerals have many essential roles in the body. Some minerals present in body fluid, such as blood, regulate the function of enzymes, maintain acid-base balance and proper blood pressure, regulate movement of nutrients, maintain proper nerve and muscle function and in some cases act as building blocks for bones and other tissues.

Although a great deal is known about vitamins and minerals, new research continues to determine chemical structures and functions of these useful substances.

Vitamins and minerals are not drugs. Thay have no caloric value and are not meal replacements. They do not have any nutritional value and are not substitutes for carbohydrates, proteins or fats. They are not pep pills and they don't give you energy. They are not diet pills. They are not used as building blocks in muscle and other tissues. You cannot stop eating vitamins and minerals in your diet and expect to stay healthy.

There are approximately 14 different vitamins that can be divided into one of two groups depending on their solubility. Vitamins that mix well with fats are called fat soluble and include vitamins A, D, E and K. Vitamins that mix well with water are called water soluble and include the B vitamins (vitamin B1, B2, B3, B5, B6, B12), biotin, folic acid and vitamin C.

There are approximately 22 different minerals that can be divided into one of two groups depending on the amount that they are required in the body. Macronutrients are required in greater quantities in the body and include minerals like calcium, magnesium, phosphorus, sodium, chloride, potassium and sulphur. Micronutrients, though required in lesser quantities, are no less important than the macronutrients. Micronutrients include minerals like iron, copper, zinc, iodine, manganese, fluoride, molybdenum, cobalt, selenium, arsenic, boron, tin, vanadium and silicon.

RDA means Recommended Daily Allowance and are recommendations by food and nutrition experts to safeguard public health. RDA's are nutritional estimates made to ensure proper growth in children and to prevent deficiencies in adults. RDA's are not recommendations for optimal intake, do not take into account ill health or sickness and are not average requirements for the general population. RDA's do not recognize the uniqueness of each individual and that the requirements for certain vitamins and minerals may differ from one individual to another.

Standard units of measurement for vitamins and minerals include grams, milligrams, micrograms, international units and retinol equivalents. 1 mg (milligram) = 1/1000 gram. 1 mcg (microgram) = 1/1000 mg. IU means International Unit and is used to measure fat soluble vitamins only (Vitamin A, D, E and K). For practical purposes 1 IU = 0.3 mcg. RE means Retinol Equivalent and is used as a substitute to measure vitamin A quantity. 1 RE = 5 IU.

Many individuals take vitamin and/or mineral combinations in large doses that greatly exceed the RDA. Vitamins and minerals are not drugs, but they do have serious side effects if they are taken at high doses for prolonged periods of time. I do not recommend that individuals administer high doses of vitamins and minerals for prolonged periods without proper medical consent.

Vitamins and minerals are available in many different forms and sizes. They are available as tablets, capsules, powders, liquids and injectables. You should choose a supplement that suits your needs, agrees with your body and provides you with a proper dosage.

If we all ate an organic, unprocessed, nutritionally balanced diet we would get all our vitamins and minerals from the food we eat. Unfortunately this not the case. The typical western diet is processed, inorganic, high in fat and sugar, low in complex carbohydrates and fiber and is often deficient in vitamins and minerals. Diseases that plague our society are reflections of our diet and lifestyle. Heart disease, high blood pressure, diabetes, stroke, tooth decay, liver disease and obesity are just a few of the common diseases that are linked to poor diet and lifestyle. Junk food including chocolate bars, chips, colas, hamburgers and hot dogs are high in calories, but are low in nutritional value and are depleted of vitamins and minerals. It comes as no surprise that we are often deficient in many of the vitamins and minerals we need for optimal health. A recent survey discovered that 90% of North Americans are deficient in chromium, 80% in vitamin B6, 75% in magnesium, 75% in folic acid, 68% in calcium, 57% in iron, 45% in vitamin C, 34% in vitamin B2, 33% in vitamin B3 and 34% in vitamin B12. Vitamin and mineral supplementation is not meant to replace a nutritionally balanced diet. Supplementation is meant to provide adequate amounts of those vitamin and minerals that we are not obtaining from our diet. Supplementation offers a way of delivering higher doses of a vitamin and mineral that may be needed when you are sick. Vitamin and mineral supplementation is simply an insurance against deficiency.

There are often unfamiliar terms associated with many vitamins and minerals. Understanding the terminology ensures that you know what you are getting.

Chelation - usually applied to minerals. Process by which one mineral is added to a substance that increases absorption. Generally, only about 10% of a mineral supplement is actually absorbed by the body. When a mineral is chelated to an amino acid the absorption increases five to ten times.

Time-release-usually only applied to vitamins. Manufacturing process in which the vitamin is broken down into little pellets and mixed with a

240

special base that prevents immediate absorption. This allows the slow release of the vitamin from the stomach and intestines over a period of 6 to 12 hours. Instead of getting a high dose all at once, this ensures slow release of lesser amounts of the vitamin over time.

Standardization-usually applied to botanical supplements. A specific chemical or group of chemicals identified as an active ingredient is measured in the herb. The active ingredient is quantified and a specific dosage is guaranteed in each batch of the supplement.

Enriched-usually applied to processed foods including flour. During the course of processing of the food the nutritional value is diminished. Certain vitamins and minerals are added back to the food after processing to ensure adequate nutritional value.

Fortified-the manufacturer adds nutrients not present in the food originally. For example, margarine is fortified with vitamin A and milk is fortified with vitamin D.

Additive-a food additive is any substance that becomes part of the food product when added directly or indirectly to the food.

Diluents or fillers-these are inert substances added to capsules or tablets to increase their bulk. This makes the material suitable for compression into a tablet or capsule. Commonly used diluents and fillers include sorbitol, cellulose, dicalcium phosphate.

Binders-these are inert substances that help powdered materials stick together. Binders are usually used to make tablets and include cellulose, acacia, algin and lecithin.

Colors-additives used to make a substance more cosmetically appealing to the consumer. A natural source of color added to some health products is chlorophyll.

Coating materials-used to coat a tablet to protect it from moisture and to make the tablet easier to digest. A natural coating material used on some tablets is zein from corn.

Cold pressed-usually applied to oils. Manufacturing process the limits the amount of heat used to process on oil. This ensures that the original oil is not altered by the heat and remains in its natural form.

Emulsified-process by which a substance is used to help mix ingredients that would not otherwise mix well together. Commonly used emulsifying agents include lecithin and pectin.

Hydrolyzed-means it mixes well with water and thus makes absorption easier.

Predigested Protein-protein is already partially broken down making it easier to absorb.

Vitamins and mineral supplements are best stored in a cool, dark place in a well closed, preferably opaque container. Cotton inserts are added to prevent moisture from damaging the supplements. A few kernels of rice in the container can produce the same effects. Vitamins stored properly can last two to three years and minerals can last greater than ten years.

The best time to take vitamin or mineral supplements is with or just after meals to ensure the best absorption. Food is necessary for proper absorption. Fat is necessary for the absorption of fat-soluble vitamins (Vitamins A, D, E and K). Water-soluble vitamins are best absorbed with foods and are excreted more slowly than on an empty stomach. Minerals are better absorbed with protein or amino acids. It is best to take supplements three times a day with meals. If taken only once a day, supplements are absorbed best when they are taken with the biggest meal.

Any individual who has a less than optimal diet is probably deficient in one or more vitamins and/or minerals and is probably in need of a supplement. Children and pregnant women have increased need for various vitamins and minerals. Women greater than 50 years old at risk for developing osteoporosis also need vitamin and mineral supplementation. Any individual of ill health is probably in need of supplementation. In addition, smokers, dieters, coffee drinkers, alcohol drinkers, vegetarians and those individuals under more stress than normal may need vitamins and minerals beyond what they are receiving in their diet.

Vitamin and mineral supplementation is not a panacea for those suffering from ill health. Supplementation may help in certain disease states and contributes to overall good health. The best form of supplementation is through our diet. We should strive to eat an organic, unprocessed, nutritionally balanced diet. We would receive all our vitamins and minerals from the foods we eat. Increase consumption of fresh fruits and vegetables, whole grains, lean meats and fish. Decrease fats, refined carbohydrates, sugar and salt. Use vitamin and mineral supplementation as an adjunct to a healthy diet.

Vitamin A (Retinol, beta-carotene)

RDA: 4000 IU (800 RE) for females and 5000 IU (1000 RE) for men.

Natural Sources: Liver, kidney and other organ meats, milk fat, cheese, fortified margarine, egg yolk, yellow and dark green leafy vegetables, apples, canteloupe and peaches.

Stability: Stable to light, heat and usual cooking methods. Destroyed by oxidation, drying, very high temperatures and ultraviolet light.

Function: Essential for normal growth, development and maintenance of epithelial tissue. Essential for vision and required for proper night vision. Helps in normal development of bone and influences tooth formation. Required for proper immune system function.

Deficiency: Night blindness, dry eyes, dry, hardened skin and softening of bone.

Toxicity: Headache, peeling of the skin, bone thickening, abnormal enlargement of the liver and spleen. Vitamin A is toxic in high doses, whereas beta-carotene is not.

Therapeutic Dosage: 10,000-25,000 IU/day of vitamin A and 100,000-300,000 IU/day of Beta-carotene.

Vitamin B1 (Thiamine)

RDA: 0.5 mg per 1000 kcal; older individuals 2.0 mg per day.

Natural Sources: Whole grains and cereals, enriched cereals and breads, wheat germ, potatoes, nuts, dried yeast, pork, liver, organ meats. Produced in the intestines by bacteria.

Stability: Unstable in presence of heat, alkali or oxygen. Heat stable in acid. Because the body does not store thiamine, foods that are good sources of it should be included in each day's diet.

Function: Necessary for breakdown and release of energy from carbohydrates and sugar, peripheral nerve cell function and heart muscle function. Essential for normal growth, appetite and digestion. Prevents deficiency called beriberi.

Deficiency: Lack of thiamine can cause loss of appetite, nerve cell inflammation and in severe cases, beriberi which affect the brain, nerves and heart. Alcoholics who tend to decrease food intake drastically during periods of drinking, may show signs of beriberi.

Toxicity: None known.

Therapeutic Dosage: 30-100 mg/day.

Vitamin B2 (Riboflavin)

RDA: 0.6 mg per 1000 kcal. Older individuals and whendiet is less than 2000 kcal require 1-2 mg per day.

Natural Sources: Milk, cheese and other dairy products, eggs, organ meats, green leafy vegetables, enriched cereals and breads.

Stability: Stable to heat, oxygen and acids. Unstable to light, especially ultraviolet light and alkali.

Function: Essential for growth. Necessary for proper development of the eyes and vision. Important in the development and maintenance of epithelial tissue. Used in many aspects of carbohydrate and protein metabolism.

Deficiency: Fissures and inflammation at the corners of the mouth, around the nose, ears and eyes. Eye irritation, poor vision, sensitivity to light and oil gland disorders of the skin.

Toxicity: None known.

Therapeutic Dosage: 10-30 mg/day.

Vitamin B3 (Niacin, Niacinamide)

RDA: 13 to 18 mg or 6.6 mg per 1000 kcal diet.

Natural Sources: Fish, liver, meat, poultry, many wheats and grains, eggs, dried yeast, peanuts, milk, legumes, enriched grains. Produced by intestinal bacteria.

Stability: Stable to heat, light, oxidation, acid and alkali.

Function: As part of enzyme system, aids in transfer of hydrogen, aids in the metabolism of carbohydrats and amino acids. Involved in breakdown of carbohydrates and sugars, fat production and tissue respiration. Requirement related to the amino acid tryptophan.

Deficiency: Pellagra, characterized by inflammation of the tongue and skin. Digestive system disturbance, nervous system dysfunction.

Toxicity: None known. High doses of niacin may produce vasodilation and flushing of the skin.

Therapeutic Dosage: 100-1000 mg/day (Niacinamide).

Vitamin B5 (Pantothenic Acid)

RDA: Level not yet determined, but 4-7 mg is believed to be adequate to supply daily needs.

Natural Sources: Present in all plant and animal foods. Eggs, kidney, liver, salmon and yeast are the best sources. Produced by intestinal bacteria.

Stability: Unstable to acid, alkali, heat and certain salts.

Function: An integral part of co-enzyme A which is involved in the production and breakdown of many vital body compounds. Essential in the intermediate metabolism of carbohydrate, fat and protein.

Deficiency: None known.

Toxicity: None known.

Therapeutic Dosage: 100-500 mg/day.

Vitamin B6 (Pyridoxine)

RDA: 1.8-2.2 mg for females and 2.0-2.4 mg for males.

Natural Sources: Wheat, grains, cereals, wheat bran and germ, milk, egg yolk, dried yeast, oatmeal, legumes, beans, organ meats, liver, pork, beef and fish. Produced by intestinal bacteria.

Stability: Stable to heat, light and oxidation.

Function: Essential for normal growth. Necessary for proper enzyme function in carbohydrate, fat and protein metabolism. Involved in many aspects of nitrogen metabolism, including transamination and hemoglobin production, the amino acid, tryptophan, conversion into niacin and the essential fatty acid metabolism. Consumption of the amino acid, leucine, increases the requirement for vitamin B6.

Deficiency: Convulsions in infancy and childhood, anemia, nerve dysfunction and seborrheic dermatitis.

Toxicity: Peripheral neuropathy.

Therapeutic Dosage: 25-100 mg/day.

Vitamin B12 (Cyanocobalamin)

RDA: 3-6 mcg per day.

Natural Sources: Liver, kidney and other organ meats, milk, cheese and other dairy products, meat and eggs.

Stability: Slowly destroyed by acid, alkali, light and oxidation.

Function: Essential for proper production of genetic material within cells. Necessary for proper growth and development of red blood cells. Involved in nerve cell function. Involved in folate, methionine and acetate metabolism.

Deficiency: Can cause pernicious anemia. Vegetarians and vegans may require a daily supplement to prevent deficiency.

Toxicity: Dependency states.

Therapeutic Dosages: 100-1000 mcg/day.

Folic Acid

RDA: 200-400 mcg per day.

Natural Sources: Fresh green leafy vegetables, fruit, organ meats, liver, dried yeast.

Stability: Slowly destroyed by acid, alkali, light and oxidation.

Function: Essential for proper production of genetic material within cells. Necessary for proper growth and development of red blood cells. Also plays an important role in the development and maintenance of epithelial tissue.

Deficiency: May cause pernicious anemia. May cause low red and white blood cell counts, especially with pregnancy, infancy and malabsorption.

Toxicity: None known.

Therapeutic Dosage: 2-10 mg/day.

Biotin

RDA: 150-300 mcg per day.

Natural Sources: Liver, kidney and other organ meats, egg yolk, dried yeast, cauliflower, broccoli, nuts, beans and legumes.

Stability: Stable in alkali.

Function: Involved in carbohydrate and fat metabolism.

Deficiency: Skin rash, inflammation of the tongue and hair loss.

Toxicity: Dependency states.

Therapeutic Dosage: 1-3 mg/day.

Inositol

RDA: Not yet established. A mixed North American diet contains 300-1000 mg per day.

Natural Sources: Fruit, grains, cereals, vegetables, nuts, legumes. liver, kidney and other organ meats. Produced by intestinal bacteria.

Stability: Stable in heat and alkali.

Function: Related to the presence of phophatidyl-inositol and is used in cell membrane structure. It is involved in nerve conduction and regulation of enzyme activity. Has lipotropic activity and stimulates fat metabolism in the liver. Concentrated in the brain, cerebrospinal fluid, skeletal and heart tissues.

Deficiency: None known.

Toxicity: Related to excess levels.

Therapeutic Dosage: 500-1000 mg/day.

Vitamin C (Ascorbic acid)

RDA: 60 mg per day.

Natural Sources: Citrus fruits, apples, peaches, melons, strawberries, tomatoes, peppers, spinach and other green leafy vegetables, cabbage, guava and potatoes.

Stability: Unstable to heat, alkali and oxidation, except in acids. Destroyed by storage.

Function: Necessary for proper growth and development. Essential for the production, development and strength of collagen, the basic substance of connective tissue. Involved in many hydroxylation reactions of bone and connective tissue. Important role in bone and tooth formation. Maintains cementing substance between cells and blood vessels. Enhances healing of wounds and fractures and reduces infections. Increases absorption of iron. Functions as a co-enzyme in amino acid metabolism, especially phenylalanine and tyrosine. Aids in the production of steroid hormones. Enhances immune function during infection.

Deficiency: Scurvy, characterized by inflammation of the gums, loose teeth, vascular fragility and hemorrhages.

Toxicity: Acid may upset stomach and digestive system. Avoid high doses if previous kidney stones.

Therapeutic Dosage: 1000-10,000 mg/day.

Vitamin D (Calciferol)

RDA: 200-400 IU (5-10 mcg)/day.

Natural Sources: Sunlight stimulates conversion of steroid molecules in the skin into vitamin D. Food sources include vitamin D fortified milk, butter, milk fat, irradiated foods, liver, egg yolk, salmon, tuna, sardines and other fish.

Stability: Stable to heat and oxidation.

Function: Necessary for growth and development of bone and teeth. Influences absorption of calcium, magnesium and phosphorus.

Deficiency: Rickets in children and osteomalacia in adults. Soft and weak bones that are prone to deformation and fractures. May also cause muscle tetany.

Toxicity: Anorexia, kidney failure and metastatic calcification.

Therapeutic Dosage: 800-1400 IU (10-40 mcg)/day.

Vitamin E (Tocopherols)

RDA: 200-400 IU (4-8 TE) per day.

Natural Sources: Wheat germ, vegetable oils, green leafy vegetables, milk fat, egg yolk, nuts, margarine, beans and legumes.

Stability: Stable to heat and acids. Destroyed by rancid fats, alkali, oxygen, lead, iron salts and ultraviolet light.

Function: Is a potent antioxidant that in small amounts inhibits oxidation of other compounds in the body. May prevent oxidation of unsaturated oils and vitamin A in the digestive system and body tissues. Protects red blood cells from breakdown. Plays a role in reproduction. Also plays an important role in epithelial tissue maintenance and prostaglandin production.

Deficiency: Red blood cell destruction. Muscle deposits and increased muscle destruction.

Toxicity: None known.

Therapeutic Dosage: 30-100 mg/day.

Vitamin K (phylloquinone, menaquinone)

RDA: 70-140 mcg per day.

Natural Sources: Liver and other organ meats, soybean oil and other vegetable oils, green leafy vegetables and wheat bran. Produced in the intestines by bacteria.

Stability: Resistant to heat, oxygen and moisture. Destroyed by alkali and ultraviolet light.

Function: Important for normal blood clotting. Required for the production of prothrombin, a protein involved in the clotting process. Also plays a role in reducing inflammation.

Deficiency: Prolonged bleeding as a result of deficiency of prothrombin.

Toxicity: May cause high levels of bilirubin in the blood and nervous system dysfunction. Occurs in newborn infants.

Therapeutic Dosage: 2-5 mg/day.

Calcium

RDA: 800-1200 mg per day.

Natural Sources: Milk, cheese and other dairy products, eggs, fish, sardines, clams, oysters, broccoli, kale, turnip greens, spinach and other green leafy vegetables, nuts and beans.

Functions: 99% of calcium is contained in bones and teeth. Calcium in blood and body fluids is necessary for electrolyte transport across cell membranes. Calcium is also required for muscle contraction, blood clotting and heart conduction.

Deficiency: Dietary surveys indicate that many diets do not meet the recommended daily requirements for calcium. Since bone serves as a homeostatic mechanism to maintain calcium levels in blood, many essential functions are maintained, regardless of diet. Long term dietary deficiency is probably one of the factors responsible for bone thinning and osteoporosis. Deficiency also associated with muscle hyper-excitability and tetancy.

Toxicity: Associated with high blood calcium levels, digestive disturbance, kidney failure and psychosis.

Therapeutic Dosage: 800-2000 mg/day.

Chloride

RDA: 1700-5100 mg per day.

Natural Sources: Common table salt, seafoods, milk, meat, eggs, nuts and salted foods.

Function: Major negatively charged electrolyte in blood and tissue fluid. Functions in combination with sodium. Serves as a buffer in pH regulation and an enzyme activator. Component of hydrochloric acid in the stomach. Most chloride present in fluid outside cells and less than 15% is found within cells.

Deficiency: In most cases dietary intake is of little significance except in the presence of vomiting, diarrhea and profuse sweating, when a deficiency may develop.

Toxicity: Excess consumption is associated with high blood pressure.

Therapeutic Dosage: 1700-5100 mg/day.

Chromium

RDA: 0.05 to 0.2 mg per day.

Natural Sources: Corn oil, sunflower oil and other vegetable oils, clams, whole grains, cereals, brewer's yeast, meats and contained in drinking water in variable amounts.

Function: An important part of glucose tolerance factor (GTF) that helps with glucose and sugar metabolism.

Deficiency: Impaired glucose and sugar metabolism found in severe malnutrition, diabetes and some cases of heart disease.

Toxicity: None known.

Therapeutic Dosage: 1.0-5.0 mg/day.

Cobalt

RDA: 3.0 mcg of vitamin B12.

Natural Sources: Liver, kidney, oysters, clams, poultry, milk; variable amounts in vegetables and grains which usually depends on selenium content.

Function: Major constituent of vitamin B12 (cyanocobalamin). Essential to normal function of all cells, particularly cells of bone marrow, nervous system and digestive system.

Deficiency: Primary dietary inadequacy is rare, except when no animal products are consumed. Deficiency may be found in such conditions as lack of stomach acid, stomach proteins and malabsorption syndromes. May also cause anemia.

Toxicity: Associated with alcoholic heart disease.

Therapeutic Dosage: 3.0-10.0 mcg/day usually as vitamin B12.

Copper

RDA: 1 to 3 mg per day.

Natural Sources: Liver, kidney, poultry, oysters, shellfish, whole grains, cereals, cherries, legumes, chocolate and nuts.

Function: Found in all body tissues. Contained in larger amounts in liver, brain, heart and kidney. Important constituent of enzymes, proteins and hormones that stimulate production of red blood cells. Also an integral part of nucleic acids (DNA and RNA).

Deficiency: Anemia in malnourished children. Menkes kinky hair syndrome.

Toxicity: Liver degeneration and cirrhosis may be associated with excess levels.

Therapeutic Dosage: 1-3 mg/day.

Fluoride

RDA: 1.5 to 4.0 mg per day.

Natural Sources: Drinking water (1 part per million fluoride), tea, coffee, rice, soybeans, spinach, gelatin, onions and lettuce.

Function: Present in bone. In optimal amounts in water and diet, reduces tooth decay and may minimize bone loss.

Deficiency: Predisposition to dental caries and osteoporosis. In areas where fluoride content of water is low, fluoridation of water (1.0 ppm) has been found to be beneficial in reducing tooth decay.

Toxicity: High blood fluoride levels, mottling of teeth and bones, permanent pitting of teeth and increased calcification of bones.

Therapeutic Dosage: 2.0-50 mg/day.

Iodine

RDA: 100-150 mcg per day.

Natural Sources: Iodized table salt, fish, seafoods, kelp, milk, cheese and other dairy products, water and vegetables in iodine rich soils.

Function: Required for proper thyroid gland function and is an important constituent of thyroxine and other hormones. Important for regulating energy metabolism throughout the body.

Deficiency: Can cause hypothyroidism characterized by fatigue, weight gain, dryness of skin, headaches, and constipation, goiter, growth disorders, cretinism and loss of hearing. Iodized table salt is recommended in areas where food is low in iodine.

Toxicity: Can cause edema, swelling and abnormal protein deposits in the skin around the face, lips and nose.

Therapeutic Dosage: 150-250 mcg/day.

Iron

RDA: 18 mg per day for females and 10 mg per day for males.

Natural Sources: Wide distribution except in dairy products. Liver, kidney and other organ meats, beef, shrimp, oysters, clams, and other seafood, egg yolk, legumes, beans, whole or enriched grains and cereals, dark green leafy vegetables, dark molasses and peaches, pears and other fruit. Much of the iron is unavailable and less than 20% of what is eaten is absorbed.

Function: About 70% is used to make hemoglobin, the oxygen carrying molecule in red blood cells. About 25% stored in the liver, spleen and bone. Used to make myoglobin, the oxygen carrying molecule within muscle. Also associated with several enzymes.

Deficiency: Iron deficiency anemia occurs mainly in women of reproductive years, infants and preschool children and in chronic bleeding. Symptoms include fatigue, weakness, tiredness, inability to work and concentrate, difficulty swallowing, cracked fingernails and digestive disturbance.

Toxicity: May cause hemochromatosis, a disorder characterized by excessive iron deposition in the body, bronze skin pigmentation, cirrhosis of the liver and diabetes mellitus.

Therapeutic Dosage: 10-25 mg/day.

Manganese

RDA: 3.5 to 5.0 mg per day.

Natural Sources: Beet greens, blueberries, huckleberries and other dark berries, whole grains, cereals, nuts, legumes, fruit and tea.

Function: Highest concentration in bone. Also relatively high concentrations in pituitary gland of the brain, liver, pancreas, stomach and intestinal tissue. An important constituent of several enzymes. Involved in energy production in the liver.

Deficiency: Unlikely that deficiency occurs in man.

Toxicity: None known.

Therapeutic Dosage: 2.0-10 mg/day.

Magnesium

RDA: 300 mg for females and 350 mg for males per day.

Natural Sources: Whole grains, cereals, nuts, legumes, beans, milk, cheese and other dairy products, green leafy vegetables.

Function: About 50% in bone. Remaining 50% almost entirely within body cells, with only about 1.0% outside cells in body fluid. Involved in bone and tooth formation, nerve conduction, muscle contraction and enzyme activation. Functions as an activator for many enzymes.

Deficiency: Dietary inadequacy considered unlikely, but can occur with surgery, alcoholism, malabsorption, hemorrhaging and loss of body fluids, certain hormone diseases, kidney disease, liver disease and other metabolic disorders. Symptoms of deficiency include low blood magnesium levels and nerve and muscle irritation.

Toxicity: High blood magnesium levels, low blood pressure, breathing irregularities and heart disturbances.

Therapeutic Dosage: 400-2000 mg/day.

Molybendum

RDA: 0.15 to 0.5 mg per day.

Natural Sources: Legumes, beans, cereals, grains, dark green leafy vegetables and organ meats.

Function: Part of the enzyme xanthine oxidase that is involved in nitrogen metabolism and urea production. Also involved in flavoprotein which is required for energy production within cells.

Deficiency: May cause hyperactivity in children.

Toxicity: None known.

Therapeutic Dosage: 0.15-1.0 mg/day.

Phosphorus

RDA: 600-800 mg per day.

Natural Sources: Milk, cheese, egg yolk, beef, chicken, fish, whole grains, cereals, legumes, beans and nuts.

Function: About 80% of inorganic phosphorus is in bones and teeth. Phosphorus is a component of every cell and of highly important substances such as nucleic acids (genetic material) amd ATP (high energy phosphate compound) and is an important component of cell walls. Also help in pH regulation of the body and blood.

Deficiency: Dietary inadequacy not likely to occur if protein and calcium intake is adequate. Symptoms of deficiency include irritability, muscle weaknesss, fatigue, blood cell disorders, digestive system dysfunction and kidney dysfunction.

Toxicity: May cause high blood phosphorus levels associated with kidney failure.

Therapeutic Dosage: 600-1000 mg/day.

Potassium

RDA: 1875 to 5625 mg per day.

Natural Sources: Many fruits including bananas, prunes and raisins, milk, cheese and other dairy products, grains, cereals, many vegetables, legumes and beans.

Function: Major positive electrolyte of fluid within cells and only in small amounts outside cells. Major role in regulating body fluid and blood pH, acid-base balance, water retention, muscle activity and nerve conduction.

Deficiency: Low blood potassium levels, muscle weakness, fatigue, paralysis and heart disturbance.

Toxicity: High blood potassium levels, paralysis and heart disturbance.

Therapeutic Dosage: 1875-5626 mg/day.

Selenium

RDA: 0.05 to 0.2 mg per day

Natural Sources: Grains, cereals, onions, garlic, beef, chicken, pork, milk, cheese and other dairy products and many vegetables depending upon the selenium content of the soil.

Function: A potent antioxidant that helps to prevent oxidation of body tissue from free radicals. Also associated with fat metabolism and vitamin E.

Deficiency: No known deficiency disease seen in man.

Toxicity: None known.

Therapeutic Dosage: 200-800 mcg/day.

Sodium

RDA: 1000-3500 mg per day.

Natural Sources: Common table salt, seafoods, fish, animal foods, chicken, beef, pork, eggs, milk and in small amounts in many vegetables. Abundant in most foods, except fruit.

Function: 30-45% in bone. Major positive electrolyte in extracellular fluid and blood. Only in small amounts inside cells. Regulates concentration of electrolytes, pH, body fluid volume and blood. Involved in nerve conduction.

Deficiency: Dietary inadequacy probably never occurs, although low blood sodium requires medical treatment in certain disorders. Requirements may increase during pregnancy.

Toxicity: Sodium restriction should be practiced in individuals with high blood pressure, edema and heart disease.

Therapeutic Dosage: Not usually given.

Zinc

RDA: 10-15 mg per day.

Natural Sources: Milk, cheese and other dairy, liver, shellfish, herring, wheat bran, green leafy vegetables and many fruits. Widely available in fresh fruit and vegetables.

Function: Present in most tissues, with higher amounts in the liver, muscle, bone and the prostate gland. An important constituent of many enzymes and the hormone insulin. Important in normal cellular reproduction and the immune system.

Deficiency: Inhibition of normal growth and development, poor sense of taste and smell and skin rash.

Toxicity: High dosages may inhibit immune response.

Therapeutic Dosages: 25-100 mg/day.

CHAPTER 63

Food Supplements

Food Supplements are naturally occuring preparations derived from different foods. They are not vitamins and minerals and although they may have vitamin-like activity they are not considered as such. They have some nutritive value. They are not herbal medicines. Food supplements include a wide variety of preparations including amino acids, glandular extracts, plant and animal derived supplements and supplements that don't fit any category.

Amino acids naturally occur in all plants and animals and they are the building blocks of proteins. They are used throughout the body to build muscle, connective tissue, glands, to make enzymes, regulate blood volume and are used in the immune system to prevent infection. There are twenty amino acids identified in humans. Eleven amino acids can be made in the body. Nine amino acids cannot be made in the body and must be obtained from the diet. These nine essential amino acids include histidine, iso-leucine, leucine, lysine, methionine, phenlyalanine, threonine, tryptophan and valine. Protein foods that provide the balance of essential amino acids required by the human body are known as complete proteins. These include proteins from animal sources such as meat, eggs, fish and milk. Proteins that cannot supply the body with the balance of essential amino acids are called incomplete proteins. These include proteins from plant sources such as peas, beans and certain forms of grains. Specific amino acids have very different and specific effects on the human body. Amino acids discussed here include glutamine, lysine, methionine, phenylalanine, taurine and tyrosine.

Glandular extracts are derived from various animal glands and organs. They contain many active and inactive ingredients that are meant to nourish and support the corresponding human glands. Adrenal glandular extract is meant to support and nourish the function of the adrenal gland. Liver glandular extract is meant to support and nourish the function of the liver. Thymus glandular extract is meant to support and nourish the function of the thymus gland, an important gland in the immune system. Thyroid glandular extract is meant to support and stimulate the function of the thyroid gland.

Other food supplements are derived from food sources and they have profound medicinal effects on the body. These include dietary fiber, evening primrose oil, flaxseed oil, Lactobacillus acidophilus and lecithin. Vitamin-like food supplements that have profound biochemical effects on the body include carnitine, choline and co-enzyme Q-10. Other food supplements that are derived from plant and animal sources include bee pollen, beewax, blue-green algae, propolis and royal jelly. Other food supplements cannot be categorized, but do have medicinal effects on the body including caprylic acid.

Adrenal Glandular Extract

Description: The adrenal glands are a small pair of triangular glands located directly above either kidney. The adrenal glands are responsible for helping the body respond to stress. They produce small amounts of adrenaline that stimulates the nervous system, increases heart rate and blood pressure, dilates pupils in the eyes and increases blood sugar levels. The adrenal glands are also responsible for producing other hormones including cortisone, aldosterone and small amounts of sexual hormones. Cortisone helps to decrease utilization of sugar and to conserve sugar throughout the body. Cortisol has profound anti-inflammatory effects throughout the body. Aldosterone helps to conserve water and salt in the blood and increases blood pressure. Small amounts of male hormones including testosterone and female hormones including estrogen are also produced in the adrenal glands.

Actions: Adrenal glandular extract helps to support and stimulate adrenal gland function. It is a rich source of nutrients including various B-complex vitamins and steroidal compounds that are utalized by the gland. It also contains antihistamine substances.

Uses: Useful in treating Addison's disease (hypo-adrenalism) and sub-clinical hypo-adrenalism. May be useful in treating fatigue caused by overworked and over-stressed adrenal glands. Can increase energy levels and help the body respond to stress. Also may be useful as an antihistamine in treating allergic disorders and as an anti-inflammatory.

Toxicity: Few adverse side effects have been reported. Occasional allergic reaction may occur.

Dosage: 500-1000 mg/day of purified adrenal glandular extract.

Bee Pollen

Description: Bee Pollen consists of plant pollens collected by worker bees, combined with plant nectar and bee saliva. This is packed by the bees into small dust pellets, which are used as a food source for the male drones. Commercially, the pollen is gathered at the entrance of the hive by forcing the bees to enter through a portal partially obstructed with wire mesh, thus brushing off the hind legs into a collection vessel.

History: The use of pollen increased during the late 1970's following testimonials by athletes that supplementation increased stamina and improved athletic ability.

Active Ingredients: Bee pollen contains protein, amino acids, sugar and small amounts of vitamins, minerals and enzymes. Bee pollen is a good nutritional source for drone bees.

Actions: The specific functions of bee pollen are not entirely understood.

Uses: There are conflicting reports that bee pollen may increase athletic stamina and improve recovery time and increase appetite in the sick and debilitated.

Toxicity: Adverse effects include allergic reactions, hayfever, skin rash and in severe cases anaphylaxis.

Therapeutic Dosage: 1000 to 3000 mg/day.

Beeswax

Description: Beeswax is the wax obtained from the honeycomb of the honeybee. Beeswax is a pale yellow solid with a mild, sweet and oily odor reminiscent of good linseed oil with a trace of honey.

Active Ingredients: Beeswax contains a large amount of fats, aromatic oils and lipids.

Uses: In Chinese medicine beeswax is used to treat diarrhea and hiccups and to relieve pain, among other uses. For internal use it is usually dissolved in hot alcohol or wine. It is a common ingredient in emollient creams, lotions and ointment.

Toxicity: Allergic reactions have been reported.

Therapeutic Dosage: 3-6 capsules/day.

Blue-Green Algae

Description: Blue-green algae is relatively simple plant that grows in ponds and lakes throughout the world. There are many different species of Blue-green algae. Two common species are Chlorella and Spirulina. Technically Chlorella is a green algae and Spirulina is a blue-green algae.

History: Blue-green algae has been used by many cultures throughout the world, but its medicinal benefits have been popularized in the Orient. It has been used to treat bad breath, indigestion, flatulence, hypoglycemia, appetite suppression to aid weight loss, stress reduction, increase athletic performance and enhance immune response.

Active Ingredients: Blue-green algae contains proteins, amino acids, carbohydrates, sugars, variable amounts of vitamins and minerals including relatively high amounts of beta-carotene and vitamin B12. It also contains 2 to 3% chlorophyll by weight.

Actions: Chlorophyll found in Blue-green algae is a natural deodorant and chelator that aids in the elimination of toxins. A few complex sugar molecules in the algae have demonstrated immune stimulating and antibacterial effects.

Uses: Blue-green algae can be used to deodorize bad breath, beltching, flatulence, indigestion and ulcerative lesions throughout the body. It may also help to chelate toxins in the digestive system. Its reported use to improve athletic performance, aid in appetite suppression and weight loss and usefulness in treating hypoglycemia is not substantiated.

Toxicity: Blue-green algae is relatively non-toxic. Occasional allergic reactions have been reported by some people.

Therapeutic Dosage: Blue-green algae - 1-3 grams/day.

Caprylic Acid

Description: Caprylic acid is a naturally occuring medium chain fatty acid that inhibits the growth of fungi and yeast in the digestive system.

Actions: Caprylic acid dissolves the cell wall of yeast and fungi and helps to normalize the normal flora of the digestive system.

Uses: Caprylic acid is used as a broad spectrum antifungal to eliminate yeast and candida from the digestive system. Caprylic acid may be used in conjunction with antibiotics and Lactobacillus acidophilus to balance the normal flora of the digestive system.

Toxicity: High doses of caprylic acid can promote rapid elimination of yeast and fungi. As a result, high levels of by-products of this process may be absorbed by the body and cause ill health. Adverse effects to rapid elimination include nausea, indigestion, fatigue, headache, muscle weakness and generalized flu-like symptoms. Its use during pregnancy is not recommended.

Therapeutic Dosage: 1000 to 2000 mg/day of time release preparations. Caprylic acid is rapidly absorbed in the intestines and time release preparations are recommended for slow, uniform releases throughout the entire length of the digestive system. Caprylic acid should be consumed with moderate amounts of dietary fat such as milk, butter and salad oil to enhance its availability.

Carnitine

Description: Carnitine is produced in humans from two amino acids, lysine and methionine.

Function: Carnitine is used to transport large fat molecules into mitochondria within cells. Mitochondria are the dynamoes within cells responsible for producing energy in the form of adenosine triphosphate (ATP). Heart and skeletal muscle, as well as other tissues, depend on the oxidation of fat as a source of energy. Carnitine is needed to supply the mitochondria with fat.

Uses: Carnitine supplementation is indicated in virtually all cardiovascular diseases including angina pectoris, heart attack and congestive heart failure. It may also be used as a supplement in atherosclerosis and obesity.

Deficiency: Carnitine deficiency has been associated with heart disease, angina pectoris, heart attack, mitral valve prolapse, heart arrhythmias and endocardial fibroelastosis.

Toxicity: None known. High doses are not recommended during pregnancy.

Therapeutic Dosage: Carnitine - 1000-2000 mg/day.

Choline

Description: Choline is derived from the amino acids methionine and serine. It has been considered to be related to the B vitamins.

Sources: Choline is derived from the diet from lecithin, egg yolk, liver and other organ meats, beans and legumes.

Functions: Choline is used in liver cells and in the production of the neurotransmitter, acetylcholine.

Uses: Choline is a strong lipotropic that decreases fat in the body by increasing fat breakdown in the liver.

Deficiency: Choline deficiency can produce fatty degeneration of the liver.

Toxicity: None known. High doses during pregnancy is not recommended.

Therapeutic Dosage: Choline - 500-1500 mg/day.

Coenzyme Q10

Description: Coenzyme Q10 or ubiquinone is similar in structure to vitamin K and and found in the mitochondria, the dynamoes within cells responsible for the production of energy. It is widely used in Japan, Russia and Europe.

Function: It is a hydrogen accepting molecule in the electron transport chain and is involved in the production of energy in the form of adenosine triphosphate (ATP).

Uses: Coenzyme Q10 can be used as a supplement in virtually all cardiovascular diseases including angina pectoris, congestive heart failure, heart disease, mitral valve prolaps and hypertensive heart disease.

Deficiency: Deficiency is associated with angina, heart disease and congestive heart failure.

Toxicity: None known. High doses are not recommended during pregnancy.

Therapeutic Dosage: Co-enzyme Q10 - 30-60 mg/day.

Evening Primrose Oil (Oenothera biennis)

Description: Evening primrose is a beautiful flowering plant of the Nightshade family. It is native North America, Central America and South America. It was used medicinally by the American Indians to treat asthma and enhance wound healing.

Active Ingredients: The seeds of this plant contain 2 to 5% oils. These oils are exceptionally high in omega-6 (linoleic acid) concentration, an essential oil required by the body. Evening primrose oil contains up to 72% omega-6 oils.

Actions: Omega-6 oils (linoleic acid) are an essential oil that is required by the body. Our body cannot make this oil from other dietary fats and we must get it from our diet. Essential fats and oils are utalized in cell membranes, nerve function and to make short lived, but extremely powerful chemicals called prostaglandins. Omega-6 oils are used to make prostaglandins of the 1 and 3 series, that have profound anti-inflammatory effects on the body.

Uses: May be useful in the treatment of eczema, psoriasis and other skin conditions, premenstrual stress, chronic fatigue syndrome, high cholesterol, rheumatoid arthritis, sjogren's syndrome and asthma. The oil may also be beneficial in treatment of diabetes.

Toxicity: Excess dosages may cause nausea, vomiting and indigestion. Excess use during pregnancy is not recommended.

Therapeutic Dosage: Evening primrose oil - 2-4 grams/day.

Fiber

Description: Fiber is the portion of plant foods that is not digested in the human digestive system. Vegetables and fruits are the main sources of dietary fiber. Although wheat bran is advertised as an excellent source of fiber, it is not unique nor is it as nutritious as fruits and vegetables and some other whole unprocessed cereals.

Active Ingredients: Fiber is composed of cellulose, which is the "skeleton" of plants, hemicellulose, lignin, pectin, gums, mucilages, algae seaweeds and other carbohydrates, indigestible in humans.

Actions: Fiber increases stool bulk and increases transit time; the time it takes food to pass through the digestive system. Fiber increases water absorption, binds minerals, absorbs organic wastes and toxins, stabilizes blood sugar levels, lowers cholesterol and triglycerides and benefits the friendly bacteria lining the intestines.

Uses: Dietary fiber supplementation is useful in treating constipation, diarrhea, obesity and diabetes. It is important in treating gout, gall stones, kidney stones, high blood pressure, stroke, heart disease, peptic ulcers, hemorrhoids, varicose veins, tooth decay, multiple sclerosis, pernicious anemia, hypoglycemia and auto-immune disorders. Fiber is especially important in preventing diseases of the digestive system including Ulcerative colitis, Crohn's disease, diverticulitis, diverticulosis, irritable bowel syndrome and appendicitis.

Toxicity: High doses of fiber can aggravate abdominal bloating, gas and indigestion and can cause constipation. High doses can bind vitamins and minerals and prevent their absorption.

Therapeutic Dosage: Fiber - 5-10 grams/day.

Flaxseed oil (Linum usitatissimum)

Description: Flax is a small, annual plant that grows from 0.5 to 1 meter in height and is found abundantly throughout North America and is cultivated throughout the world. Flax was widely used by many ancient cultures including

Active Ingredients: The seeds of this plant contain an 2 to 5% oils. The oil provides a exceptionally rich source of essential oils that are required

266

by the body. Flaxseed oil contains a high amount of omega-3 and omega-6 oils. Flaxseed oil contains 50 to 60% omega-3 oils (linolenic oil) and 15 to 25% omega-6 oils (linoleic oil).

Actions: Omega-3 and omega-6 oils are essential oils that are required by our body. Our body cannot make these oils from other dietary fats and oils and we must get these oils from our food. Essential fats and oils are utalized in cell membranes, nerve cell function and to make prostaglandins, short lived, but extremely powerful chemicals. Omega-3 and omega-6 oils are used to make prostaglandins of the 1 and 3 series, that have powerful anti-inflammatory effects.

Uses: May be beneficial in the treatment of eczema, psoriasis and other skin conditions, premenstrual stress, rheumatoid arthritis, osteoarthritis, chronic fatigue syndrome, sjogren's disease, auto-immune disorders, high cholesterol and asthma.

Toxicity: None known. Excess dosages may cause nausea, indigestion and stomach upset.

Therapeutic Dosage: Flaxseed oil - 5-30 grams/day.

Glutamine

Description: Glutamine is a form of the naturally occuring non-essential amino acid, glutamic acid, found in most proteins throughout the body.

Actions: Glutamic acid, in addition to glucose, is used as the primary fuel for the brain. It is also a inhibitory neurotransmitter in the central nervous system and increases another inhibitory neurotransmitter, GABA. Glutamic acid does not pass across the blood-brain barrier, but glutamine does readily pass across the barrier. It is also used to make monosodium glutamate (MSG), the flavor enhancer added to foods and tobacco, that may responsible for allergic reactions.

Uses: May be beneficial in treating mental and emotional diseases including certain cases of depression, schizophrenia and alcoholism. Supplementation appears to be beneficial in treating alcoholics and helps to reduce alcohol cravings. It is believed that some imbalance in the brain involving glutamine is associated with alcohol cravings.

Toxicty: Glutamine is relatively non-toxic and few adverse reactions

267

have been reported. Allergic reactions and headaches have been reported. Excess dosages should not be consumed for prolonged periods of time.

Dosage: Glutamine - 2000-4000 mg/day.

Lactobacillus acidophilus

Description: Lactobacillus acidophilus is one of a group of naturally occuring bacteria that populate the gastrointestintal tract of humans and the vagina of females. These bacteria are capable of digesting and fermenting undigestible material in the colon, forming vitamin K, B1, B2 and B12 and producing antibacterial and antifungal substances.

Actions: Lactobacilli inhibit bacteria and fungi by competing for nutrients, lowering pH, oxygen utilization, prevention of attachment and production of antibiotic substances. Lactobacilli produce a number of antibiotic substances including adidolin, acidophilin and lactocidin. They also improve digestion and nutrient absorption, improve bowel regularity and enhance immune function.

Uses: Lactobacilli can be used to treat disorders of the digestive system including indigestion, abdominal bloating, gas, bad breath, beltching, bloating, flatulence, diarrhea, constipation, irritable bowel syndrome, ulcerative colitis, crohn's disease and other disorders. It is also useful in treating vaginitis and candida infections.

Toxicity: None known.

Therapeutic Dosage: 1 to 3 capsules per day containing the equivalent of 4 billion active bacteria per capsule.

Lecithin (Phosphatidyl choline)

Description: Lecithin is a naturally occuring phosphate containing fat that is found in high concentrations in egg yolk, liver and soybeans. It is also found in other organ meats and other beans and legumes.

Active Ingredients: Lecithin contains choline, glycerol and fat. Commercial lecithin sources contain 10 to 95% phosphatidyl choline. Average levels in commercial sources are between 20 and 35%.

Actions: Lecithin is used as a choline source by the body. Choline is used by the liver to make bile and aids in the digestion and absorption of fats. Choline is also used to make the neurotransmitter, acetylcholine, a chemical used in nerve cell function in the brain and nervous system.

Uses: Lecithin may be used to enhance memory function in the brain and aid in the digestion and absorption of dietary fats. May be useful in the treatment of poor memory, memory loss, Alzheimer's disease, Parkinson's disease, tardive dyskinesia, liver problems, jaundice and gallstones.

Toxicity: None known. Excess dosages for prolonged periods of time and used during pregnancy is not recommended.

Therapeutic Dosage: Lecithin - 5 to 30 grams/day.

Liver Glandular Extract

Description: The liver is a large, dark red gland located in the upper right portion of the abdomen, just beneath the diaphragm. It is one of the largest and most active organs in the entire body. It has over 500 different functions including the storage and filtration of blood, breakdown of carbohydrates into energy, production of proteins, enzymes and clotting factors, production of bile that aids in fat absorption, removal of organic wastes and toxic material, removal of foreign material such as bacteria, fungi, drugs, alcohol and other toxic substances, storage of proteins, glycogen, vitamins and minerals.

History: Liver has been recommended for centuries to help build the blood, support liver function and treat fatigue.

Actions: Liver glandular extract is a rich source of fat soluble vitamins A,D,E and K, B-complex vitamins including vitamin B12, folic acid, vitamin C, trace minerals including easily absorbable iron (heme iron) and other nutrients that help to support and enhance liver function.

Uses: Can be used as a rich source of vitamins and minerals including B-complex vitamins and iron. May be effective in treating a variety of liver disorders including both acute and chronic hepatitis, jaundice, fatty infiltration of the liver, fibrosis, cirrhosis and drug induced liver damage. May be effective in treating fatigue caused by anemia or liver congestion.

Toxicity: Few adverse side effects have been reported. Occasional allergic reaction may occur.

Dosage: 500-1000 mg/day of purified liver glandular extract.

Lysine

Description: Lysine is a naturally occuring essential amino acid required for optimal growth in human infants and for maintenance of nitrogen equilibrium in adults.

Actions: Lysine inhibits the growth of herpes simplex viruses responsible for cold sores, fever blisters and genital sores. It appears that the inhibitory effect of lysine is due to its structural similarity to another amino acid, arginine, that is required by the virus for proper replication. The virus cannot distinguish the difference between the two amino acids and uses lysine in place of arginine. The virus mistakenly incorporates lysine into its growing structure and as a result, viral function is lost and viral growth stops. Lysine may also inhibit other viruses from the herpes family including Herpes zoster, Rubella, Varicella, Variola, Adenoviruses and Cytomegalovirus.

Uses: May be beneficial in suppressing active herpes outbreaks and preventing further outbreaks on the skin including cold sores, fever blisters and genital sores. May also be beneficial in inhibiting other viral diseases caused by members of the Herpes family including shingles, chicken pox, mononucleosis and the common cold.

Toxicity: Lysine is relatively non-toxic and few adverse side effects have been reported.

Dosage: Lysine - 2000-4000 mg/day.

Methionine

Description: Methionine is a sulfur containing amino acid occuring in proteins and is an essential component of the diet.

Function: Methionine is a major source of other sulfur containing amino acids in the body including cysteine, taurine and the antioxidant, glutathione. It forms a compound called S-adenosylmethionine (SAM) that is responsible for detoxification of organic wastes, toxic chemicals and other foreign substances in the liver.

Uses: Can be used as a dietary supplement to aid the liver in detoxification and hasten the breakdown and removal of fat.

Toxicity: None known. Its use during pregnancy is not recommended.

Therapeutic Dosage: 1000-2000 mg/day.

Phenylalanine

Description: Phenylalanine is a naturally occuring essential amino acid that is required for optimal growth in infants and for nitrogen equilibrium in adults.

Actions: Phenylalanine is used to make protein throughout the body. Phenylalanine is used to make the neurotransmitters dopamine, noradrenaline and adrenaline. Phenylalanine blocks certain enzymes in the central nervous system responsible for breaking down naturally occuring morphine-like hormones called endorphins and enkephalins.

Uses: Supplementation may be beneficial in treating certain cases of depression, Schizophrenia and Parkinson's disease. May also be beneficial in treating chronic pain of osteoarthritis, rheumatoid arthritis, low back pain, joint pains, menstrual cramps, whiplash and migraine headache.

Toxicity: Phenylalanine is relatively non-toxic and few adverse side effects have been reported. Taking excess dosages for prolonged periods of time is not recommended.

Dosage: Phenylalanine - 2000-4000 mg/day.

Propolis

Description: Propolis is the resinous product collected from the buds of conifers and used by bees to fill cracks in their hives.

History: Propolis has been used in folk medicine as early as 300 BC for medical and cosmetic purposes.

Active Ingredients: Propolis contains resins, wax, oils, essential and aromatic oils, pollen and small amounts of vitamins and minerals.

Action: Propolis has been reported to possess such versatile biologic activity as antibacterial, anti-viral, fungicidal, local anesthetic, estrogenic, anti-ulcer, anti-inflammatory, immuno-stimulating, hypotensive and anti-cancer properties. Many of the actions of propolis are not confirmed by clinical research.

Uses: Propolis is used as a base in many ointments, creams and emollients. It may be used as a supplement in the treatment of menopause and female related disorders.

Toxicity: Adverse effects include allergic reaction and skin rash.

Therapeutic Dosage: 250 to 500 mg/day.

Royal Jelly

Description: Royal jelly is a milky-white jelly produced by worker bees to develop and nurture the queen bee.

History: Queen bees are fed mostly royal jelly. Because of this specialized nutrition, queen bees differ from worker bees in several ways. Queen bees are about twice the size as regular bees, they lay about 2000 eggs a day (female worker bees are infertile) and they live 5 to 8 years, about 40 times longer than worker bees. These differences led to the marketable assumption that ingestion of royal jelly will have the same effect on humans as it does for bees. Royal jelly has been sold to increase size, improve fertility and prolong longevity. It has also been sold as a skin tonic and hair growth stimulant.

Active Ingredients: Royal jelly is a complex mixture of proteins, sugars, fats, variable amounts of vitamins and minerals and pheromones (sexual hormones). About 15% of royal jelly is an acid which is thought to play an important role in bee growth regulation.

Actions: Royal jelly has been found to possess specific anti-tumor and antimicrobial activity. Its estrogenic effect in regulating female hormones is questionable.

Uses: There is no evidence that royal jelly increases size, fertility and prolongs longevity. It may be used as a supplement in women with menopause and other female related disorders. It is a good source of various vitamins and minerals, including B-complex. It may help in treating some skin conditions.

Toxicity: Other than skin irritation, there are no reports of toxicity.

Therapeutic Dosage: 250 to 500 mg/day.

Taurine

Description: Taurine is a naturally occuring non-essential amino acid that is a chief constituent of bile in the liver and is found in small amounts in the lung, heart and brain.

Actions: Taurine is a natural constituent of bile, a clear yellow or orange fluid produced in the liver and stored in the gall bladder. Bile helps in emulsification, digestion and absorption. Taurine is also found in small amounts in the membranes of lung, heart and brain tissue. It may reduce membrane excitability in these tissues.

Uses: Supplementation may be beneficial in treating individuals with gall stones, high cholesterol and atherosclerosis. Taurine helps to increase the solubility of bile and may help to decrease stone formation. Taurine stabilizes heart muscle and may be beneficial in treating congestive heart failure, arrhythmias and angina. Taurine may also be beneficial in stabilizing the blood-brain barrier and reducing hypoglycemia, hyperactivity and epilepsy.

Toxicity: Taurine is relatively non-toxic and few side effects have been reported. Excess dosages for long periods of time are not recommended.

Dosage: Taurine - 1000-3000 mg/day.

Thymus Glandular Extract

Description: The thymus gland is a small gland located in the upper chest region just beneath the sternum. It plays a very important role in the development of a healthy immune system. It reaches its maximum development during puberty and continues to play an important role in the immune system throughout life.

Actions: The thymus gland is responsible for entrapping immature white blood cells called T-lymphocytes (T-cells) arising from the bone marrow and circulating in the blood. The thymus processes these cells causing them to become sensitized and capable of developing into active part of the immune system. The thymus gland produces several hormones including thymosin, thymopoetin and thymic factor. These hormones stimulate thymus gland activity and the development of mature T-cells.

Uses: Can be used as a supplement to support the function of the thymus gland and the immune system. It may be useful in treating any infection and is particularly effective to is conditions caused by poor immune function.

Toxicity: Few adverse side effects have been reported. Occasional allergic reaction may occur.

Dosage: 500-1000 mg/day of purified thymus glandular extract.

Tyrosine

Description: Tyrosine is a naturally occuring non-essential amino acid present in most proteins.

Actions: Tyrosine is used to make neurotransmitters in the nervous system, thyroid hormones and melanin, a dark pigment substance found in the hair, skin and retina of the eye. Tyrosine is produced as an intermediate metabolite in the conversion of the amino acid, phenylalanine into the neurotransmitter, nor-adrenaline. It is also a precursor to the neurotransmitters, adrenaline and dopamine.

Uses: Useful in supporting the function of the thyroid gland and can be used to treat hypothyroidism is conjunction with other therapies. May be useful in treating individuals with hypo-melanosis, a condition characterized by lack of skin pigment. May also be useful in treating certain cases of depression and schizophrenia.

Toxicity: Tyrosine is relatively non-toxic and few adverse side effects have been reported. Avoid taking excess doses of tyrosine for prolonged periods of time.

Therapeutic Dosage: Tyrosine - 2000-4000 mg/day.

CHAPTER 64

Herbal Medicines

Herbal medicine is experiencing a renaissance in Europe and North America. The modern use of plants and plant derivatives in the treatment of disease is being validated by scientific research. The World Health Organization (WHO) has estimated that 80% of the world population of 5 billion relies on traditional medicines for their primary health care needs. Over 25% of all prescription drugs in North America have contained active constituents derived from plants. One of the great fallacies and misconceptions being perpetuated by the conventional medical establishment is that herbal medicine has no scientific proof. One of the goals of this book is dispel the myths and skepticism surrounding natural medicine, including herbal medicines and bridge the gap between folk medicine and modern science.

There are many advantages of using herbal medicines. As a rule of thumb, they are less toxic than their synthetic counterparts and offer less risk of adverse effects. Herbal preparations consist of many different synergistic factors that act together, demonstrating that the whole plant of crude plant extract is superior in action than an isolated constituent. The mechanism of action of many herbal medicines is to correct the underlying cause of dysfunction. Herbal medicines are often cheaper than their synthetic counterparts.

Traditionally that pharmaceutical industry has paid little attention to the herbal industry. Since a plant or herbal medicine cannot be patented and no profit generated, little research has been done on traditional herbal medicines. However, don't be mislead, herbal medicine is a powerful and effective medicine.

Herbal medicines contain many pharmacologically active chemical constituents. One of the problems in the herbal industry has been the lack of quality control. There has been no way of ensuring the quality of an herbal product the consumer is using. Substitutions, adulterants and misrepresentations have been widespread in the industry. As an example, the Health and Welfare branch of the Canadian government analyzed taheebo or pau d' arco (Tabebuia avellandeae), Brazilian tree bark, widely promoted in the natural health industry for its antibacterial, antifungal and anti-cancer properties. Quinone derivatives, mainly identified as lapachol, found in the bark of this tree were believed to be responsible for this plant's medicinal effects. However, after chemical analysis it was determined that nine out of ten pau d' arco products sold in health food stores throughout Canada contained no quinone derivatives at all. This study further confirms the lack of quality control and misrepresentations that are widespread throughout the natural health field.

Fortunately, in Asia and Europe several pharmaceutical firms became re-interested in traditional botanical medicine and a new chapter in herbal medicine was opened. Through modern technology, new techniques became available to measure and quantify the active chemical constituents responsible for each plants medicinal action. Many active chemical constituents were isolated and identified for the first time. New techniques including thin-layer chromatography (TLC) and high pressure liquid chromatography (HPLC) are now being used to isolate and quantify active chemical constituents. Additionally, improvements in cultivation, harvesting, curing procedures, storage and shelf life added to the resurgence of this field. Standardized herbal medicines containing a specified amount of active constituents responsible for the pharmacologic effects of each medicine are now available.

Let's use Ginseng as an example. Ginseng is one of the most popular herbs in the market place and is widely used for its tonifying and tranquilizing effects. There have been many different ginseng preparations commercially available in the health food stores. Modern technology has been responsible for identification and isolation of chemicals in the crude plant responsible for its reported therapeutic effects. Ginsenosides are a group of chemically related compounds that are believed to be responsible for the pharmacologic action of this plant. The usual concentration of ginsenosides in ginseng root has been determined to range from 2.0 to 5.0%. Using modern technological procedures, high quality ginseng extracts are now available guaranteeing a specific concentration of active ginsenosides, 5.0% ginsenosides by weight.

Another major improvement in herbal medicines has been in the area of extraction and concentration. By knowing the active chemical constituents in herbal preparations, an effort was made to concentrate these constituents to produce a higher potency preparation. These high quality preparations are typically produced from four times the quantity of the original herbal material. A 4:1 concentration means that 4 parts of the crude herbal material is equivalent to 1 part of the concentrated standardized extract. Using Ginseng as an example; in a concentrated

276

preparation the active ginsenosides are concentrated above and beyond the range that they are normally found in the original plant. Preparations containing 14% ginsenosides are now being produced. New and improved herbal medicines containing specified amounts of active chemical constituents are being produced as standardized herbal extracts. Also, improvements in the study of toxic side effects of herbal medicines has paralleled the improvement of the quality of herbal medicines being produced. It is an exciting time in the herbal medicine field.

Alfalfa (Medicago sativa)

Description: Alfalfa is a perennial herb that grows to a height of 1 meter and is cultivated throughout the world for animal forage.

History: The Arabs fed alfalfa to their horses claiming it made the animals swift and strong, naming the legume, "al-fal-fa" meaning the "father of all foods." Alfalfa has been used medicinally in the treatment of kidney, bladder and prostate disorders. Leaf preparations have been used to treat arthritis, diabetes, asthma and indigestion.

Active Ingredients: 2 to 3% steroidal saponins, alkaloids and flavonoids.

Actions: Alfalfa saponins reduce cholesterol absorption from the digestive system. Certain flavonoid derivatives in Alfalfa have demonstrated estrogenic activity.

Uses: May be useful in reducing high blood cholesterol levels. May be used in the treatment of premenstrual stress, dysmenorrhea and menopause.

Toxicity: May cause allergic reactions and contact dermatitis in some individuals. Should be used with discretion in individuals with systemic lupus erythematosus (SLE) and may aggravate lupus. Alfalfa may contain a toxic amino acid, canavanine.

Dosage: Alfalfa (4:1) - 500-1000 mg/day.

Angelica (Angelica sinensis)

Common names: Dong quai.

Description: Angelica is a stout biennial or perennial plant growing up to 2 meters in height. It is native to the Orient.

History: Angelica has been used for thousands of years in the Orient. Angelica is a very popular medicinal herb and is second in reputation only to ginseng. It has been used medicinally to treat a variety of female disorders.

Active Ingredients: Coumarin derivatives at 0.2 to 0.5% and volatile oil at 0.3 to 1.0% of the dry weight of the plant.

Actions: Coumarin derivatives have demonstrated analgesic, anti-inflammatory, uterine smooth muscle relaxing, estrogenic and immune stimulating properties.

Uses: May be used to treat premenstrual syndrome (PMS), menstrual pain and cramping, dysmenorrhea and menstrual cycle irregularities. Also can be used to relieve intestinal bloating and gas and as an expectorant to break up lung congestion.

Toxicity: Few side effects have benn reported including contact dermatitis, stomach upset, muscle cramping and photosensitivity.

Dosage: Angelica sinensis (4:1) 500-1000 mg/day.

Bearberry (Arctostaphylos uva-ursi)

Description: Bearberry is a low growing evergreen shrub that forms a dark green carpet of leaves on the forest floor. The plant grows abundantly throughout the northern hemisphere in Asia, Europe and northern United Stated and Canada.

History: Bearberry has been used medicinally for centuries as a diuretic, astringent and urinary antiseptic. It has been used to treat urethritis, cystitis, urinary tract infections, kidney stones and bronchitis.

Active Ingredients: Arbutin in the leaves at a concentration of 5.0 to 18.0% of the dry weight of the plant. Also contains high amount of tannins and flavonoids.

Actions: A urinary antiseptic and antibiotic effective against common bacteria that invade the bladder and urinary tract. Also has a mild diuretic action.

Uses: Bearberry has been used effectively to treat urinary tract infections.

Toxicity: Excess doses may cause indigestion, nausea and vomiting. Excess of doses of isolated arbutin may have more serious side effects.

Dosage: Bearberry (4:1) - 750-1500 mg/day.

Bilberry (Vaccinium myrtillus)

Description: Bilberry is a low growing shrub native to northern Europe and Asia. It is a cousin to the North American blueberry and huckleberry.

History: Bilberry has been used to make jam for hundreds of years. Medicinal use of bilberry became popular during World War II when British R.A.F. pilots consumed bilberries prior to night flying to improve their night vision.

Active Ingredients: Anthyocyanoside flavonoids in the berries at a concentration of 0.1 to 0.25% of the crude weight of the berry.

Actions: Bilberry anthocyanosides stabilize connective tissue around blood vessels, relaxes smooth muscle around blood vessels, decreases blood vessel fragility, decreases blood clotting and decreases inflammation. Also stimulates dark adaption and improves night vision.

Uses: Bilberry has been used effectively in the treatment of a variety of visual problems including night blindness, visual fatigue from eye strain, diabetic retinopathy, cataracts and macular degeneration.

Toxicity: Bilberry is virtually non-toxic and few side effects have been reported.

Dosage: Concentrated bilberry extracts are standardized to contain 20 to 25% anthocyanoside content. Bilberry (4:1) - 100-200 mg/day.

Bitter melon (Momordica charantia)

Description: Bitter melon is a perennial plant that has bitter tasting fruit and is cultivated throughout Asia, Africa and South America.

History: Bitter melon has been used for hundreds of years in traditional medicine to treat diabetes, blood sugar abnormalities, increase appetite and stimulate hydrochloric acid production in the stomach.

Active Ingredients: 0.2 to 0.5% short protein molecules called peptides, specifically polypeptide P.

Actions: Bitter melon contains several small proteins including polypeptide P. Polypeptide P from Bitter melon decreases blood sugar levels by inhiting sugar uptake from the digestive system.

Uses: May be beneficial in treating diabetes, hyperglycemia and other blood sugar abnormalities.

Toxicity: Bitter melon is relatively non-toxic and few side effects have been reported.

Dosage: Bitter melon (4:1) - 250-500 mg/day.

Chamomile (Matricaria chamomilla)

Description: Chamomile is a fragrant, low annual herb that grows up to 0.6 meters in height and is native to North America, Europe and northern and western Asia.

History: Chamomile has been used medicinally since the Roman times to treat digestive and rheumatic disorders. It has been widely consumed as a medicinal tea for hundreds of years. It is widely used in the cosmetic industry in shampoos, creams and perfumes.

Active Ingredients: 0.24 to 1.9% of a volatile oil found mainly in the flower head. The volatile oil is composed mainly of bisabolol and chamazulene.

Actions: The volatile oil of Chamomile has anti-spasmodic actions on the gastro-intestinal system, antibacterial and antifungal activity, anti-inflammatory activity and anti-ulcer activity in the stomach.

Uses: Chamomile helps to relax spasm and relieve gas in the gastro-intestinal system and is recommended for treatment of indigestion, gastritis, peptic ulcers, ulcerative colititis, irritable bowel syndrome and other disorders of the digestive system. Topical preparations may be effective in reducing inflammation, preventing infection and enhancing wound healing.

Toxicity: Chamomile is relatively non-toxic and few side effects have been reported. Occasional allergic and contact dermatitis reactions have been reported.

Dosage: Chamomile (4:1) - 500-1000 mg/day.

Chinese ginseng (Panax ginseng)

Description: Chinese ginseng is a small, woody perennial plant that grows abundantly throughout China and Korea. It is a member of the Araliaceae family.

History: Chinese ginseng is the most popular and widely used medicinal plant throughout the orient. It has been used for thousands of years for its tonic and rejuventating effects on the body.

Active Ingredients: The root of this plant contains 2 to 5% triterpenoid glycosides called ginsenosides.

Actions: Supports and stimulates the adrenal glands and helps the body respond to stress, decreases elevated blood sugar, decreases cholesterol levels, increases DNA and protein production, displays antiviral effects, displays both stimulant and depressant effects on the nervous system, acts as an antioxidant and decreases the effects of radiation and displays specific antitumor effects.

Uses: Helps to decrease the effects of stress and fatigue and improves work capacity. May also be used to protect the body from the damaging effects of radiation.

Toxicity: Reported side effects at high doses include nervousness, insomnia, irritability, anxiety, heart palpitations and indigestion.

Dosage: Chinese ginseng (10:1) standardized for ginsenoside content - 100-200 mg/day.

Coleus (Coleus forskohlii)

Description: Coleus is an aromatic perennial plant that grows up to 0.6 meters in height and is native to India, Africa, Arabia and Brazil. The tubers of this plant are used as a condiment and for its medicinal properties.

History: Coleus has been used for thousands of years in Indian Ayruvedic medicine in the treatment of heart diseases, abdominal colic, respiratory disorders, painful urination, insomina and convulsions.

Active Ingredients: Contains approximately 0.5% of a diterpene derivative called forskolin.

Actions: Forskolin is a powerful activator of the enzyme adenylate cyclase in various tissue of the body. Forskolin inhibits platelet aggregation, dilates smooth muscle around blood vessels, dilates smooth muscle in the lungs, reduces intra-ocular pressure and inhibits the growth of certain tumors.

Uses: Coleus may be useful in the treatment of high blood pressure, atherosclerosis, glaucoma, asthma and certain cancers.

Toxicity: Coleus is relatively non-toxic and few adverse side effects have been reported.

Dosage: Coleus (4:1) - 50-100 mg/day.

Dandelion (Taraxacum officinale)

Description: Dandelion is a common perennial weed that grows up to 0.5 meters in height and is common to meadows, lawns and roadsides of North America. The leaves of this plant may have a saw-tooth appearance giving rise to its name, dandelion.

History: Dandelion has been used medicinally for centuries. The root has been used to brew a coffee-like beverage. The bitter leaves have been used in salads, in wine making and cooked like spinach. The leaves have also been used to lower high blood sugar, appetite stimulant, stimulate bile flow from the liver and as a laxative.

Active Ingredients: Several triterpenes compounds, up to 25% inulin, bitter compounds and a very high concentration of vitamin A.

Actions: The bitter compounds stimulate production of hydrochloric acid in the stomach and stimulate production of bile in the liver. Bile is released from the liver and flushed out into the intestines. Inulin is responsible for the diuretic properties of this plant. Dandelion is one of the most potent herbal diuretics known and due to its high potassium content acts as a potassium sparing diuretic. Inulin also slows sugar release from food and helps to prevent blood sugar abnormalities.

Uses: Dandelion may be beneficial in treating liver and gall bladder disorders including hepatitis, cirrhosis, gallstones, high cholesterol, fat indigestion, flatulence and constipation. May be beneficial in treating diabetes and disorders of blood sugar abnormalities. May be beneficial in treating kidney and bladder disorders and kidney stones.

Toxicity: Dandelion is relatively non-toxic. Allergic reaction and contact dermatitis have been occasionally reported.

Dosage: Dandelion (4:1) - 500-1500 mg/day.

Devil's Claw (Harpagophytum procumbens)

Description: Devil's claw is a flowering plant native to the Kalahari desert and Namibian steppes of southwest Africa.

History: Devil's claw has been used medicinally by Africans to treat a variety of disorders including liver and kidney problems, allergies, headaches, muscle aches and arthritis.

Active Ingredients: Harpagoside, primarily found in the roots of this plant ranging from 1.0 to 2.0% of the dry weight.

Actions: Decreases swelling and inflammation, especially around joints.

Uses: May help to reduce swelling and inflammation in rheumatoid arthritis, osteoarthritis and other rheumatisms.

Toxicity: Harpagoside has been found to have low toxicity. Side effects include headaches, ringing in the ears and poor appetite.

Dosage: Devil's claw (4:1) 500-1500 mg/day.

Ephedra (Ephedra sinensis)

Description: Ephedra a shrub native to mainland China and is cultivated commercially throughout the world.

History: Ephedra has been used medicinally in the Orient for thousands of years. It has been used to treat respiratory infections, asthma and hayfever. Ephedra was intorduced into western medicine in 1924.

Active Ingredients: Alkaloids including ephedrine, pseudoephedrine and nor-pseudoephedrine at 1.0 to 3.0% of the dry weight of the plant.

Actions: Ephedra alkaloids dilate the bronchi in the lungs, constrict blood vessels, decrease localized congestion and swelling as in the nose, stimulate the nervous system, dilate pupils and increase blood pressure.

Uses: Widely used as a nasal decongestant and broncho-dilator in allergic reactions, asthma and hayfever. Also used to increase fat breakdown and aid in weight loss.

Toxicity: Excess use may cause headaches, dizziness, insomnia, high blood pressure, heart palpitations, sweating and other disorders. Prolonged use for nasal congestion can actually cause reactive nasal swelling.

Dosage: Ephedra (4:1) 400-800 mg/day.

Feverfew (Tanacetum parthenium)

Description: Feverfew is a short perennial plant that grows along fields and roadsides throughout North America and Europe.

History: Feverfew has been used medicinally for hundreds of years to treat headaches, arthritis, asthma and menstrual disorders. According to legend, the ancient Greeks called feverfew "parthenium" because it was used to save the life of someone who had fallen from the Parthenon, the Doric temple in Athens.

Active Ingredients: 0.1 to 0.5% sesquiterpene lactones commonly known as parthenolides.

Actions: The parthenolides inhibit platelet aggregation in the blood and prevent blood vessel constriction, internal clotting and inflammation.

Uses: Feverfew may be beneficial in treating migraine headaches and may be useful in reducing both the severity and duration of headaches. It may also be useful in treating inflammation due to arthritis, asthma and menstrual disorders.

Toxicity: Feverfew is relatively safe and non-toxic. High doses of feverfew may cause tongue irritation, indigestion, headache and diarrhea. Occasional allergic reactions have been reported.

Dosage: Feverfew (4:1) - 50-100 mg per day.

Garlic (Allium sativa)

Description: Garlic is a strong scented perennial plant with long, flat and firm leaves, widely used as a culinary spice in cooking.

History: Garlic has been used medicinally for thousands of years by various cultures to treat colds, respiratory infections, whooping cough, bronchitis, toothache, earache and many other conditions too numerous to list here.

Active Ingredients: Allicin and other sulfur containing compounds at 0.1 to 0.5% of the dry weight of the bulb.

Actions: Garlic has broad spectrum antibiotic activity against bacteria, viruses, fungi and parasites. Garlic decreases atherosclerosis in arteries, inhibits clot formation, decreases blood cholesterol and decreases blood pressure. It also has some anti-tumor effects.

Uses: Garlic may be used as a broad spectrum antibiotic to treat common infections of the digestive system, urinary tract, respiratory system and ears. Garlic may be used to treat high blood pressure and high cholesterol. It can also be used to inhibit blood clot formation in individuals with atherosclerosis.

Toxicity: Garlic is virtually non-toxic and safe to use, although the pungent odor of this plant may be offensive to some individuals. Allergic reactions including contact dermatitis and stomach upset may occur.

Dosage: Allium sativa (fresh garlic) - 10-30 gm/day.

Ginger (Zingiber officinalis)

Description: Ginger is a perennial plant that grows up to 1 meter in height and is native to southern Asia and the tropics including India, China, Jamaica, Haiti and Nigeria. The root is highly aromatic and is the source of the dried powdered spice widely used as condiment for food.

History: Ginger root has been used for thousands of years in the Orient. It has been used medicinally to treat indigestion, diarrhea, nausea, toothache, poisoning, snakebite and rheumatisms. It also induces sweating,, relieves intestinal gas and stimulates the appetite.

Active Ingredients: Volatile oils at 0.25 to 3.5% of the dry weight of the root.

Actions: The volatile oil inhibits the growth of bacteria and parasites, reduces fever, decrease pain, decreases coughs, decreases nausea and improves digestion. Also has some immune stimulating effects, anti-cancer effects and reduces blood cholesterol.

Uses: Reduces symptoms of motion sickness, vertigo (spinning sensation) and dizziness. Also reduces stomach upset, indigestion and nausea.

Toxicity: Ginger is relatively non-toxic and few side effects have been reported. It may cause stomach upset and in large doses may cause nervous system irregularities and heart arrhythmias.

Dosage: Zingiber officinale (4:1) - 1000-3000 mg/day.

Ginkgo (Ginkgo biloba)

Description: Ginkgo is a perennial tree that once grew abundantly more than 200 million years ago. Individual trees grow up to 50 meters in height and may live as long as 2000 years.

History: Ginkgo is a living fossil and considered to be the world's oldest living tree and has been used medicinally for thousands of years.

Active Ingredients: Flavonoids including Ginkgo heterosides. Concentrated extracts are standardized to contain up to 24% Ginkgo heterosides.

Actions: Ginkgo heterosides inhibit the formation of clots and

286

atherosclerotic plaques, stabilize the blood-brain barrier, dilates blood vessels in the brain, increases cerebral blood flow, increases nerve transmitters and is a potent antioxidant preventing free radical damage.

Uses: Can be used to treat individuals with cerebral vascular insufficiency, stroke victims and mental and cognitive impairment. Can also be used to treat tinnitus (ringing in ears), high blood pressure and senility.

Toxicity: Ginkgo is safe and non-toxic. Few adverse side effects including digestive upset and headaches have been reported. Allergic reaction may cause a topical, red, itchy rash.

Dosage: Ginkgo biloba (4:1) - 100-200 mg/day.

Goldenseal (Hydrastis canadensis)

Description: Goldenseal is a small perennial plant that grows up to 30 centimeters in height in damp woods and meadows of eastern United States and Canada. Goldenseal is cultivated in parts of the west coast. It has a rough, wrinkled root with a distinctive odor and bitter taste.

History: The Cherokee indians used goldenseal root to treat skin ulcers and arrow wounds. The root has been used medicinally as an antiseptic, diuretic, hemostatic, bitter, laxative and tonic to relieve inflamed mucous membranes.

Active Ingredients: Isoquinoline alkaloids including hydrastine (1.5 to 4.0%), berberine (0.5 to 6.0%), berberastine (2.0 to 3.0%).

Actions: Berberine and other alklaloids of goldenseal have demonstrated antimicrobial effects against bacteria, fungi and protozoa. Stimulates specific white blood cells and increases blood supply to the spleen. Also lowers body temperature in fever.

Uses: Effective against common bacterial, fungal and protozoal infections. Especially effective in treating infectious diarrhea.

Toxicity: Berberine and other alkaloids of goldenseal are safe and non-toxic. Berberine and other berberine containing plants are not recommended during pregnancy.

Dosage: Hydrastis canadensis (4:1) 500-1000 mg/day.

Gotu kola (Centella asiatica)

Description: Gotu kola is a slender, creeping perennial plant that prefers a watery habitat and is native to India, Madagascar, China, South Pacific and southern and middle Africa.

History: Gotu kola has been used medicinally for thousands of years in China and India to treat a variety of disorders including wound healing, skin inflammation and leprosy. It has also been used as an herbal tonic and to increase mental alertness. Gotu kola was used daily by the Chinese herbalist, Li Ching Yun, who is reported to have lived to 256 years.

Active Ingredients: Leaves of this plant contain 1.1 to 8% (average concentration 2.2 to 3.4%) triterpene compounds known as asiaticosides.

Actions: Asiaticosides have remarkable wound healing properties. They increase the strength and formation of connective tissue in the skin, nails, hair and blood vessels. They also appear to activate the part of the immune system responsible for filtering and eliminating waste products in the body.

Uses: Gotu kola may be beneficial in the treatment of skin disorders including keloids, scleroderma, burns, skin ulcers, surgical wounds, cellulite, varicose veins, hemorrhoids, periodontal disease, fissures, leprosy, lupus and may be used to enhance wound healing in the skin. Gotu kola may also be useful in the treatment of cirrhosis, tuberculosis, bladder ulcers and mental senility.

Toxicity: Gotu kola is relatively non-toxic and few side effects have been reported. Occasionaly allergic reaction and contact dermatitis may occur.

Dosage: Gotu kola (4:1) - 60-120 mg per day/day.

Hawthorn (Crataegus oxyacantha)

Description: Hawthorn is a shrub or tree that grows up to 6 meters in height and is native to Europe, east Asia and eastern North America. Hawthorn has white flowers that bloom in spring, bright red fruit containing one to three nuts and long slender thorns along its stems.

History: Hawthorn tree has been the focus of May time rituals in England and the fruits has been used throughout Europe to make jam and wine. It has been used medicinally to treat heart disorders, anemia, indigestion, respiratory ailments and as a diuretic and astringent in menstrual complaints.

Active Ingredients: Contains flavonoids. Over thirty different flavonoids have been isolated in Hawthorn. Flavonoid content ranges from 0.05 to 5.0% of the dry weight of the plant.

Actions: Flavonoids increase coronary blood flow, increase peripheral blood flow, increase the force of heart contraction, decrease oxygen use by the heart, decrease blood pressure and can increase or decrease heart rate.

Uses: Helps to improve heart function in individuals with heart disease, angina, heart attacks and congestive heart failure. May also help to decrease high blood pressure.

Toxicity: Hawthorn and its extracts are virtually non-toxic and completely safe for long term use. Few side effects have been reported.

Dosage: Crataegus oxyacantha (4:1) - 400-800 mg/day

Horehound (Marrubium vulgare)

Description: Horehound is a perennial aromatic plant that grows up to about 1 meter in height and is native to Europe and Asia and has been naturalized to North America.

History: Horehound has been used medicinally to treat sore throats, colds, coughs and other respiratory ailments. It has also been used as a bitter tonic to stimulate digestion and as a diuretic. It is now primarily used as flavorings in liqueurs, candies and cough drops.

Active Ingredients: 0.3 to 1% of a bitter volatile oil called marrubiin.

Actions: Marrubiin is a strong expectorant that helps to break up mucous and congestion in the throat and chest. It also stimulates bile acid secretion from the liver and gall bladder and has mild blood vessel dilating properties.

Uses: May be used to treat sore throats, coughs, colds and other respiratory ailments.

289

Toxicity: Horehound is relatively non-toxic and few adverse side effects have been reported. At high doses it may cause stomach upset, indigestion and may induce heart beat irregularities.

Dosage: Horehound tincture (1:5) - 3-5 ml three times per day.

Indian tobacco (Lobelia inflata)

Description: Lobelia is a hairy annual or biennial plant that grows up to 1 meter in height and is native to parts of North America.

History: American indians used lobelia as a tobacco substitute. It has been used medicinally as an anti-spasmodic, anti-asthmatic, diaphoretic, expectorant, emetic and sedative.

Active Ingredients: Piperidine alkaloids primarily as lobeline at approximately 0.5 to 1.0% of the dry weight of the plant.

Actions: Nervous system stimulant, one-third as potent as nicotine. Helps to break up congestion in lungs.

Uses: Widely used as an expectorant to break up congestion in the lungs. May be used as a substitute for cigarette smoking and as a smoking deterrant.

Toxicity: Lobeline can be toxic in large doses. Symptoms of toxicity include depression, nausea, sweats, stupor, convulsions and coma. Excessive ingestion of lobeline can cause respiratory arrest and may be fatal.

Dosage: Lobelia inflata (4:1) 400-800 mg/day.

Licorice (Glycyrrhiza glabra)

Description: Licorice is a perennial plant that grows between 1 to 2 meters in height and is native to Asia, Europe, parts of the Middle East and naturalized to North America.

History: Roots and rhizomes of this plant have been used for centuries as a condiment to flavor candies and tobacco. Licorice has been used treat a variety of illness including asthma, bronchitis, diabetes, inflammation, indigestion and constipation.

Active Ingredients: 1 to 27% (average 7 to 15%) of a group of triterpenoid glycosides known as glycyrrhizin. Glycyrrhizin is responsible for the sweetness of licorice and is 50 to 100 times sweeter than sugar.

Actions: Licorice supports and stimulates adrenal gland function and helps the body to reduce inflammation and respond to stress. Licorice coats the stomach and intestines and prevents inflammation of the digestive system. Licorice is a mild expectorant and helps to break up throat and chest congestion. Glycyrrhizin has estrogenic activity and may be useful in treating female disorders.

Uses: Licorice may be beneficial in treating indigestion, inflammation of the digestive system, irritable bowel syndrome, constipation and peptic ulcers. Topical application of licorice may help to reduce inflammation and swelling. Licorice may be useful in treating premenstrual syndrome, dysmenorrhea and menopause. Licorice may be useful in helping the body respond to stress and aiding adrenal gland function.

Toxicity: High doses of licorice for prolonged periods of time may cause a condition known as pseudo-aldosteronism, marked by electrolyte imbalance, swelling, edema and hypertension. Deglycyrrhizinated licorce (DGL) preparations do not cause this condition.

Dosage: Licorice (1:1) - 500-1500 mg/day.

Milk Thistle (Silybum marianum)

Description: Milk thistle grows throughout Europe and North America. It grows from 1 to 3 meters in height and has large prickly leaves and attractive red and purple flowers.

History: During the middle ages monks introduced this plant into Europe. Milk thistle has been used medicinally to treat liver disorders, jaundice, gallstones, abdominal inflammation, bronchitis and varicose veins. During the 18th century milk thistle as the treatment of choice for liver disorders.

Active Ingredients: Contains flavonoids including silymarin at 4.0 to 6.0% of the dry weight of this plant. Concentrated extracts are standardized to contain 70 to 80% silymarin content.

Actions: Stabilizes and strengthens liver cell walls and prevents toxins from penetrating into the cells, increases protein production and liver cell regeneration and acts as an antioxidant in preventing free radical damage.

Uses: Can be used to treat jaundice, acute and chronic hepatitis, cirrhosis, liver damage caused by toxic chemicals and inflammation of the gall bladder.

Toxicity: No adverse side effects have been reported. Long term use during pregnancy is not recommended.

Dosage: Silybum marianum (10:1) - 400-800 mg/day.

Mistletoe (Viscum album)

Description: Mistletoe is a parasitic, woody perennial plant commonly found growing on oak and other deciduous trees throughout Europe.

History: Early pagan customs required hanging mistletoe over doors and in hallways to inspire passion during the pagan holiday, "Hoeul". Today, these evergreen plants are used as a christmas ornament and the custom of kissing under the plant is a keyed-down version of this ancient pagan practice.

Active Ingredients: The chemical constituents of mistletoe reflect the host plant on which this parasite grows. Contains alkaloids, amines, steroids, flavonoids and proteins.

Actions: Mistletoe extracts dilate blood vessels, decrease heart rate and decrease blood pressure. Specific mistletoe extracts have anti-tumor effects.

Uses: Can be used to treat high blood pressure. Also can be used to treat certain types of cancer.

Toxicity: Adverse effects include nausea, vomiting, decreased heart rate, digestive upset, allergic reactions and diarrhea. May be fatal in high doses and should be administered with proper medical consent.

Dosage: Viscum album (5:1) - 100-200 mg/day.

Peppermint (Mentha piperita)

Description: Peppermint is an aromatic perennial herb that grows up to 1 meter in height and is native to Europe and North America.

History: Peppermint has been widely used for centuries as a medicinal tea to treat bad breath, colds, bronchitis, sinusitis, indigestion, abdominal bloating, abdominal cramps, constipation and diarrhea.

Active Ingredients: Peppermint contains up to 2% of a volatile oil containing menthol, menthone and jasmone.

Action: Peppermint oil inhibits smooth muscle contraction in the stomach and intestines. Peppermint oil can be used as an expectorant to break up throat and chest congestion. Topical application of the oil is an effective antibiotic and antifungal and has been used as a counter-irritant to reduce itching.

Uses: Peppermint may be beneficial in treating indigestion, stomach cramps, abdominal bloating, irritable bowel syndrome, constipation and other ailments of the digestive system. Peppermint may be useful in treating colds, bronchitis, sinusitis and other ailments of the respiratory system. Topical application of peppermint oil may be useful in preventing skin infection and reducing itching.

Toxicity: Peppermint is relatively safe and non-toxic. It may be irritating to the skin, eyes and other mucous membranes. Internally, the oil can be irritating to the digestive system and can decrease heart rate.

Dosage: Peppermint oil - 0.6-1.2 ml/day.

Purple coneflower (Echinacea angustifolia)

Description: Echinacea is a perennial flower native to the great plains of North America. It grows from 20 to 100 centimeters in height.

History: Echinacea was one of the most widely used medicinal plants of the plain indians. They used the plant to treat toothaches, coughs, colds, sore throats, snakebites and as a painkiller.

Active Ingredients: Echinacin and echinacoside at approximately 1.0% of the dry weight of the plamt.

Actions: Echinacin stabilizes connective tissue, inhibits connective tissue breakdown, promotes the breakdown of clots, stimulates the immune system and has demonstrated antiviral activity.

Uses: Effective immune stimulant in colds, flus and other common infections. Used to enhance immune function in individuals with poor immune systems and diseases that inhibit immune response.

Toxicity: Echinacea is safe and non-toxic. There appears to be no side effects with long term use and its use during pregnancy is unknown.

Dosage: Echinacea angustifolia (6.5:1) - 500-1000 mg/day.

Saint John's wort (Hypericum perforatum)

Description: Saint John's wort is a woody perennial plant that is native to Europe, Asia, Africa and is naturalized to many other parts of the world including North America and Australia.

History: Saint John's wort has been medicinally used by the Greeks to treat a variety of illness including infections, wounds, respiratory problems, kidney dysfunction and depression. The plants's common name, St. John's wort, is in reference to biblical apostle St. John. Early christians believed that red spots appeared on the leaves of this plant on the exact day of the saint's beheading.

Active Ingredients: Hypericin and pseudo-hypericin at a concentration of 0.0095 to 0.5% of the dry weight of the plant.

Actions: Inhibits breakdown of neurotransmitters in the brain and nervous system. Inhibits viral growth. Extracts of Hypericum have also demonstrated antibacterial and wound healing activity.

Uses: Effective in treating mild cases of depression. Also used for bedwetting and nightmares in children and stomach inflammation in adults. The oils may be used externally to aid in burn and wound healing. May also be used to inhibit viral growth including HIV infection.

Toxicity: May be photo-toxic in large doses. Exposure to sunlight may induce an allergic skin rash.

Dosage: Hypericum perforatum (4:1) 1500-3000 mg/day.

294

White Willow (Salix alba)

Description: White willow is a tree common throughout the temperate climates on North America, Europe and the mediterranean.

History: Willow bark has been used medicinally for centuries to treat arthritis, inflammation and fever. It has been used by Egyptians, Assyrians, Greeks and has been mentioned in writings of Galen, Hippocrates and Dioscorides. Natural salicylates in this plant were used in the 19th century to make aspirin.

Active Ingredients: Salicin ranging from 2.0 to 7.0% of the dry weight of the plant.

Actions: Salicin is a precursor to acetylsalicylic acid or aspirin as it is commonly known. Salicin can reduce pain, inflammation and fever.

Uses: May be used to treat pain, inflammation and can reduce fever. Effective in treating moderate aches and pains including acute trauma, arthritis and headaches. Helps to reduce swelling and inflammation and reduce fevers.

Toxicity: Excessive doses may cause stomach upset, nausea and vomiting.

Dosage: Salix alba (8:1) - 1000-2000 mg/day.

Saw palmetto (Serenoa repens)

Description: Saw palmetto is a small dwarf tree native to the West Indies and the south-east coast of North America.

History: The indians used the berries of this plant for food. They also used this plant medicinally to treat colds, bronchitis, asthma, irritated mucous membranes, bladder infections and prostate problems in men. It has also been used as an aphrodisiac.

Active Ingredients: Fatty acids at 1.0 to 2.0% of the dry weight of the berries. Concentrated extracts are standardized to contain 75 to 95% fatty acid content.

Actions: Fatty acids inhibits activation of testosterone in males which inhibits prostate gland enlargement.

Uses: Effective in treating prostate enlargement in older adult males. Also can be used to treat hirsutism in females

Toxicity: Standardized extracts of Saw palmetto berries are well tolerated and no side effects have been reported.

Dosage: Serenoa repens (80-95% liposterolic extract) - 250-500 mg/day.

Siberian Ginseng (Eleutherococcus senticosus)

Description: Siberian ginseng is a perennial shrub that grows to a height of 2 to 3 meters and is native to eastern Russia, Korea, China and Japan.

History: Used as a cheap and abundant alternative to Chinese ginseng. Used medicinally as a tonic and for its rejuventating effects on the body.

Active Ingredients: The root of this plant contains 0.6 to 1.5% steroidal compounds called eleutherosides.

Actions: Supports and stimulates the adrenal glands, normalizes both high and low blood pressure, decreases elevated blood sugar levels, immune activation, radiation protection and specific anti-tumor effects.

Uses: Widely used as an "adaptogen." Helps the body deal with stress and helps to increase energy levels and work capacity.

Toxicity: Excess dosages may cause insomnia, irritability, anxiety and headaches.

Dosage: Eleutherococcus senticosus (20:1) standardized for eleutheroside content - 100-200 mg/day.

Tea tree oil (Meleleuca alternifolia)

Description: Tea tree is a small tree that is native only to the North-east coastal region of New South Wales, Australia.

History: Leaves of tea tree have been used to make a tea that has been used to treat sore throats, colds and sinusitis. Oil from tea tree has been used by aborigines in Australia to prevent skin infection.

Active Ingedients: 1 to 3% of a volatile oil known simply as tea tree oil.

Actions: Tea tree oil is a potent antiseptic and antifungal. Antiseptic activity has been demonstrated against common bacteria and antifungal activity has been demonstrated against many fungi including Candida.

Uses: Topical application of tea tree oil may be used as an antiseptic to clean skin wounds and prevent infection. It may be used to treat impetigo, boils, athlete's foot and other fungal infections. Dilute prepartions of the oil may be used to treat sore throats, colds and sinusitis.

Toxicity: Topical application of tea tree oil may be irritating to the skin and can cause inflammation and contact dermatitis. Internal use of the oil may cause severe indigestion, stomach upset and increased heart rate. Oral consumption of the oil is not recommended.

Dosage: Tea tree oil - 1-3 ml per day.

Tumeric (Curcuma longa)

Description: Tumeric is a perennial plant of the ginger family that is a major ingredient in curry powder.

History: Widely used as a culinary spice in Oriental and Indian foods throughout the world.

Active Ingredients: Curcumin, an orange or yellow oil at 0.5 to 7.0% of the dry weight of the plant.

Actions: Curcumin decreases swelling and inflammation. Anti-inflammatory action is comparable to conventional drugs including ibuprofen and cortisone.

Uses. May be used to decrease swelling and inflammation throughout the body.

Toxicity: Excess doses may cause indigestion, nausea and vomiting. May be allergic to some individuals.

Dosage: Tumeric (10:1) - 50-100 mg/day.

Valerian (Valerian officinalis)

Description: Valerian is a perennial plant that grows up to 1.5 meters in height and is native to the temperate zones of North America, Europe and Asia. Valerian has a very distinctive odor.

History: Valerian has been called "the valium of the 19th century" and has been widely used as a natural sedative for hundreds of years.

Active Ingredients: Valepotriates found in highest concentration in the root ranging from 0.1 to 2.0% of the dry weight of the root.

Actions: Valepotriates have antispasmodic, muscle relaxant and nerve depressant actions. Valerian extracts compare favorably with synthetic sedatives such as Xanax and Valium.

Uses: Reduces the time required to fall asleep, increases the quality of sleep and has no effect on nocturnal movement.

Toxicity: Excess doses can cause headaches, irritability, drowsiness, lethargy, low blood pressure and slow heart rate.

Dosage: Valerian (4:1) - 250-500 mg/day.

Index

"Don't loaf and invite inspiration; light out after it with a club and if you don't get it, you nonetheless get something that looks remarkably like it. Work all the time. Find out about this earth, this universe, this force and matter from the maggot to the godhead. And by this I mean work for your philosophy of life. It doesn't hurt how wrong your philosophy is, so long as you have one and have it well."

Jack London

Useful Addresses

Association of Naturopathic Physicians of British Columbia
204-2786 W. 16th Avenue
Vancouver, British Columbia   V6K 3C4
(604)-732-7070

or

Canadian Naturopathic Association
P.O. Box 4520 Station C.
Calgary, Alberta   T2T 5N3
(403)-244-4487

or

American Association of Naturopathic Physicians
P.O. Box 33046
Portland, Oregon   97233
(503)-255-4863

or

Bastyr College of Natural Health Sciences
144 N.E. 54th St.
Seattle, Washington   98105
(206)-523-9585